PSALMS 73–150

ABINGDON OLD TESTAMENT COMMENTARIES

PSALMS 73–150

RICHARD J. CLIFFORD

Abingdon Press
Nashville

ABINGDON OLD TESTAMENT COMMENTARIES
PSALMS 73–150

This book is printed on recycled, acid-free, elemental-chlorine–free paper.

Library of Congress Cataloging-in-Publication Data

Clifford, Richard J.
    Psalms 73-150 / Richard J. Clifford.
        p. cm.—(Abingdon Old Testament commentaries)
Includes bibliographical references.
    ISBN 0-687-06468-6 (alk. paper)
    1. Bible. O.T. Psalms LXXIII-CL—Commentaries. I. Title: Psalms seventy-three to one hundred fifty. II. Title. III. Series.

    BS1430.3.C56 2003
    223'.207—dc21
                                                                    2003011318

All italics within scriptural quotations are the author's emphasis.

The Hebraica® font used to print this work is available from Linguist's Software, Inc., PO Box 580, Edmonds, WA 98020-0580 tel (206) 775-1130.

All scripture quotations unless noted otherwise are taken from the New Revised Standard Version of the Bible, copyright © 1989, by the Division of Christian Education of the National Council of the Churches of Christ in the United States of America. Used by permission. All rights reserved.

Scripture quotations marked NJPS are from *The Tanakh: The New JPS Translation According to the Traditional Hebrew Text.* Copyright © 1985 by the Jewish Publication Society. Used by permission.

Scripture quotations marked NIV are taken from the HOLY BIBLE, NEW INTERNA-TIONAL VERSION®. NIV®. Copyright © 1973, 1978, 1984 by International Bible Society. Used by permission of Zondervan Publishing House. All rights reserved.

Scripture quotation marked NJB is from THE NEW JERUSALEM BIBLE, copyright © 1985 by Darton, Longman & Todd, Ltd. and Doubleday, a division of Random House, Inc. Reprinted by Permission.

Scripture quotations marked REB are taken from the Revised English Bible © Oxford University Press and Cambridge University Press 1989.

03 04 05 06 07 08 09 10 11 12 — 10 9 8 7 6 5 4 3 2 1

MANUFACTURED IN THE UNITED STATES OF AMERICA

CONTENTS

Book 4 (Psalms 90–106)

Book 5 (Psalms 107–150)

FOREWORD

The Abingdon Old Testament Commentaries are offered to the reader in hopes that they will aid in the study of Scripture and provoke a deeper understanding of the Bible in all its many facets. The texts of the Old Testament come out of a time, a language, and socio-historical and religious circumstances far different from the present. Yet Jewish and Christian communities have held to them as a sacred canon, significant for faith and life in each new time. Only as one engages these books in depth and with all the critical and intellectual faculties available to us, can the contemporary communities of faith and other interested readers continue to find them meaningful and instructive.

These volumes are designed and written to provide compact, critical commentaries on the books of the Old Testament for the use of theological students and pastors. It is hoped that they may be of service also to upper-level college or university students and to those responsible for teaching in congregational settings. In addition to providing basic information and insights into the Old Testament writings, these commentaries exemplify the tasks and procedures of careful interpretation.

The writers of the commentaries in this series come from a broad range of ecclesiastical affiliations, confessional stances, and educational backgrounds. They have experience as teachers and, in some instances, as pastors and preachers. In most cases, the authors are persons who have done significant research on the book that is their assignment. They take full account of the most important current scholarship and secondary literature, while not attempting to summarize that literature or to engage in technical academic debate. The fundamental concern of each volume is analysis and discussion of the literary, socio-historical, theological, and ethical dimensions of the biblical texts themselves.

The New Revised Standard Version of the Bible is the principal translation of reference for the series, though authors may draw upon other interpretations in their discussion. Each writer is attentive to the original Hebrew text in preparing the commentary. But the authors do not presuppose any knowledge of the biblical languages on the part of the reader. When some awareness of a grammatical, syntactical, or philological issue is necessary for an adequate understanding of a particular text, the issue is explained simply and concisely.

Each volume consists of four parts. An *introduction* looks at the book as a whole to identify *key issues* in the book, its *literary genre* and *structure,* the *occasion and situational context* of the book (including both social and historical contexts), and the *theological and ethical* significance of the book.

The *commentary* proper organizes the text by literary units and, insofar as is possible, divides the comment into three parts. The *literary analysis* serves to introduce the passage with particular attention to identification of the genre of speech or literature and the structure or outline of the literary unit under discussion. Here also, the author takes up significant stylistic features to help the reader understand the mode of communication and its impact on comprehension and reception of the text. The largest part of the comment is usually found in the *exegetical analysis,* which considers the leading concepts of the unit, the language of expression, and problematical words, phrases, and ideas in order to get at the aim or intent of the literary unit, as far as that can be uncovered. Attention is given here to particular historical and social situations of the writer(s) and reader(s) where that is discernible and relevant as well as to wider cultural (including religious) contexts. The analysis does not proceed phrase by phrase or verse by verse but deals with the various particulars in a way that keeps in view the overall structure and central focus of the passage and its relationship to the general line of thought or rhetorical argument of the book as a whole. The final section, *theological and ethical analysis* seeks to identify and clarify the theological and ethical matters with which the unit deals or to which it points. Though not aimed primarily at contemporary issues of faith and life, this section should provide readers a basis for reflection on them.

Each volume also contains a select bibliography of works cited in the commentary as well as major commentaries and other important works available in English. A subject index is provided to help the reader get at matters that cut across different texts. Both of these sections can be found in volume 2 of the Psalms.

The fundamental aim of this series will have been attained if readers are assisted not only to understand more about the origins, character, and meaning of the Old Testament writings, but also to enter into their own informed and critical engagement with the text themselves.

Patrick D. Miller
General Editor

List of Abbreviations

CAT	Commentaire de l'Ancien Testament
CD	*Damascus Document*
Haer.	*Adversus haereses*
m. Mid	Mishnah *Middot*
m. Sukkah	Mishnah *Sukkah*
MT	Masoretic Text
WSA	Works of Saint Augustine. *The Confessions.* Translated by Maria Boulding. Hyde Park, N.Y.: New City Press, 2000–2003.

BOOK THREE
(PSALMS 73–89)

PSALM 73

Literary Analysis

Psalm 73 is usually classed as a wisdom psalm, for it ponders a common topic in the Wisdom literature: the problem of evil. In the Bible, the problem of evil is usually posed as scandalous *events:* the prospering of the wicked and the suffering of a just individual. Like the similarly reflective Pss 32, 37, 49, and 139, the psalm views the unfairness and opaqueness of life as a personal and public reality. The psalmist, for instance, admits having at one time considered going public about the problem of evil (v. 15), though in the end decides to make a public proclamation of God's wonderful works (v. 28). The emotional dimension of the problem is seen in the expression of inner anguish. (Note the frequent use of the Hebrew emphatic first-person singular pronoun in vv. 2, 22, 23, 28.) As in Ps 32, the topic is explored by a conversion story: the movement from shock at injustice to peaceful rest with God. Unlike many conversion stories, however, it is thoroughly *theo*centric and applicable to every person. It is God who gives the illumination in the Temple; the movement from scandalized confusion to peaceful proclamation can be every believer's story.

Several formal features of the poem provide clues to the structure, the most notable being repetitions of key words. Examining these words makes possible an "objective" entry into the dense thought of the poem. The Hebrew particle *'ak* is the most important structuring word. It begins the three verses (vv. 1, 13, 18; rendered "truly" in vv. 1 and 18; translated indirectly in v. 13) that introduce the three main sections of the poem, verses 1-12, 13-17, and 18-28. Also important is the Hebrew phrase *wa'ănî* ("[as] for me," "I"), which begins verses 2, 22, 23, and 28. The occurrence of "for me" in the final line (v. 28) brings closure to the beginning (v. 2), because "for me" and two other words from verses 1-2 ("God" and "good") are repeated in verse 28. Moreover, verses 1-2 and verse 28 have approximately the same number of Hebrew words, another indication that the ending is meant to restate the opening axiom of faith.

The placement of the Hebrew markers *'ak* and *wa'ănî* plus the change of topics mark off the subsections of the poem. The opening and closing lines (vv. 1-2, 28) are, as noted, set off by their vocabulary and similar word count. Verses 3-12 form a section because of their single topic (portrait of the wicked) and also by the fact that the Hebrew words rendered "prosperity of the wicked" in verse 3 occur again in reverse order in verse 12 ("wicked; always at ease"). Topically, the section falls into two parts (vv. 3-7, 8-12). The first part describes the physical appearance of the wicked ("I *saw* the prosperity of the wicked," v. 3. N.B.: Italics within scriptural quotations are the author's emphases.) and the second describes their arrogant words ("They . . . *speak* with malice," v. 8; "And they *say* . . . ," v. 11). In other words, verses 3-7 record what the psalmist sees, verses 8-11 what the psalmist hears. Speech is exceedingly important in Wisdom literature because words are the defining human act, expressing the kind of person one is. Verse 12 is a summary statement.

The middle section of the poem (vv. 13-17), describing the psalmist's reaction, begins with *'ak* ("*all* in vain," v. 13a). The final large section beginning with *'ak* (vv. 18-27) is divided, like the first (vv. 3-12), into two parts: verses 18-22 and 23-27. The Hebrew phrase *wa'ănî* ("I," vv. 22a, 23a) serves as the division between the two parts. The topic of the first part (vv. 18-22) is the "end" or destiny of the wicked, and the topic of the second (vv. 23-27) is the "end" or destiny of the just psalmist.

The following structure appears: opening statement of faith and scandal (vv. 1-2); the prospering wicked (vv. 3-12); the anguished psalmist seeks a solution (vv. 13-17); the final state of the wicked and of the just (vv. 18-27); summary statement and promise to proclaim God's deeds (v. 28).

Exegetical Analysis

Opening statement of faith and scandal (vv. 1-2)

The psalmist begins by stating the principle that God is good to the pure of heart, that is, protects and rewards them, yet in the very next verse admits to having been scandalized by the experience of the opposite—God is not good to the just. One must therefore interpret the opening verse as the psalmist's present belief in God's trustworthiness, a belief that came through a process of education or discipline. The axiom is repeated in the last verse, thus framing the poem by statements of faith. In between, the psalmist tells us the story of coming to faith from doubt.

The prospering wicked (vv. 3-12)

In verses 3-7, the psalmist *sees* the affluence of those who live evil lives. Their well-fed bodies signify success; trouble touches others but never them; they wear beautiful clothes and exude confidence. In verses 8-11, the psalmist *hears* their malicious words and bullying threats. Verse 9 is a marvelous description of arrogance. They even deny that God has a clue about what is going on (v. 11). Verse 12 notes in exasperation that they take whatever they desire.

For the psalmist, life as a physical and social reality comes from God. When people live healthy and long lives, see their children prosper, have goods and property, and enjoy a good reputation in the community, they can only conclude that God is pleased with them. Thus the prospering wicked are a continual scandal, for they advertise the view that it does not matter how one lives. Might rules, and Yahweh is silent. This is exactly what the wicked conclude: "Is there knowledge in the Most High?" (v. 11*b*).

The anguished psalmist seeks a solution (vv. 13-17)

In contrast to the *many* wicked of verses 3-12, the psalmist must bear alone the bitterness of being punished for loyalty (v. 14). What response can one make to such inequality and divine silence? Verses 15 and 16 express the two options that immediately present themselves, but no sooner are they proposed than the psalmist rejects them as too costly. One possibility is to abandon all restraint and tell the whole community of God's injustice as Job did (cf. Job 15:17), but this is rejected on the grounds that it would scandalize the community (v. 15). A second option is to resolve the problem through reflection and study, but this is rejected as too costly physically and psychically (v. 16). Then, without explanation, another alternative presents itself: Go directly to God by visiting the Temple (v. 17). It is the climax of the series of options. There, "I perceived their end." "End" in Wisdom literature means the outcome in the light of which the whole is evaluated, for example, "Sometimes there is a way that seems to be right, / but in the end it is the way to death" (Prov 16:25; cf. Sir 21:10; Matt 7:13). The "end" will be developed in the next section.

The final state of the wicked and of the just (vv. 18-27)

Resolution of the problem through God's revelation in the Temple takes place in the last section of the poem (vv. 18-27), introduced by the third occurrence of *'ak*. The true situation of the wicked is described in verses 18-22 and the true situation of the just in verses 23-27. The wicked are walking on a slippery slope (v. 18); they can fall to ruin in a moment (vv. 19-20). What happens suddenly, "in a moment," is by definition abnormal and presumably of divine origin. A good parallel is Prov 24:19-20:

Do not fret because of evildoers.
 Do not envy the wicked;
for the evil have no future;
 the lamp of the wicked will go out.

Having no firm hope, the wicked are on the brink of annihilation. The psalmist admits previously not appreciating the precariousness of the wicked, having had, in fact, the understanding of a brute beast. The Hebrew verb "to know" in verse 16 ("understand") and verse 22 ("ignorant") frames the passage.

The second half of the section, verses 23-27, develops the psalmist's realization that God is always there, always at one's side. God's presence permeates verses 23-27, which has at least eleven references to "you." The psalmist, once plagued all day long (v. 14), can say now "you guide me with your counsel" (v. 24a). The statement in verse 24b, "and afterward you will receive me with honor," has intrigued readers. Some understand it as reception into heavenly glory. The Hebrew verb "to receive, to take" can indeed refer to elevation of a righteous person to God's domain. Enoch in Gen 5:24, Elijah in 2 Kgs 2:11-12, and the righteous psalmist in Ps 49:15 are biblical examples. The elevation of Enoch into heaven (itself modeled on nonbiblical accounts of human beings taken up) became a model for any divine rescue. Another interpretation is that the psalmist was brought so low by the experience of injustice that the revelation of God's presence constituted a veritable resurrection to life with God. A third interpretation translates the phrase, "you will receive me with honor," in the sense of bringing me to your divine presence. Perhaps the psalm has deliberately used open-ended language. The psalmist at any rate has learned to trust God, who is never far away: When I am with you, I need nothing more. Even in the face of death, the psalmist trusts (v. 26a); nearness to God is the only good, absence from God, the only evil.

In one sense, the divine visitation does not alter the situation; the wicked are still carefree and the righteous are still afflicted. Rather, the new understanding makes it possible to bear these afflictions, for God is now recognized to be there.

Summary statement and promise to proclaim God's deeds (v. 28)

The last verse (v. 28) restates the axiom of faith that began the poem ("Truly God is good to the upright") but in a more personal way: "but for *me* . . . / *I* have made." One example of the change is that the psalmist who refused to "talk on" *(sippēr)* in verse 15 about "my" injustice now resolves in verse 28*c* "to tell of all *[sippēr] your* [God's] works." The assurance of divine closeness enables the psalmist not simply to endure but to see a new divine reality and declare God's praises.

Theological and Ethical Analysis

To maintain our religious beliefs by disregarding counterindications and repeating traditional formulations is all too easy. The psalmist is someone who came within a hairsbreadth of rejecting God as powerless and uncaring. Living in a world where enemies of God flourish, while the loyal seem plagued by the very God they serve, generated intense frustration. The psalmist asked: Should I rage publicly against the injustice and thereby disturb the faith of others, or should I try to figure it out? Fortunately, the decision to face the Lord directly by going to the Temple brought a life-changing insight: The wicked live precariously; they can fall in a moment; no god stands at their side. But as for me, I am with God who is there even when my path goes through the valley of darkness. That is enough for me.

The poem is for those who are not afraid of noticing what is around them, even if it disturbs their faith. Such clear-sightedness takes in not only the beauties of nature but also its horrors, such as famine, floods, and earthquakes. Willing to look squarely at injustice in individuals and institutions and unmerited suffering, the psalm affirms the Lord's abiding presence. It models how honest observations can become prayer and lead to a more profound relationship with God.

PSALM 74

Literary Analysis

To live trustingly before God is always difficult, but never more so than when basic symbols of faith are destroyed with no assurance they will ever be restored. The faith symbol can vary: an inspiring person who has failed us, a principle that turns out to be false, or, as in this poem, God's dwelling place reduced to ruins by enemies. The Jerusalem Temple symbolized God's presence to Israelites, and its destruction signified, according to ancient ways of thinking, God's withdrawal "in anger" from them. Painful as that withdrawal is to the people, even greater pain and confusion comes from the silence that follows the destruction, for the community has had no word about when the Temple will be restored (vv. 1, 9); perhaps it never will. The community longs for an oracle telling it when the affliction will end. The Hebrew phrase *(lā)neṣāḥ,* "without limit of time, forever," echoes through the poem (vv. 1, 10, 19), and the question "how long?" is repeated twice (vv. 9, 10).

The poem seems to have been written during the period in the sixth century BCE when the Temple lay in ruins; the "impious people" (v. 18) are therefore the Babylonians who destroyed the Temple in 587 BCE. The community lament petitions God to return and rebuild. Similar laments are Pss 44, 77, 80, 83, and 89.

The poem proceeds in three stages, the first stage approximately twice the length of the other two (vv. 1-11, 12-17, 18-23). Part 1 (vv. 1-11) expresses the community's pain and anxiety over the *unlimited* divine punishment and abandonment symbolized by the ruins at the Temple site. Part 2 (vv. 12-17) remembers liturgically God's primordial victory that created the world of which the Temple is a central part, posing the question, will you allow your creation victory to be annulled by a hostile force? Part 3 (vv. 18-23) transposes that question into a triple prayer that God act now (vv. 18-19, 20-21, 22-23).

Exegetical Analysis

Complaint at the unlimited divine anger (vv. 1-11)

The psalmist infers from the destruction of the Temple that God is angry, for ancient peoples customarily ascribed massive afflictions to the gods. The reason might be divine anger at human sins, the inscrutable ways of heaven, or the eclipse of one's personal or national god. What bothers the psalmist, however, is not so much that the Temple has suffered attack, but rather that the people remain without an authoritative word telling them whether God will rebuild it and punish its destroyers. One can bear a temporary set back but not one without a time limit. In antiquity, great afflictions were often accompanied by an oracle or a sign letting the people know how long they would have to suffer. An example in Akkadian literature is an omen text on the capture of the statue of the god Bel: "It is said that after thirty years vengeance will be exercised, and the gods will return to their place" (Roberts 1977, 478). A biblical example of a fixed time of suffering is the seventy-year exile foretold by Jeremiah (Jer 25:11-12; 29:10). Psalms 39:4 and 90:11-12 are also concerned with fixed periods of suffering (see the commentary on those passages). In Ps 74, the absence of oracular assurance might suggest to the people that their God has no power to alleviate the distress or, worse, no longer cares enough about them to do so. Verses 1-11 thus constitute an anxious plea to know how long God will let this shameful situation continue (vv. 1-2). They beg God to march forth as a warrior (v. 3, "direct your steps") and put a stop to the reckless destruction of the holy place.

The opening plea asks whether the destruction of the sacred precincts is a rejection of Israel (v. 1). Divine anger means that God has withdrawn and that the people have been left to their own devices—a dangerous situation, particularly when neighboring states' armies are powerful and there is no indication when divine favor will return.

Verse 2 asks God to remember the intimate bond long ago established between God and Israel. Divine remembering is important in the Bible. In Gen 8:1, God remembered Noah and his entourage and made the flood subside. The psalmist hopes for a similar "remembering." "Tribe of your heritage" means the tribe you possess and further develops the phrase in verse 1, "the sheep of your pasture." The latter phrase means the flock whose care you delegate to no other shepherd, for the sheep are your very own (similarly Pss 95:7 and 100:3).

The mention of Mount Zion in the third clause of verse 2 makes the verse into a tricolon, a three-line verse, the only such in the poem. Its extra length highlights the name "Mount Zion." The sacred mountain can be seen as an integral part of Israel's origins, as in the ancient hymn Exod 15:17-18 (Hebrew words identical to the psalm passage are in italics):

> You brought [Israel] in and planted them *on the mountain of*
> *your own possession,*
> the place, O LORD, that you made your abode,
> the sanctuary, O LORD, that your hands have established.
> The LORD will reign forever and ever.

See also Ps 78:52-55.

In verse 3, the phrase *"Direct your steps* to the perpetual ruins" marks the solemn beginning of a journey like that of Jacob who "lifted up his feet and went" (Gen 29:1, my translation; NRSV: "Jacob went on his journey"; cf. Gen 41:44). Ugaritic literature has a similar formula, "to me let your feet run, to me let your legs race." The stately phrase "direct your steps" is a suitable beginning of the divine march from the southern mountains, like those in Deut 33:2-3; Judg 5:4-5, 20-21; Hab 3, and Ps 68. These ancient poems presuppose that God's mountain dwelling is in the south of Palestine (variously called in the poems Seir, Edom, and Mount Paran). The traditional location of the mountain of God is the Sinai Peninsula, well to the southwest of Palestine, but that identification is no older than the fourth century CE. The ancient poems cited above locate the mountain dwelling directly southeast of Palestine—Seir and Edom—from which God marches forth to rescue Israel. These poems ask God to march forth with the heavenly army (as in Deut 33:3; Judg 5:20), equipped with the weapons of war (sometimes personified as in Hab 3:5; Ps 68:17), to rescue Israel (as in Ps 68:12, 18, 21-23), which is portrayed as "poor" (as in Hab 3:13-14; Ps 68:9-10). God will be victorious and be celebrated in the sanctuary (Deut 33:29; Judg 5:9; Ps 68:24-35; Hab 3:18-19). Psalm 74 does not, however, share the ancient assumption that Yahweh dwells in the southern mountains. Yahweh has evidently transferred his dwelling to a new holy mountain: Zion (Ps 74:2). As an utterly transcendent deity, however, Yahweh "appears" there, "comes" there, and it is for such an appearance that the psalmist prays.

Verses 4-11 depict with great vividness the desecration of the once-beautiful Temple. In verses 4 and 9, the word "signs" ('ôt; NRSV: "emblem") is important, though its meaning is not obvious. NRSV takes the word as referring to military emblems or insignia, but such a meaning does not fit verse 9. A clue to the correct sense is Ps 86:17, "Show me a sign ['ôt] of your favor, / so that those who hate me may see it and be put to shame." The sign is a foretaste of the divine power that will appear fully later. "Sign" in Ps 74:9 has a similar sense: a word from a prophet telling when the divine power will come (or how long the divine affliction will last). But, complains the psalmist, there is no one who can give such an assuring word. "Sign" in verse 4 has the same meaning as in verse 9. The enemy has declared that its own signs (presumably oracles or omens predicting victory) are *the* authentic interpretation of the present situation, proving its gods are triumphant. Part 1 ends with a question: How long will you permit your name to be reviled?

Hymn to God the Creator (vv. 12-17)

Part 2 is a hymn to the God who overcame chaos and brought the world into being. At first reading, the triumphant tone of part 2 seems an abrupt shift from the anxious reflections that concluded part 1. Indeed, several prominent scholars believe the entire section was added later to offset the persistent silence of God. Part 2, however, fits perfectly with ancient thinking about creation and temple building. The description of the primordial battle in verses 13-17 is also found in Isa 51:9-11; Pss 77:16-20; and 89:9-10. Ugaritic literature uses similar language of the great battle between the storm-god and the forces of chaos:

> Did I not crush Sea, the beloved of El?
> Did I not finish off the El's Flood Rabbim?
> Did I not muzzle the dragon?
> I did crush the twisting Serpent,
> Shalyat with its seven heads. (My translation)

In antiquity, creation was often imagined on the model of human activity: building (a house), molding (clay); begetting (offspring), or, as here, conquering the chaotic (or inert) forces that held back order and fertility. The last act of the cosmic combat is the building of the god's palace, which ever thereafter symbolizes the god's supremacy.

In Ps 74:12, the speaker addresses God in hymnic fashion, "my King is from of old, / working salvation [= achieving victory] in the earth," that is, proving yourself king in the heavenly and earthly realms by conquering cosmic enemies. Verses 13-14 list those enemies, and verses 15-17 detail typical creation tasks: organizing the cosmic waters to fertilize the earth (v. 15; cf. Gen 1:6-10; Ps 104:5-9; Prov 3:19-20; 8:27-29), arranging darkness into a beneficial night-day sequence (v. 16; cf. Gen 1:3-4), and demarcating the agricultural year (v. 17; cf. Ps 104:19-23). The opening phrase "God my King" in verse 12a sums up the prayer in a nutshell: I believe you are *my* God and can do all things.

In seeking to persuade God to act, the psalmist appeals to the divine honor: *You* were the one who conquered primordial forces to create the world (of which your Temple is a part). How can you sit idly by while that creative work is dismantled by your enemies? Why do you hesitate to defend your own house and people?

Prayer that God act here and now (vv. 18-23)

The remembrance of the creation victory symbolized by the Temple prompts the psalmist to petition God in a final and formal way. Verse 18 reconnects to the anguish of verse 10 by using its vocabulary: "the enemy," "scoffs," "reviles," and "your name," and links to verse 2 by asking God to remember. The devastating vision of verses 1-11 and the exalted remembrance of the creator God in verses 12-17 are woven together in the final prayer. The prayer repeats three times the ardent wish that God come to the people (vv. 18-19, 20-21, 22-23). Each petition begins with a positive imperative verb ("remember," "have regard for," "rise up") and is brought to completion by a negative second-person singular verb ("do not").

In verse 19, the word "dove" in the sentence, "Do not deliver the soul of your dove to the wild animals" (if a correct reading), has not been satisfactorily explained. Is it an affectionate reference to the king or to the people? "Dove" may simply be a symbol of vulnerability, as birds often are in the Psalms (Pss 11:1; 102:7; 124:7). The several references to "poor" and "needy" (vv. 19, 21) are common in passages about the march from the south (Ps 68:9-10; Hab 3:13-14) and refer to the beleaguered community.

Theological and Ethical Analysis

The psalm is driven by enormous anguish and frustration. The very place where the community gathers to meet their God has been destroyed. Where can the people assemble and meet God? The grandeur of the Temple buildings represented the grandeur of God (Ps 48:12-14; Isa 60–62). Their ruin suggests the eclipse of Yahweh and the rise of another deity. Such conclusions need not be articulated in words; they were already symbolized by the wrecked sanctuary and the exulting enemy.

The psalm is particularly suited to communities whose loyalty to God has created enemies. It is also suitable for communities whose own misdeeds have brought humiliation and misfortune upon them and have nowhere else to turn. The poem allows the community to express freely its frustration and shame and, more important, to channel those negative feelings in a way that deepens their faith in Yahweh. Our God, it confesses, will never delegate the care of us to another "shepherd." Our God has proved to be the only deity by defeating chaotic forces and creating a beautiful world. The people insist that the Lord be their God.

PSALM 75

In the present arrangement of the Psalter, Ps 75 serves as a transition between Pss 74 and 76. All three develop the problem posed in Ps 73: How can the just God allow the wicked to prosper? Psalm 73 finds a solution by entering the sanctuary of God and pondering the destiny of the wicked (v. 17). Psalm 74 then laments the destruction of the sanctuary itself and poses the question of justice from a communal point of view. In response, Pss 75 and 76 show God judging the nations and winning the epochal victory on the holy mountain.

Literary Analysis

Psalm 75 is recognizable as a thanksgiving from its opening line, "We give thanks to you, O God." Giving thanks in the Bible is not simply saying "thank you," but rather publicizing the divine benefit so that others may know and acknowledge the excellence of the benefactor. In this psalm, however, it is not clear for what divine act the singer is giving praise. Instead of the description of the divine act, there is a speech (v. 2, in the first person) in which God judges the wicked (vv. 2-5). In verses 6-8, a human speaker expands the divine speech. Possibly, God could be the speaker even here, because Hebrew style allows sudden shifts in grammatical person from first to third. In verses 9-10 a human speaker responds with joy to the divine speech and resolves to continue the divine act of judgment.

The simplest solution to the problem of the dramatic logic is to assume a liturgical context: Before the gathered community, the divine voice (spoken by an official speaker) utters a judicial condemnation of the wicked of the earth. The second speaker

(vv. 6-10), perhaps the king, rejoices to hear the authoritative voice of the Lord and resolves to act as God's agent carrying out on earth the divine verdict. It is also possible that a liturgical official is the speaker in verses 6-10 and promises in the name of the community that they will carry out divine justice. Precise identification of the human speaker is not essential, however, for the king and the official would speak for the community.

The above interpretation is not universally held. Some scholars are generally reluctant to assign a role to the king except in explicitly royal psalms such as 2, 18, 20, 21, 45, 72, 101, 110, and 144:1-11. It must be remembered, however, that in the Bible the king was responsible for administering justice (e.g., 2 Sam 8:15; 15:4; 1 Kgs 3:28). He was the primary human agent of divine justice, the instrument by which God or the gods ruled the world. It seems reasonable to assume that situation here. Here, then, the psalm records God's words establishing divine justice on earth and the king's joyous and willing acceptance of carrying out that task. The psalm is similar in spirit to that of Ps 101 where the king promises to walk with integrity, employing only the blameless as officials and excluding the wicked, so that he may cut off evildoers from the city of God (Ps 101:8). Two other psalms similarly depict God's judgment of the wicked: Pss 58 and 82.

The outline is as follows: Invitation to the community to praise God (v. 1); God judges the wicked of the world (vv. 2-5); only God can lift up and put down (vv. 6-8); shout of exaltation and vow to carry out divine justice (vv. 9-10).

Exegetical Analysis

Invitation to the community to praise God (v. 1)

The entire assembly is invited to "give thanks," that is, to proclaim publicly what God has done. Such proclamations widen the circle of God's admirers. By giving praise one returns the gracious act that God has done. The next phrase in verse 1, "your name is near," occurs nowhere else in the Hebrew Bible. Some judge it corrupt and emend it (changing only one consonant) to "we call upon your name" on the basis of the Greek and Syriac renderings. Psalm 105:1 has a similar phrase. NRSV retains the Masoretic Text, understanding it, it seems, in an anticipatory sense: your just verdict (v. 2) indicates that your presence (= name) is in the midst of this community. The phrase itself ("Your name is near") has links to similar words in neighboring psalms: "near" in Ps 73:28 and "your name" in Ps 74:7, 10, 18, and 21. The final sentence in verse 1, "People tell of your wondrous deeds," links the community's present thanksgiving with the thanksgiving of others.

God judges the wicked of the world (vv. 2-5)

God appoints a time for judgment and then pronounces a verdict. Judgment in the biblical sense is generally not an impartial verdict to be carried out by someone else, but a "lifting up" of the righteous person or group and a "putting down" of the unrighteous. The judge, God, is the one who carries out the judgment. The exact meaning of "the set time" in verse 2 is hard to determine. Most scholars think of a future event, either the time of universal judgment and redemption or an unspecified intervention that will save the congregation from its present crisis.

An attractive alternative to the above is to translate Hebrew *môʻēd* ("set time") as "assembly," which is the meaning it has in Num 16:2; Job 30:23; Ps 74:4 ("holy place"); Isa 14:13; and in Ugaritic texts. The Hebrew verb translated as "appoint," *lāqah* can also mean "to summon" as in Num 23:11 and 1 Sam 16:11. The line would then read "I will summon the assembly" (so also Dahood in his commentary). The advantage of this rendering is that it preserves the parallelism with the second line: To summon the judicial assembly is to exercise judgment.

In either case, God's act of judgment is a public act, for it makes the earth and its inhabitants "totter." The literal meaning of the verb is "to wave or undulate, to be moved by the wind or the sea." In Ps 46:6 God reveals his presence in the city besieged by enemies: "The nations are in an uproar, the kingdoms totter; / he utters his voice, *the earth totters*" (NRSV: "melts"). God's act—the judgment of the wicked—makes the earth and its inhabitants totter. The quaking of earth is only temporary, for God intervenes before it collapses into primordial chaos.

Who are "the boastful" and "the wicked" judged in verse 4? They are not further identified. A clue to their identity is offered by Pss 58 and 82, which are also about divine judgment. The group judged in Pss 58:1 and 82:1, 6 is "the gods," that is, heavenly beings who were thought to exercise authority over certain human communities on earth. According to Deut 32:8-9, each of the nations has a god assigned to it, but Israel has Yahweh, the Most High.

> [God] fixed the boundaries of the peoples
> according to the number of the gods;
> the LORD's own portion was his people,
> Jacob his allotted share.

Israelite thinkers tended to demote and even dethrone these gods for incompetent and malicious judging (= ruling). Psalm 58 is particularly instructive, for its verses 1-2 condemn these gods, and verses 3-5 mention "the wicked [people]," who evidently are considered the human instruments of the errant heavenly forces. Psalm 82 does not specifically distinguish between superhuman and human agencies, but it does blame the gods for failures of *earthly* justice. The view that heavenly powers influenced human behavior was common in antiquity as is shown by the widespread interest in astrology. A New Testament example of belief in heavenly powers is Eph 6:12: "For our struggle is not against enemies of blood and flesh, but against the rulers, against the authorities, against the cosmic powers of this present darkness, against the spiritual forces of evil in the heavenly places" (cf. Col 1:16). Psalm 75, it seems, presupposes such malevolent authorities in the universe, but prefers to focus on the human agents who further the work of the iniquitous powers in the heavens. Who exactly are these human agents in our psalm? Were they anyone dedicated to evil, or were they specific, for example, kings hostile to Israel? For an answer we must look at the opening words of the divine speech (v. 2).

Verse 2a ("At the set time that I appoint") is unfortunately unclear, as noted above, forcing us to begin where there is some clarity, in verse 2b: " I will judge with equity *(mîšārîm)*." Psalms use *mîšārîm* several times in parallel with "justice, righteousness" *(ṣedeq* or *ṣedāqāh*, e.g., Pss 9:8; 58:1; 99:4) in contexts of making visible and establishing the kingship of God. One can assume that Ps 75:2 likewise reflects a ceremony that celebrates God's kingship over Israel and dethrones or "judges" rival deities or powers. This interpretation is supported by the reference in the next line to the earth tottering, for in Exod 15:15; Ps 46:6; and Nah 1:5; 2:6 the earth and its inhabitants totter in fear at the coming of the Lord.

What happens when God judges with equity? In the similar Pss 58 and 82, God strips the gods and their human agents of their authority to rule over the earth. This psalm does not mention any gods, but only human beings. They are given a general command: not to lift up their horns, that is, act arrogantly. "Lift up" occurs five times. The context of enthronement gives specific meaning to "lift up one's horn": It refers to those who resist the sovereignty of God. Verses 6-7 make it clear that only God can lift up.

Only God can lift up and put down (vv. 6-8)

No human being, no matter how powerful, has the power to lift up or bring down. Hebrew, like English, expresses exaltation and collapse with the spatial metaphors of up and down. These verses perhaps refer to the great empires of the East (Assyria and Babylon) and to Egypt (the wilderness in the south). Even they do not have ultimate power to harm the Lord's people. A play on words occurs in verse 6: One would expect a mention of "the north" after "wilderness" (i.e., east) to round out the four directions. Instead one finds *hārîm*, which can mean both "mountains (to the north)" and "lifting up." Only God can put down and lift up, a phrase that nicely sums up the biblical view of justice. Verse 8 develops the phrase "putting down one" of the previous verse by the metaphor of forcing someone to drink a cup. "Cup of wine" is a metaphor of divine judgment (e.g., Ps 60:3; Isa 51:17;

Jer 25:15, 28), since alcohol takes away one's power to act and makes one reel and stagger.

Shout of exaltation and vow to carry out divine justice (vv. 9-10)

The speaker, perhaps the king, accepts the daunting task with great joy, eager to put God's just decrees into effect to the ends of the earth. Horn is a symbol of strength and power. To cut off the horns of the wicked is to destroy their power to harm others, and to raise the horns is to enhance someone's power and prestige.

Theological and Ethical Analysis

The wondrous act of creating the world also included endowing it with justice; to give thanks for the world is at the same time to give thanks for its justice. The "set time" in the psalm could therefore be any critical time in history: the act of creation, the granting of the Torah to Israel at Sinai, or whenever the holy people or the universe seems near collapse from the injustice of the wicked. At such times, God appears to initiate order. Such an appearance is not simply a restatement of laws but an act that puts down the arrogant and lifts up the lowly. The act of putting down and raising up is what the Bible means by justice.

The holy community of God has a role in carrying out that justice in the world. It too, in its own way, lifts up the righteous lowly and puts down the lofty wicked. It does so by taking on joyously the task of justice. Faith and ethics are an inseparable pair. Like its Lord, the community speaks a word of equity and acts with justice.

PSALM 76

Psalm 74 lamented the destruction of the Temple by enemy armies, and Ps 75 rebuked those enemies. Psalm 76 celebrates the victory over the enemies, which is symbolized by the Temple on Mount Zion. Psalm 77, however, laments the defeat of the Lord's people. The juxtaposition of psalms of celebration and lament suggests that the kingdom of God is not present in its definitive fullness. People must live in a shadowed world and hope for its final coming.

Literary Analysis

Like Pss 46 and 48, this poem is classed as a song of Zion, glorifying the city where the Lord dwells. The singer does so by telling the story of its origins—how the Lord came to dwell on Zion. It happened by a decisive victory over the kings of the earth and (by implication) over their patron gods. That victory demonstrated that Yahweh is sole God in the universe. The city with its glorious buildings memorializes that decisive victory, a symbol of the sole divinity of the Lord and his intent to dwell in Zion, the holy city of Israel. The implication for Israel is that they can encounter the only God in the Temple in the city.

Verses 1-3 make clear that the victory was won in the holy land of Canaan ("Judah" // "Israel") and the divine dwelling established in the holy city of Zion ("Salem" // "Zion"). By mentioning the battle, verse 3 shifts the scene from the dwelling to the act of victory that made that dwelling possible (vv. 4-7). The latter verses are framed by a nearly identical sound pattern in verse 4a (nā'ôr 'attāh, lit. "Glorious are you") and verse 7a ('attāh nôrā', lit. "you are awesome"). Verses 8-10 should be considered part of this section, for God proclaims the freshly won victory to the world; the proclamation functions as the rescue of "the oppressed" (v. 9b). The last section (vv. 11-12) exhorts all to pay worship (in the form of vows of obeisance and gifts) to the God who has outperformed all deities and powers. Honoring the holy city Zion honors the saving God who dwells there.

Exegetical Analysis

The glorification of the city (vv. 1-3)

Verse 1 declares that God is revealed in the holy land of Judah and Israel. As in 1 Kgs 4:20, 25; Ps 114:2; and Jer 23:6, the pair Judah // Israel designates the entire sacred land; it matches the pair Salem // Zion in verse 2. The verb "is known" (v. 1*a*) conveys more than the fact that Yahweh is generally acknowledged as God in these areas, for the same conjugation of the verb in Ps 9:16 describes an act of judgment against the wicked. In Ps 48:3, the same form of the verb refers to the defeat of the enemy kings attacking Zion. In Ps 76:1, God is revealed as a conqueror at Zion; the conquest will be described in verses 3-7.

Other phrases in verses 1-3 fit this interpretation. As in Ps 99:3, the nominal sentence, "great is his name," means that God's authority is acknowledged by the nations. "Abode" and "dwelling place" can mean "tent," which is a venerable and traditional designation of the divine dwelling (e.g., Pss 15:1; 27:5, 6; 61:4; 78:60). That the word "tent" should be used of the Lord's dwelling should occasion no surprise, for the pre-Temple divine dwelling was a tent (NRSV: "Tabernacle" in Exod 25–31). Reference to the tent-dwelling of God is not a vestige of a "nomadic phase" of Israel's history as some scholars suggest. Ugaritic texts, which reflect urban culture, show the high god El living in an elaborate tent structure, containing "seven enclosures, yea eight." The image of tent-dwelling in Ps 76 is a borrowing from traditional iconography.

The Temple is built on the site of the victory over enemies. Verse 3 mentions only the victory as if to suggest the battle was so one-sided that it was not worth mentioning. The Lord sits majestically in his palace after all enemies are defeated. The Temple itself thus is a symbol of the victory of God, bespeaking divine authority and unique divinity. Another Zion psalm, Ps 48:12-14, is explicit about the symbolism of the buildings, for it urges people to

> walk about Zion . . .
> that you may tell the next generation
>   that this [edifice] is . . .
> our God.

The reference to the battle in verse 3 serves as a transition to the next section.

The victory of God (vv. 4-10)

Verses 4-7 describe the battle and victory simply by describing the corpses of the enemies, illustrating how effortlessly the victory was won. Verses 8-10 contain the proclamation of the kingship achieved by the victory. The enemies perished "at your rebuke" (v. 6), a phrase used elsewhere of cosmological victories (Job 26:11; Pss 18:15; 80:16). Verse 8 shifts the perspective to heaven. God rises up in judgment, a phrase that blends military and forensic imagery.

Who are the enemies? Are they historical enemies such as the ninth-century BCE Arameans, the eighth-century BCE Assyrians, or the sixth-century BCE Babylonians? Or are they "mythological," that is, representatives of malevolent heavenly figures or symbols of evil generally? It is probable that the original reference is mythological, that is, a cosmic battle between Yahweh and his enemies in the heavenly world that ends in an acclamation of sovereignty symbolized by the building of a palace. Language of the cosmic myth is used of historical kings' attacks on the Lord's people and sacred city, for earthly enemies were in effect attacking the Lord by attacking the Lord's people and city. The Davidic dynasty was based on the kingship of Yahweh, its patron. The Davidic king's victories reflect the primordial victories of Yahweh. One can readily understand why the charter myth or story meant so much to Israel. When beset by enemies, they confidently called for a renewal of that great victory in primordial time. How could the Lord let anyone defeat them?

In verse 8, God's "judgment" is a part of the victory. In comparable Ugaritic texts, the storm-god Baal expresses his victory in thunder that terrifies the inhabitants of the world (CAT 1.4.vii.27-37). Yahweh is often portrayed in the guise of the storm-god in battle (e.g., Exod 15:1-18; Judg 5; Ps 18 [= 2 Sam 22]). The judgment is the proclamation of his kingship like Baal's proclamation in the Ugaritic texts. The "oppressed of the earth" who receive the proclamation with joy are the people of the Lord.

Verse 10 is corrupt. NRSV translates the Masoretic Text, only adding "your." The text is often emended. This commentary suggests the emendation: "Even wrathful Edom will praise you, / the remnant of Hamath will celebrate your feast." "Celebrate your feast" is based on the Septuagint. Edom was a nation on Israel's southeast and Hamath was a district to the north, between Aleppo and Damascus. In all probability, verse 10 continues the thought of verse 9, for verses 11-12 introduce a new topic, exhorting the nations.

Pay obeisance to the Lord your God (vv. 11-12)

The final verses are a natural conclusion to the poem. Because Jerusalem is the place where Yahweh's victory took place and where it is enshrined, all nations must come there to pay homage. Those summoned are preeminently kings and princes, for Yahweh is superior to their divine patrons. The pilgrimage of the nations is a prominent theme in the Bible (Isa 2:1-4 // Mic 4:1-3; Isa 60–62; 66:20-21).

Theological and Ethical Analysis

As in the other Zion psalms, the sovereignty of the Lord has to be achieved. The Bible imagines it as achieved through defeating rival divine claimants to sovereignty. The common assumption of the ancient Near East was polytheism. There were many gods, among whom certain ones periodically rose to ascendancy by virtue of their deeds. The most frequently mentioned act of ascendancy was military victory, often enough victory over a chaotic monster threatening the stability of the world. That victory was cosmic, that is, it restored the earth to its original orderly state and it made the particular god who did it supreme over the other gods. Often enough, the other gods were portrayed as helpless before the threat. This psalm seems to imagine such a scene. The language of Ps 76 is restrained, evidently removing detail and lessening the narrative suspense of the old myths.

Psalm 76 declares that the victory has been achieved and is celebrated among a particular people. One can have access to the world-stabilizing authority of the Lord in a specific place: Jerusalem. The psalm does not praise God in a generic way; it has in mind a particular deed. Though the deed took place in mythic time, its effect is real and palpable in a particular place and time. Christian readers have imagined that the divine victory culminates in the resurrection of Jesus, which has established a new world. The "site" of the victory is the body of Christ, and its fruits can be glimpsed in the church.

PSALM 77

Psalm 73 pondered the triumph of the wicked and found an answer in the Temple (v. 17). Psalm 74 mourned the destruction of the Temple, and Ps 76 celebrated it as the symbol of the Lord's triumph. Psalm 77 continues the Psalter's alternation of triumph and sorrow by lamenting the silence of God in a crisis. Psalm 78 will declare Mount Zion to be God's own choice and Ps 79 will again lament the destruction of the Temple. To live before God involves shadow and light.

Literary Analysis

The poem is one of the great laments in the Psalter. Most commentators regard it as the lament of an individual because of the first-person references in verses 1-10 such as "my trouble," "my soul" (v. 2) and indications of sleeplessness and depression (vv. 2-4). Interpreting the references as purely private, however, does not comport with the national concerns expressed in the second half of the poem, verses 11-20. The apparent disparity in outlook between the two halves of the poem has not gone unnoticed by commentators, who have proposed three solutions. The most common is to suppose that an individual seeks solace in personal distress by remembering the Lord's fidelity to the entire people in the exodus. A second solution is to suppose that two originally distinct psalms have been combined or that an ancient psalm has been supplemented with verses in the course of transmission. Seybold, for example, suggests that the psalm documents an individual's movement from a crisis of faith to a heightened awareness of the faithful God, like Ps 73. In his view, verse 10 states the psalmist's dilemma ("the right hand of the Most High has changed"), which is resolved by the recital of salvation history in verses 11-20 that renews the psalmist's faith in the "unseen" ways of God (v. 19). Fragments from old hymns were added later, according to Seybold, and, later still, the refrains of verses 3a, 5, and 11. A third solution is that verses 1-10 portray the psalmist as the model sufferer who expresses the nation's plight in terms of personal anguish. Remembering the founding event of the exodus in verses 11-20 brings the sufferer to a deepened faith in God as savior. Jeremiah did something of the sort when he made his inner anguish public in order to instruct the people about their future suffering.

Of the three interpretations, the first is unlikely, for the narrative of public salvation would not relieve a purely personal grief. The second, that verses were gradually added to a document describing a personal journey, properly takes note of the dramatic tensions but gets rid of them prematurely by postulating later additions; it neglects the way the poem itself resolves them. The third view is the most satisfactory. The anguish of the speaker in the opening verses, though quite real, is corporate and representative; it is resolved by recital of Yahweh's primordial act of founding in the liturgy. The speaker may even be the king. Several factors suggest the poem was a unity from the beginning: The number of Hebrew words in each of the two halves (vv. 1-10 and 11-20) is almost identical (73 words in part 1 and 74 words in part 2); 'ĕlōhîm ("God") occurs seven times; verbs of "remembering" occur in both parts with a different set of objects in each half of the poem.

Another indicator of unity is the poem's coherent logic. In the first part, the psalmist cries out to God, refusing all comfort (vv. 1-2). What is the cause of such anguish? It is the cognitive dissonance that comes from remembering a past when God was favorable and experiencing the present when God is absent. The psalmist remembers divine favor (vv. 3-5), steadfast love, and fidelity to promises (vv. 6-10). My misery, says the psalmist, has one root cause: God's attitude toward us has changed (v. 10). In the second part (vv. 11-20), the psalmist remembers again but this time the object of memory is not the absence of God but the act that defeated chaos itself. Recalling those primordial deeds invites God to renew them in this unhappy time.

Exegetical Analysis

The memory of the past and the experience of the present (vv. 1-10)

Verses 1-2 describe insistent prayer, accompanied with loud cries and hands outstretched in prayer. "Aloud" is, literally, "my voice," which seems to be an ellipsis: "[I lift up] my voice." The psalmist in verse 2c, like the patriarch Jacob grieving over the loss of his son Joseph (Gen 37:35; cf. Jer 31:15), refuses comforting alternatives to the bitter pain. It has not been clear up to this point what is bothering the psalmist. Verses 3-6 reveal the problem: the painful realization that God is no longer with the people. Remembering God brings moans and dizziness, for the object of remembering is no longer present. The psalmist's remembering is done in private, for it takes place at night (vv. 2 and 6) as the psalmist suffers from sleeplessness (v. 4a) and communes "with my heart" (v. 6). These mental exertions have, quite understandably, brought the psalmist to depression and hopelessness. Verse 10 summarizes the sufferer's state. "And I say" in verse 10, like the same expression in Job 29:18 ("then I thought") and Ps 95:10 ("and said"), expresses a final decision or conclusion. The shock of verse 10 is that God "has changed." God is not supposed to change. In Mal 3:6, God declares, "For I the LORD do not change; therefore you, O children of Jacob, have not perished." Psalm 89:34 reads "I will not violate my covenant, / or alter the word that went forth from my lips."

Before going on to the second half of the poem, one should note the extraordinary number of references to the Song of the Sea in Exod 15:1-18. Exodus celebrates the great act by which Israel came into existence as a people, and it is that act that the psalmist wishes to remember before God. "Steadfast love" (Ps 77:8) occurs in Exod 15:13; "the right hand" of God (Ps 77:10) alludes to the three-times repeated "right hand" of the Lord in Exod 15:6, 12; the unusual form of the divine name *yāh* ("LORD"; Ps 77:11) occurs also in Exod 15:2; the Hebrew phrase *baqqōdeš*, "is holy" (Ps 77:13) appears also in Exod 15:11; "What god is so great as our God?" (Ps 77:13) is nearly identical to Exod 15:11; the statement in Ps 77:14 that God has declared his might among the peoples seems to allude to Exod 15:14, where "the peoples heard" of the might of Yahweh; the divine name *ʾēl* in Ps 77:14*a* is found also in Exod 15:2; the phrase "who works wonders" (Ps 77:14) appears in Exod 15:11; "redeemed" in Ps 77:15 appears in Exod 15:13; and, most important of all, the enemy of Yahweh in our psalm is personified Sea, who also appears in Exod 15 (though demythologized as the site of the battle rather than the enemy as such).

The liturgical remembrance of the exodus (vv. 11-20)

Four verbs of remembering cluster in the first two verses of the second half of the poem, alerting the reader to the extraordinary importance of remembering. This time the object of the verbs is not, as in the first half of the poem, the present misery of a once-favored people, but the ancient salvation story of the exodus. The "deeds," "wonders" (singular in Hebrew), "work," "mighty deeds" in verses 11-12 all refer to the exodus, which is then described in verses 13-20.

Verses 13-20 describe a single event. NJPS and NAB recognize this by making no stanza divisions. The exodus is told from two perspectives. The earthly perspective is indicated by the mention of historical personages, "the descendants of Jacob and Joseph" (v. 15) and "Moses and Aaron" (v. 20). The heavenly or mythic perspective is indicated by the reference to cosmic waters ("the waters saw you," v. 16*a*). Modern readers know the exodus from the prose accounts in the Pentateuch, which are largely couched in historical language that features Moses and Aaron, Pharaoh, and the people. Poetic accounts, however, such as Exod 15:1-18 and Ps 114, interpret the exodus victory of Yahweh mythically, as a combat myth in which the warrior god defeats the forces of chaos and creates a universe that includes people. The victory establishes the supremacy of the victorious god in the pantheon. Psalm 77 employs the traditional mythic framework and language. Verses 13-15 preface the account of the battle and victory in verses 16-20 by praising the God who performs the "wonder" (*pele* in v. 14*a* is singular in Hebrew), the creation victory that makes Yahweh the only real god in the pantheon. Blending heavenly and earthly perspectives, the verses declare that the victory redeems Jacob and Joseph (v. 15) and announce that fact to the nations and their patron gods (v. 14*b*). Verses 16-19 depict the battle and victory in terms of the storm-god battling the monster Sea. For the combat myth, see the Introduction, "Observations on the Theology in the Psalms: Implied Narratives," in *Psalms 1–72*. The victory itself is told in verse 19 when Yahweh, using the weapons of the Storm God—wind, lightning, thunder, rain—makes a way through Sea, in effect removing Sea's power to keep Yahweh's people from their native land. Israel is freed from Sea's grip to take possession of their land.

The description of the victory highlights two points that would be meaningful to a grieving nation: (1) even in the splendid cosmic victory Yahweh's "footprints" or tracks were not visible (v. 19*b*), a detail of great significance for a people who tended to interpret divine absence as abandonment; (2) the people were led through defeated Sea not by Yahweh personally but by Moses and Aaron (v. 20). Moses and Aaron founded institutions still vital for the people's identity—torah and worship; they can thus still guide the people.

Theological and Ethical Analysis

It was probably a false dichotomy between private and public domains that led to the psalm being categorized as an individual lament. Anyone can feel intense personal anguish over the fate of one's city, nation, or church. The first few verses of the psalm describe intense physical and emotional pain—groans, tears, sleeplessness, inability to communicate with others ("I am so troubled that I cannot speak," v. 4*b*)—and recurrent negative memories. Such symptoms need not arise from private problems alone, but from the realization that God's community is in deep trouble. Moses had to bear the suffering of the people's disobedience when (according to Deut 3:25-29) he could not enter the promised land. Jeremiah and the Second Isaiah anguished over the people's stubbornness. Paul listed his anxieties over the community as proof that his call was authentic (2 Cor 11:28-29).

One's final response to indications that God seems absent from the community cannot, however, be the conclusion that God has departed forever. One may have to pass through a stage of absence, as the speaker does in verses 1-10 of the psalm, but the stage cannot be the final one. Faith and responsibility urge a second step: to remember publicly the divine act that formed the community in the first place in the hope that God will renew it. One hopes that God has not changed. Such proclamation is essential if the community is to survive. It is the mark of true leadership to bring the community back to its foundation. This psalm does just that.

PSALM 78

As if in answer to the community laments of Pss 74 and 77, Ps 78 tells how the community recovered from devastation, graced with a new shrine and a new dynasty. See the opening paragraph of the commentary on the previous psalm for the relation of this poem to the surrounding poems.

Literary Analysis

Psalm 78, like Pss 105, 106, 135, and 136, retells national traditions with a specific goal—in this case to reveal that God's choice of Zion and the Davidic dynasty is the completion of the mighty acts of the exodus. This psalm, second only to Ps 119 in length, challenges modern readers with its subtle reinterpretation of the national story. A schematic outline showing the two parallel narratives contained in the psalm best shows its rhetoric and purpose. In the introduction (vv. 1-11), the speaker promises to reveal the meaning of the national traditions so that hearers might properly respond now and avoid the folly of earlier generations.

First recital	Second recital
Red Sea and wilderness	*From Egypt to Canaan*
(vv. 12-31)	(vv. 40-64)
Gracious act (vv. 12-16)	Gracious act (vv. 40-55)
Rebellion (vv. 17-20)	Rebellion (vv. 56-58)
Divine Anger and Punishment	Divine Anger and Punishment
(manna and quail, vv. 21-31)	(destruction of Shiloh,
	vv. 59-64)
God's readiness to forgive	God's readiness to forgive
and begin anew (vv. 32-39)	and begin anew (vv. 65-72)

The psalm arranges traditions of the exodus and the desert journey into a new pattern: God's gracious act, Israel's rebellion, divine punishment, and divine readiness to forgive and begin anew. Ancient hearers evidently could recognize subtle resetting of familiar traditions.

The speaker claims authority to reveal unnoticed aspects of the tradition and indict Israel (in the person of the Ephraimites) for infidelity (vv. 9-11). Though the speaker is not identified, the language of Ps 78 is reminiscent of the Deuteronomic portrait of Moses in Deut 29:1–30:20 and 32:1-43. According to Deut 18:18-19 (cf. Deut 5:1–6:3), the office of Moses could be passed on to future leaders: "I will raise up for them a prophet like you from among their own people; I will put my words in the mouth of the prophet, who shall speak to them everything that I command." In the name of Moses, the speaker expounds the tradition to all Israel.

The best clue to the date of composition is its message to believe that God has chosen Zion and the dynasty of David as a replacement for the destroyed northern shrine of Shiloh and the northern kingdom. Historically, the capital of Israel, Samaria, was destroyed by the Assyrians in 722 BCE. The reason, according to 2 Kgs 17:7 was "because the people of Israel had sinned against the LORD their God, who had brought them up out of the land of Egypt from under the hand of Pharaoh king of Egypt." Shortly thereafter, according to 2 Chron 30:1-27, King Hezekiah of Judah sought to unite all Israel after the northern collapse:

> O people of Israel, return to the LORD, the God of Abraham, Isaac, and Israel, so that he may turn again to the remnant of you who have escaped from the hand of the kings of Assyria. Do not be like your ancestors and your kindred, who were faithless to the LORD God of their ancestors, so that he made them a desolation, as you see. . . . For the LORD your God is gracious and merciful, and will not turn away his face from you, if you return to him. (vv. 6-7, 9)

Psalm 78 originally seems to have been part of the eighth-century appeal for national unity. It now stands as a perennial appeal to believe in God who acts in new ways.

Exegetical Analysis

I will explain what our history means for you (vv. 1-11)

Formally, the introduction falls into three sections of five bicola each (vv. 1-4, 5-7, and 8-11), which are signaled by the word "ancestors" (vv. 3*b*, 5*c*, 8*a*, which moves its position progressively forward in each section) and by the mention of God's acts concluding each section (vv. 4*cd*, 7*bc*, 11). In verses 1-4, the speaker promises to reveal the true meaning of "the glorious deeds" and "the wonders" of the Lord (v. 4*cd*); in verses 5-7, the speaker reminds the people of the contractual obligations of those deeds ("they should . . . / not forget the works of God"); and in verses 8-11, the speaker cites the Ephraimites as an example of forgetting. "To forget" is characteristic Deuteronomic language for being unfaithful (e.g., Deut 4:9, 23, 31; 6:12). Ephraim was the younger of the two sons of Joseph though blessed first by Jacob (Gen 48:1-20), foreshadowing the prominence of the later tribe Ephraim. In Josh 16 and 17:14-18, the northern tribe Joseph is replaced by two tribes, Ephraim and Manasseh. "Ephraimites" is thus a designation for the northern kingdom.

"Parable" and "dark sayings" (ḥîdôt, v. 2), better translated as "lessons" (cf. NAB, NJPS), occur as a fixed pair also in Ezek 17:2 where they refer to the dealings of Kings Jehoiachin and Zedekiah with foreign kings. In Ezek 17:1-15, the prophet applies the symbolic story to the lives of his hearers. The speaker in Ps 78 intends to interpret history for the present-day needs of the people. Verses 5-7 also make clear that the speaker is giving a homily on the sacred text, for the verses assume the historical acts are not bare facts, but draw the people into a relationship with God (v. 7a, "so that they should set their hope in God"). Good preaching is concrete, and verses 9-11 give an example: the Ephraimites, who were defeated because they lost God's favor. Two defeats in northern history are treated virtually as one: the Philistine destruction of the shrine at Shiloh (eleventh century BCE, Jer 7:12-14) and the destruction of Samaria, the capital of the northern kingdom of Israel in 722 BCE. As will become clear, the psalmist believes that the once-legitimate but destroyed shrine at Shiloh (vv. 54, 59-60) continues in Zion (vv. 67-69), and the once-legitimate but destroyed northern kingdom (v. 67) has been transferred to the Davidic kingdom in Judah (vv. 68-72). Though some commentators take the reference to Ephraim in verses 9-11 simply as Judahite polemic against the northern kingdom, it is much more likely that the psalmist considers the Ephraimites as part of greater Israel and asserts that the defeat does not mean the end of the people. Verse 57 specifies the sin of verse 9 as infidelity leading God to abandon the northern kingdom and Shiloh.

First recital: the Red Sea and the wilderness (vv. 12-40)

In this section, the psalmist recasts the wilderness traditions in order to illustrate how the Lord deals with Israel. Mentioned first is the Lord's gracious act that should invite an openhearted response. When the people rebel, the Lord becomes angry and inflicts punishment. The punishment, however, is not the final stage, for the Lord gives them a second chance. In illustrating the pattern of gracious persistence, the psalmist arranges the traditions differently from the Pentateuch. Among the differences are that the people are led by the cloud and fire *after* they pass through the sea, and the episode of the poisonous quails is given an importance it does not have in the Pentateuch.

The order in Psalm 78	*The same episodes in Exodus–Numbers*
Splitting of the Sea (v. 13)	Exod 14–15
Leading by cloud and fire (v. 14)	Exod 13:21-22; 14:19-24; Num 9:17; 14:14
Water from rock (vv. 15-16)	Exod 17:1-7; Num 20:2-13
Sinful demand for food (vv. 17-20)	Exod 16; Num 11
Manna (vv. 23-24) and quails (vv. 26-29)	Exod 16; Num 11
Poisonous quail (vv. 30-31)	Num 11:33-34

The place names "Egypt" and "fields of Zoan" in verse 12 introduce both recitals (cf. v. 43), thereby underlining their parallelism. "Zoan" (present-day Tanis, Greece) is a town in the eastern Delta, the capital of the twentieth and twenty-first Egyptian dynasties; here it is simply a designation for Egypt. The pattern of gift-sin-punishment-renewal is implicit in the Pentateuch, but the psalm emphasizes it to link the two recitals. As the psalm tells it (vv. 12-16), God "splits" (NRSV: "divided") the sea so they could cross and "splits" the rock so they could drink! The people, however, take the miracle of water completely for granted (v. 20) and demand full meals with meat (implied by "to spread a table"). Such presumption and lack of trust in God (v. 22) brings down wrath. The punishment fits the crime; the people get the "meat" they demanded (vv. 20*d*, 27*a*), but it turns out to be poisonous. The gracious thing—food from God—turns into an instrument of punishment. Yet the Lord relents and offers the people a fresh start.

Second recital: from Egypt to Canaan (vv. 41-64)

This second account is parallel to the first. "In the wilderness," "in the desert" (v. 40) summarizes and concludes the first recital. References to Egypt and Zoan preface both recitals (vv. 12 and 43). The traditions in verses 41-55 follow Exod 15:1-18: A divine attack on the Egyptians is followed by a procession of the victorious Israelites to the mountain of God. The plagues in the psalm are in a series of seven bicola with the killing of the firstborn in the seventh and climactic place. The source of the psalm account seems to be the Yahwist (J) account of the plagues in the Pentateuch. There are some changes, however: Moses and Aaron are not mentioned, and the warrior God acts alone in devastating Egypt and leading the people to the holy mountain. The end of the procession in verse 54, "his holy hill," "the mountain," is not Zion but Shiloh, as is shown by the reference to verse 60. To the psalmist, Shiloh was once a legitimate shrine for Israel, but its legitimacy has been annulled (v. 60) and transferred to Zion (v. 68).

Just as the first gracious deed was followed by rebellion so also the second gracious deed. After being given choice land, the northerners turned away. There is wordplay on Hebrew *hāpak*, "turn back, turn away." In verse 9 it has the sense "were defeated," and in verse 57, it has the sense "were faithless." Like the punishment in the first account, God does not hesitate to make a gracious thing into something bad: The shrine of Shiloh becomes a ruin and symbol of rejection.

Like the first account, the story ends with a fresh offer. Though God destroyed Shiloh and its adherents, another shrine and another dynasty take their places—Zion and David. The late eighth-century BCE destruction of the northern kingdom turned out not to be a tragedy in the end.

Theological and Ethical Analysis

Few psalms seem, on first reading, to be as irrelevant to modern life as Ps 78. It assumes that retelling the story of the exodus will instruct people where God's shrine and royal representative are to be found today. A closer reading shows the psalm is very relevant, however, for its details reveal a God who leads Israel from tyrannous Egypt to a secure land and remains with the people despite their arrogance and obtuseness. God, though ever just (i.e., punishing sin) is also merciful, seemingly unable to abandon the people because of the bond forged at the beginning. Though the people's base actions turned previous gifts—food in the wilderness, a secure land—into something harmful, God found a way to begin again. Furthermore, the poem is deeply concerned with the unity of God's people; no sin however heinous can splinter the people who have a common tradition and have entered into a covenant with their God. God is willing to adapt in order to stay with the people. God's relationship with Jews and Christians has a history with its own crises and turning points. For modern believers to learn from the history is important. Only by knowing it can people today learn how to meet the living God.

PSALM 79

This poem is linked to the preceding poem by its focus on Zion/Jerusalem (v. 1; cf. Ps 78:54, 68), its reference to the people as "Jacob" (v. 7; Ps 78:71), and its metaphor of shepherd for God (v. 13; Ps 78:52-53). It is linked to the following Ps 80 by the image of the Lord as shepherd (v. 13; Ps 80:1), its question "how long?" (v. 5; Ps 80:4), and its mention of the people as scorned by their neighbors (v. 4; Ps 80:6). Nearly every prayer in Book 3 up to this point has been concerned in some way with the Temple.

Literary Analysis

This community lament urges God to avenge the destruction of the Temple and slaughter of the people and to show favor once again. The sixth-century BCE exile is the most suitable context for the poem, for the Temple was destroyed in 586 BCE by the Neo-Babylonian army (2 Kgs 24:18–25:21; 2 Chron 36:11-21;

Jer 39:1-14; 52), and there were mass executions at the time (2 Kgs 25:18-26), though none is recorded as having taken place in Jerusalem. Neighboring populations, especially Edom, took advantage of Judah's weakness. On "Asaph" in the superscription see the note on Ps 50.

NRSV arranges the psalm into four stanzas, which is supported by symmetrical word counts in the paragraphs: stanza 1, verses 1-4 (36 Hebrew words); stanza 2, verses 5-7 (29 Hebrew words); stanza 3, verses 8-10 (36 Hebrew words); stanza 4, verses 11-13 (29 Hebrew words). Stanza 1 describes the destruction of the Temple and defilement of the sacred precincts by unburied corpses; stanza 2 pleads that the divine anger be turned against the perpetrators rather than the victims; stanza 3 appeals to the divine honor for God to provide deliverance; stanza 4 promises the thanksgiving of the people when deliverance comes.

The argument is simple and clear: the slaughter of your saints and defilement of the Temple cries out to heaven for redress. Why then does your anger burn against us rather than the perpetrators who offer you no worship? We are the only ones who will give you praise once you avenge this insult. The points are made in part by repetition of words. The divine name appears once in each section, each time with a different word: "God," "LORD" *(YHWH)*, "God of our salvation," "Lord" *('ădōnāy)*. The word "nations" occurs four times (vv. 1, 6, 10 [twice]), the Hebrew verb *šāpak,* "pour out," occurs three times (vv. 3, 6, 10), and "name" occurs three times (vv. 6, 9 [twice]). Several other words occur twice: "blood," "Jerusalem," "servants," "around (us)," "come," and "taunt." Repetition of these words reinforce the vengeance theme: Do to them as they have done to your honor and your people.

Exegetical Analysis

Depiction of destruction and defilement (vv. 1-4)

The shocking thing is not the devastation and suffering but the insult given to God's house and servants; the perspective here and throughout the psalm is completely theocentric. "Your inheritance" in verse 1 is specific: It is the land that belongs to the Lord. People lived on the land to till it and enjoy its fruits, but the domain remained the Lord's. That pagans now enter it at will is an abomination. Giving the bodies of the faithful to the animals to eat in Ps 79:2, that is, leaving them unburied, is the act of a victor, as in Ezek 29:5; 39:4; Rev 19:21. Unburied corpses make a place unclean (Num 19:11-16) and desecrate the sacred precincts. Leaving bodies unburied (v. 3) is also unnatural, a failure to perform the most basic human duty (Tob 1:17-19). In the Bible, one dies *and is buried.*

The devastation allows neighboring peoples to taunt "Where is their God?" (v. 10). Edom, across the Dead Sea to the south, in fact took advantage of Judah's weakness during the Exile to encroach on its land (Ps 137:7; Ezek 35:5-15; Lam 1:20-22; Obad 10-14). The people of Judah feel shamed. In verses 1-4, the first three verses are tricola, making the bicolon in verse 4 stand out as the conclusion.

Turn your anger against the nations (vv. 5-7)

The question "how long?" is a real question in laments. It means at what point will our affliction end? The same question is asked in Pss 39:4-5; 74:9; and 90:11-12. People assumed that afflictions were sent by the gods for a specific duration and therefore sought to find out their precise length so they could endure them with some equanimity. The word "jealous" in verse 5b refers to the Lord's jealousy over Israel's infatuation with other gods. The psalmist wants God, rather, to consider the sins of the guilty party, those who have devastated God's own house and people. They, not we, are your enemies, for they besmirch your name in the sight of the nations! The phrases "know you" and "call on your name" in verse 6 are essentially synonyms, meaning to worship the Lord alone. The next section will urge God to forgive Israel, for they are the victims of impiety, not the perpetrators of it.

Consider your honor and act! (vv. 8-10)

A tricolon (v. 8) begins the section, which otherwise consists of bicola. As the preceding section urged God to pay attention to the impiety of those who attacked the Lord's house and clients, so this section completes the argument by urging God no longer to remember Israel's sins (v. 8). Verse 8a, "the iniquities of our ancestors," is better translated "our past iniquities" (so the Septuagint, Vulgate, NAB, NJPS), for the people do not deny they have sinned. Their point is rather that their enemies have sinned even more, while they are paying the price for it. Verse 8b asks that divine mercy (personified as a messenger) arrive in God's presence to offset the effect of remembering the people's sins. "Forgive our sins" means not only to wipe the slate clean but also, as often in the Bible, to take away the terrible situation our sins have brought on us. The motive presented to God is that of preserving the divine honor. "Where is their God?" is a taunt, equivalent to saying the Lord is powerless, as in Pss 42:3, 10; 115:2; Joel 2:17; and Mic 7:10. Avenging the blood of your servants will show the nations that God is powerful.

Rescuing us will guarantee that you receive praise (vv. 11-13)

The people are imprisoned, unable to move freely because of their captors, and doomed to die because of the loss of Temple land. Verse 12 asks for God to work vengeance on the taunters. Though the plea has something of the all-too-human instinct to inflict pain on those who have caused pain, it is more than that. According to the psalm's own words, the plea arises chiefly from the desire for justice on earth, that is, that Yahweh be seen by all as the sole powerful deity and that those who refuse to give Yahweh honor be punished. At bottom, the plea is "thy kingdom come."

The first word of the final verse (v. 13) should perhaps not be rendered "then" (though virtually all translations have it). The sentence should read simply "we are your people." The people's thanksgiving is not merely a quid pro quo for the expected rescue. The thanksgiving rather characterizes Yahweh's people as different from the nations: We are the flock of your pasture, the people whom you personally guide (so also Ps 100:3), and so only we can give you fitting praise. Given the down-to-earth humanity of the psalmist, the verse is no doubt a promise of praise for the hoped-for rescue, but not only that. It expresses the essence of Israel, always hoping and ready to praise its God.

Theological and Ethical Analysis

It is easy to read the psalm as a cry for revenge on those who have inflicted terrible damage on the people. Desire for revenge is no doubt present. To claim that revenge is the only, or the chief, motivation overlooks, however, the underlying aim: to redress the grievous wrong that the people are deprived of God's presence because of the destruction of the Temple and deprived of their gift of their land as well. They are being slaughtered and even denied burial. The nations who do this scorn the one powerful God and suffer no consequence. As a result, God is not properly recognized and given due honor.

Many Christians today may feel uncomfortable praying this psalm for the church. They realize that sometimes church members behave in such a way that invites disrespect. Christians should of course be ready to admit their own and the church's sins. Willingness to admit fault does not, however, mean one ceases to regard the church as God's holy people. When the community is attacked and ridiculed by those who reject God, it is appropriate to sing this psalm. The aim ultimately is to make the community a worthy and credible witness to God in the world. It is all too easy to turn the psalm into an expression of revenge. Instead, the prayer seeks a redress of wrongs done to God's honor and rule on earth.

PSALM 80

Psalm 80 uses shepherd imagery of the Lord (v. 1) like the immediately preceding Pss 77:20; 78:52; and 79:13. Like them, it seeks to assuage divine anger, asks "how long?" (Ps 80:4; cf. Ps 79:5), and complains that the people are scorned by their neighbors (Ps 80:7; cf. Ps 79:6).

Literary Analysis

This community lament asks God's help to restore tribes who have suffered enemy attacks. An unusual feature is that the appeal to the Lord "enthroned upon the cherubim" (presumably in the Jerusalem Temple, v. 1) comes from *northern* tribes—Joseph, Ephraim, Manasseh, and Benjamin (the last sometimes reckoned as northern). These tribes separated from Judah and Jerusalem in 922 BCE. The psalm prays for the northern tribes, probably after the fall of Samaria to the Assyrians in 722 BCE. It presumes that Israel is one people, the Jerusalem Temple is the dwelling of the God of all Israel, and the king is the Davidic king. Such views were not only held in the south. The northern prophet Hosea expressed the hope that Israelites would one day seek David their king (Hos 3:5), and King Hezekiah (2 Chron 30:1-12) and King Josiah (2 Chron 35:18; cf. Jeremiah 30–31) appealed to northerners to regard the Temple and the king as their own.

The poem is structured by refrains in verses 3, 7, 14, and 19; verse 14 uses different wording, but it too employs the key Hebrew verb *šûb*, "to turn." The word counts of the sections marked by the refrains show a pattern: in part 1, verses 1-2*a* have nineteen words and verses 4-6 have twenty words; in part 2, verses 8-13 have thirty-eight words and verses 14-18 have forty words. The two sections of part 2 (vv. 8-13, 14-18) have exactly double the number of words as the two sections in part 1 (vv. 1-2*a*, 4-6).

The logic of the psalm is clear: Part 1 asks the Enthroned One in the Temple to come to the aid of the northern tribes suffering the effects of God's anger in becoming objects of ridicule to their neighbors (vv. 1-7). In part 2, verses 8-13 narrate the founding event that is called into question by the crisis. In this psalm, the founding event is the exodus and conquest. It is imagined metaphorically as the transplanting of a vine. To recite the founding event in a community lament is equivalently to ask God: Will you allow someone to destroy what you have founded? The second section of part 2 (vv. 14-18) contains the petition, which is couched in negative terms (destroy the enemies) and positive terms (protect the vine and the one you have chosen).

Exegetical Analysis

Petition and first refrain: come to our rescue, O Enthroned One (vv. 1-3)

God is invoked as Shepherd, a divine title also found in Gen 48:15; 49:24; Pss 23:1; 28:9; Isa 40:11; Ezek 34:15; and John 10:1-18. Like other ancient Near Eastern kings, the Israelite king was called a shepherd (2 Sam 5:2; 1 Chron 11:2; Ps 78:71). Some texts (e.g., Ezek 34:8) contrast fallible human shepherds with the trustworthy divine shepherd. The invocation thus contains an implicit plea: Rescue your very own flock! As is clear from Deut 33:2; Pss 50:2; and 94:1 (and from Ps 80:1*bc*), the verb "shine forth" invites God to appear with the luminosity proper to a god and to march out as a warrior, armed with brilliant light, to fight for the troubled tribes. Though the nature of the crisis is not known for certain, it could well have been Assyrian attacks on the northern kingdom leading to the destruction of Samaria in 722 BCE. The superscription in the Septuagint, in fact, mentions the Assyrian crisis.

The refrain in verse 3 asks that God restore us (lit. "cause us to return"), an expression that can have the specific meaning of return from exile (1 Kgs 8:34; Jer 27:22). A shining face is a face brightened by a smile that welcomes and provides blessings (cf. Ps 4:6 and especially Num 6:24-26); the opposite of a shining face is a hidden face (e.g., Pss 10:11; 13:1; 30:7).

First complaint and second refrain (vv. 4-7)

"How long?" is a real question (as in Pss 39:4-5; 74:9; 90:11-12): How long will the present wrath of God last? People assumed that serious afflictions were sent by God for a specific time and naturally sought to know their duration. It is difficult to bear an affliction if one has no idea when it will end. In verse 5, the reference to tears plays on the normal idiom of giving someone food to eat and water to drink (as in 1 Sam 30:11; Prov 25:21; 2 Chron 28:15). In Jer 9:15 (cf. 23:15) God is "feeding this people with wormwood, and giving them poisonous water to drink." Here, the poet uses the idiom to accuse God of punishing people instead of nourishing them. Their weakness elicits scorn and ridicule from their neighbors, a statement designed to stir God to action on behalf of the divine honor. The refrain asks God to grant victory. The phrase, "that we may be saved," has a military nuance, as in Num 10:9; Deut 33:29; and Ps 18:3.

The transplanting of the vine from Egypt to Canaan (vv. 8-13)

Essential to community laments is a recital of the divine act that established the world and the people Israel. Though recitals can take many forms, each is tailored to the purpose of the lament. In Ps 74, for example, the community remembers the day of creation, when the Temple was built, in order to ask God to rebuild it; Ps 77 remembers the exodus, which is told both in historic and cosmic form: exodus from Egypt and Yahweh's victory over Sea. Though Ps 80 begins traditionally enough with the exodus ("brought out," v. 8a) and the conquest ("drove out the nations," v. 8b), the poem takes an original direction by comparing Israel to a vine. The metaphor is unusual but not without parallel. In Exod 15:17, Israel is planted. Ps 44:2 tells how God "drove out the nations, / but them you planted" (the same verb as in Ps 80:15). In Jer 2:21; 6:9; and Hos 10:1, Israel is a vine. In Ezek 17:1-6 the great eagle (the Lord) takes a seed, plants it, and watches it become a vine with branches turning toward him. In Ezek 17:22-24, a sprig from a lofty cedar is transplanted to the mountain height of Israel where it becomes a great cedar, sheltering birds and towering over other trees. Ezekiel 19:10-14 is the best example, however, where a vine is transplanted to Canaan and its strongest stem becomes a ruler's scepter. Psalm 80:17 also associates the ruler with the vine. Isaiah speaks of Israel as a vine-yard rather than a vine in 5:1-7 and 27:2-6. In the New Testament, John 15:4-5 places the image of Israel as a vine within an "I am" saying, "Just as the branch cannot bear fruit by itself unless it abides in the vine, neither can you unless you abide in me. I am the vine, you are the branches."

In Ps 80, the transplanted vine is deeply rooted, reaches lofty heights, and spreads abroad to the ends of the earth (vv. 8-11). The language is mythic rather than literally geographic. "The mighty cedars" (v. 10b) is literally "the cedars of El (God)." Some scholars see here a reference to the sacred garden that was part of the Temple complex in Jerusalem. Though "sea" and "river" can sometimes refer to the Mediterranean and the Euphrates (the boundaries of the Davidic Empire), they here refer to the outer limits of the universe, the cosmic waters surrounding the disk of earth (as in Jonah 2:3; Zech 9:10). What has caused the destruction of this world-filling vine? Verses 12-13 lay the blame squarely on God, who has deliberately broken down the walls of the vineyard to let in predators.

Petition: protect the vine and your chosen one. Third and fourth refrain (vv. 14-19)

Verse 14, though different in wording from the refrains in verses 3, 7, and 19, functions as the third refrain, summing up the preceding verses in a prayerful way. Its variant wording and cli-mactic position call attention to itself. Its three imperative verbs, "turn again," "see," "have regard," also occur in the description of God's noticing the people's misery in Exod 2:23–4:31 and God's forgiveness of their apostasy in chapters 32–34. "Turn again" occurs in Exod 32:12 ("Turn from your fierce wrath"); "see" occurs in Exod 2:25; 3:7; 4:31; and 34:10; "have regard" occurs in 3:16 and 4:31. The petition "look down from heaven" (Pss 33:13; 102:19; Isa 63:15) assumes that God dwells in heaven and looks down upon the prayers uttered in the Temple. Solomon's great prayer at the dedication of the Temple in 1 Kgs 8 has the same perspective: "Hear the plea of your servant and of your people Israel when they pray toward this place; O hear in heaven your dwelling place; heed and forgive" (v. 30). The claim is that the mere sight of the devastated vine will move God to intervene (Ps 80:14-16). Verse 17 mentions the king for the first time in the poem. Ezekiel 19:10-14 likewise associates the transplanted vine with the king. Some assume that the people Israel is meant here, but the association of king and Temple is more appropriate, for the Temple was the palace of the king's patron god. The divine patron watched over the dynasty.

NRSV's translation of verses 17-18 is too wooden: "the one whom you have made strong for yourself" is better rendered "chosen as your own"; "give us life" is better rendered "give us the means of survival." The section offers a series of motives for God to act: Only you are powerful enough to help (v. 14); it is *your* vine (v. 15); your enemies have desecrated your handiwork (v. 16); it was you who chose the king (v. 17); if you enable us to survive, we will be your people (v. 18). Once again, the refrain sums up the preceding section.

Theological and Ethical Analysis

When trouble comes to a community, people often turn to their own affairs as an escape. At least one can control one's personal and family life. Trouble has come to the northern kingdom at a particular moment in their history: Their capital city has been destroyed, and the tribes are dispersed. The singer does not turn away, feeling an obligation to pray for them all. What is the singer's strategy? How does one persuade God to help the people? Instead of presenting an argument, the singer parades a series of images before the reader: a shepherd, the divine face smiling in welcome, feeding people with tears, and a vine transplanted from Egypt to Canaan. These images largely make the argument. As Shepherd of Israel, the Lord can never forget his flock, will smile upon the people in accord with the ancient blessing (Num 6:25), will no longer feed the people with tears but with bread, and will see to it that the vine is protected.

The psalm invites people today to stay with their community, praying for its needs especially when times are bad. It further invites pray-ers to look confidently at the ancient symbols of their faith and believe that God will honor the promises inherent in them. Several important symbols have already been mentioned in the poem: the shepherd, the vine, the feeding in the wilderness, God's face smiling in acceptance. Christians will see new dimensions in these and even add new symbols to the list: the cross, the fish, the handshake of peace, bread and the cup, the book. Though the symbols are not guarantees, they inspire and unify the community. Moreover, they contain a pledge and promise that God will be there especially in time of need.

PSALM 81

Literary Analysis

Psalm 81, like Ps 50, summons the people to a liturgy celebrating the Lord enthroned as king. Though some doubt the unity of a psalm that begins with an invitation to celebrate a great deed of the Lord (vv. 1-5b) and ends with confronting the people with their sins and those of their ancestors (vv. 5c-16), the liturgical situation is a sufficient explanation. The psalm recalls the rebellion and punishment of the first hearers only to impress upon the present hearers their need to obey God's commands now. The psalm does not denounce so much as challenge the congregation to respond to the living Lord.

Rituals enabled the Israelite community to experience the exodus. Some ancient narratives of the exodus had liturgical responses built into them. Exodus 12:43–13:6, for example, mandates rituals for the Passover lamb, unleavened bread, and consecration of the firstborn so that subsequent generations could experience the event. Exodus 19:16-19 alludes to rites by which later congregations might enact the Sinai theophany (allusions to rituals are in italics).

On the morning of the third day there was thunder and lightning, as well as a thick cloud on the mountain, and a *blast of a trumpet* so loud that all the people who were in the camp trembled. Moses brought the people out of the camp to meet God. They took their stand at the foot of the mountain. Now Mount Sinai was wrapped in smoke, because the LORD had descended upon it in *fire; the* smoke went up *like the smoke of a kiln,* while the whole mountain shook violently. As the *blast of the trumpet* grew louder and louder, Moses would speak and God would answer him in thunder.

The theophany could, it seems, be reenacted by a trumpet blast (Ps 81:3a) representing the thunder of the storm theophany; by fire representing lightning (cf. Ps 50:3); and by smoke ("from a kiln") representing a storm cloud. The rites need not have been elaborate; they could have consisted of a few simple gestures. The psalm seems to reflect a ceremony in which Israel encountered the God of the exodus and affirmed its loyalty.

The call to worship (vv. 1-5b), spoken by the officiant, is followed by a divine speech in the first person (vv. 5c-16). The speech uses single incidents to signify the entire exodus, the movement from Egypt to Canaan. The exodus included a constitutive command (the first commandment, vv. 9-10a) that is repeated to the present congregation, successors of the first generation.

Formal indicators of structure can be helpful in understanding the poem: "the God of Jacob" in verse 4b repeats the same phrase in verse 1b; "the land of Egypt" in verse 10b echoes verse 5b. "Hear, O my people" in verse 8a points ahead to "But my people did not listen (hear)" in verse 11a and "O that my people would listen" in verse 13a. Names for Israel (Israel, Jacob, Joseph) appear seven times. It is also helpful to notice transitional phrases. Though scholars differ on the point, verse 5a, "he made it a decree in Joseph," seems to be a transition from the invitational verses to historical recital. Verse 4 bases the invitation to celebrate the feast in the stipulations of pentateuchal law ("statute" and "ordinance"). "I tested you" (v. 7c) is a transition from historical narrative to the liturgical confrontation in verses 8-10. "Open your mouth" (v. 10c) is a transition to the divine desire to give Israel everything.

COMMENTARY

Exegetical Analysis

Call to worship (vv. 1-5b)

Despite its seriousness, the feast is marked by joy and music. A tambourine consisted of small bronze cymbals four to six inches in diameter that were shaken together. A lyre, used to accompany singing, was a portable rectangular instrument with two arms, sometimes of unequal length and curved, joined at the top by a crosspiece. Its strings were approximately the same length. A harp was a stringed instrument, though its precise shape is not certain. The term "festal day" could be applied to any of the three annual pilgrimage feasts: Passover, Weeks, and Tabernacles. In this psalm, the feast is probably Tabernacles, which, according to Lev 23:33-43, was characterized by public rejoicing that memorialized the exodus. Though some suggest verse 5a, "he made it a decree in Joseph," is not parallel to the preceding verse 4 (rather anticipating the commandment in verse 9), it is most natural to take verses 4-5a as parallel statements. The three words "statute," "ordinance," and "decree" do not merely mandate a festival but command Israel's recommitment to God in the festival. Feasts were established so that Israel might encounter its Lord.

The divine voice challenges Israel to live up to its original commitment (vv. 5c-16)

The speaker quotes a strange speech, that is, communicates a divine oracle. Verse 5c, "I hear a voice I had not known" (lit. "I hear [šāmaʿ] a language I did not know [yādaʿ]"), is puzzling. The most frequently attested idiom for knowing a language is "to hear a language" (Gen 11:7, "to understand speech"; Deut 28:49, "to understand a language"). Jeremiah 5:15ef ("a nation whose language you do not know [yādaʿ], / nor can you understand [šāmaʿ] what they say") uses the verb "to know" exactly as does Ps 81.

The alternation of second and third person pronouns helps unify the section. The first part of the speech (vv. 6-10) refers to Israel in the second-person singular, and the second part (vv. 11-16) refers to Israel in the third-person singular. Exceptionally, verse 6 also refers to Israel in the third-person singular. In the Masoretic Text, the final verse (16) refers to Israel in the third person in colon A and in the second person in colon B. The blending of grammatical persons in verse 16 brings the two parts of the speech together. NRSV makes all the grammatical persons in verses 6 and 16 second person for the sake of clarity.

Though the events referred to appear in the books of Exodus and Numbers, Ps 81 interprets them differently. To describe the liberation of the Hebrew slaves ("I relieved your shoulder of the burden," v. 6a), the psalm uses language similar to Isa 9:4; 10:27; and 14:25. One important difference from the account in Exodus should be noted. In Exodus, the rescue itself from Pharaoh's dominion does not make them the Lord's people. They have to go to Sinai, where they are invited to give their assent to the Lord's offer to be their God: "You have seen what I did to the Egyptians. . . . Now therefore, if you obey my voice and keep my covenant, you shall be my treasured possession out of all the peoples" (Exod 19:4-5). Psalm 81, on the contrary, compresses the events. It assumes the Hebrews became the Lord's people at the moment they were freed from slavery.

Verse 7a, "in distress you called, and I rescued you," condenses and interprets Israel's experience in the wilderness. The phrase does not refer to one specific event, but to the period when the Lord became Israel's God. Verse 7bc condenses matters further: the Lord "answers" the people at Sinai and scrutinizes their conduct in the wilderness. The "secret place [sēter] of thunder" is Mount Sinai where God appeared in thunder (Exod 19:16, 18; 20:18). Psalm 18:11 uses the word "secret place" for the storm theophany: "[the Lord] made darkness his covering [sēter] around him, / his canopy thick clouds dark with water." In Exod 17:1-7 and Num 20:2-13, Israel tests God by doubting whether God can quench their thirst in the wilderness. Here, differently, God tests Israel by scrutinizing their conduct to see whether it is wicked or righteous. Such scrutiny is entirely appropriate. It is concerned with Israel's obedience to the first commandment, which is quoted in verses 9-10 immediately after the mention of testing.

Though some scholars are uncomfortable with the placement of verse 10c ("open your mouth wide and I will fill it") and relocate it after verse 5c or verse 7, it makes good sense in its present position. At Meribah in Exod 17:1-7 and Num 20:2-13, the people doubted that the Lord could give food and water to the people in the desert. They doubted the Lord's power. In Ps 81:10c, "open your mouth" expresses lordship over all powers. To allow the Lord to feed them in the wilderness is equivalently to accept the Lord as their God.

Verses 11-16 tell their story concisely. The first generation did not listen to God's voice and did not follow God's instructions to attack Canaan from the south (Num 14 and Deut 1:19–2:15). With poetic justice, the people were left to follow their own hearts (Ps 81:12), embarking on a self-willed campaign with disastrous results. If the people had listened, that is, acted as the Lord's people, the Lord would have acted as their God, subduing their enemies and feeding them. Alas, it was never to be, and the first generation did not enter the land. The journey stalled for forty years until the first generation died out.

The undertone of divine passion and jealousy is unmistakable. The Lord is a disappointed lover in verses 13-16:

> O that my people would listen to me, . . .
> I would quickly subdue their enemies. . . .
> I would feed you.

The yearning tone was already set in verse 8b, "O Israel, if you would but listen to me!" The final verse (v. 16) echoes and transposes the pentateuchal phrase "land of milk and honey" to "milk of the wheat" (NRSV: "finest of the wheat") and "honey from the rock."

Theological and Ethical Analysis

Rituals enable a community to experience the founding moment. Exodus 12:43–13:6, for example, is a text that makes it possible for Jews today to celebrate the exodus. Psalm 81 (and 50 and 95) enables the holy community to experience again the founding event of the exodus and recommit itself to its Lord. In few other psalms is God's passion for the people so prominent as in Ps 81. Divine desire is on display especially in verses 8 and 13-16. The psalm narrates the historical failure so that the invitation in it may be heard today. It is not so much a command as it is an invitation to hear, to pay attention to, a familiar voice. The verb "to hear" occurs four times. Turn to me in order to flourish, says God, so much is at stake in our relationship. The contemporaneity of the liturgy allows the two perspectives, past failure and present passion, to be held at the same time. Israel only becomes truly itself when it encounters the Lord on Mount Zion.

PSALM 82

Literary Analysis

Psalms 50 and 73–83 are attributed to Asaph, a musician employed by David and Solomon (1 Chron 6:39; 2 Chron 5:12). Like Ps 29, and to a lesser extent Pss 58 and 75, this psalm is set in the assembly of the gods. As is widely recognized, Israel came only gradually to a "theoretical" monotheism that affirmed belief in one god and the denial of divinity and even existence to other gods. At an earlier stage Israel operated with the assumption that each nation had its own god or gods who ruled it under the supreme rule of the Most High, Yahweh. A good statement of the monotheism of an earlier stage is Deut 32:8-9:

> When the Most High apportioned the nations,
> when he divided humankind,
> he fixed the boundaries of the peoples
> according to the number of the gods;
> [but Yahweh's] own portion was his people,
> Jacob his allotted share.

Psalm 82 tells the story of the dethronement of the so-called gods.

The divine assembly, which is so prominent in Ps 82, also appears in such texts as 1 Kgs 22:19-22; Isa 6; and 40:1-9. In these texts, Yahweh, the Most High, rules unchallenged over a thoroughly obedient court. Like any earthly royal court, courtiers perform their duties according to a strict hierarchy. In Ps 82, the assembly of the gods has been summoned by Yahweh, the Most High God, to stand trial. (This section of the Psalter, the so-called Elohistic Psalter, Pss 42–83, generally prefers the divine name 'ĕlōhîm, "God," to YHWH, "the LORD.") God finds the heavenly beings guilty of failure to meet their responsibilities of governing the world justly. Their punishment is mortality, that is, loss of divine status and expulsion from heaven. Though it is not said, one may assume the Most High takes over their responsibilities and will henceforth rule all nations directly. A variant of this judgment scene is found in Ps 58.

The vivid mythology in the psalm may surprise readers who assume that mythology characterizes Canaanite religious literature, whereas history characterizes biblical literature. It is a mistake, however, to make a dichotomous distinction between history and myth in the ancient Near East and to suppose that biblical writers did not employ the language and imagery of the day for their God. Does the psalm reflect a particular myth? It may refer to the revolt of a member of the heavenly assembly against the high god that led to the rebel being cast out of heaven. Such a myth seems to be fragmentarily preserved in Gen 6:1-2; Isa 14:12-21; and Ezek 28:1-19.

Exegetical Analysis

The trial in the assembly (vv. 1-5)

God rises from the throne ("God has taken his place") in the midst of the assembly to question the accused and pronounce judgment. The parallel verb, "he holds judgment," makes clear the event is a legal trial that includes questioning (vv. 2-4) and a verdict (vv. 6-7). Verses 2-4 constitute a single charge, for verses 3-4 describe the duties that the gods have failed to carry out. The defining duties of the deities are presented in the form of imperatives ("Give justice to the weak. . . . / maintain the right"). The gods did not carry out the duties of governing the earth entrusted to them.

Roles that in modern legal procedures are assigned to two different officials—the prosecutor who questions and the judge who decides—are combined into one in this trial. God is both prosecutor and judge, gathering the evidence, examining the defendants (v. 2), stating the laws that have been violated (vv. 3-4), and announcing the verdict (vv. 6-7).

"How long?" (v. 2) implies "for too long," as in Exod 10:3 and Ps 74:10. Biblical judging was often conceived as deciding *between* righteous and unrighteous claimants. The questions in verse 2 presume a conflict (wicked versus righteous); justice is achieved by upholding the right of aggrieved members of society against their enemies. The gods are charged with not coming to the aid of the aggrieved innocent.

As noted, verses 3-4 define the standard of justice. The language of protecting the poor is traditional (e.g., Lev 19:15; Deut 24:14; Isa 11:4). These are the "laws" that the gods are accused of neglecting. No less than six terms are used to describe the poor. The terms are here virtually synonymous; the accumulation conveys a sense of gross malfeasance. There are nonetheless distinctive terms in the cluster: An "orphan" is a fatherless minor who is not a member of a household and therefore lacks the support and protection of "the house of the father"; the "destitute" and the "needy" are economically poor; the other terms refer to those afflicted by others without the means of defending themselves.

Lacking knowledge and walking in darkness (v. 5) describe the culpably negligent gods; they cannot mount a credible defense against the divine judge. The verse could have been uttered by the divine prosecutor; it may also be the psalmist's description of them. The shaking of the foundations (v. 5c) is a sign of a great crisis, for when God blesses and protects, the world stands firm (Pss 46:5, 6; 93:1; 96:10).

The verdict (vv. 6-7)

The Most High pronounces the gods guilty and expels them from heaven. No longer gods, they will one day die like human beings. To be a god is to be immortal; to be human is to be mortal.

Prayer for justice on earth (v. 8)

Those who have suffered from the gods' malfeasance plead that the Lord personally take charge of the earth. The prayer is an instance of the familiar biblical tension between the already and the not yet. Though the powers have been dethroned in the heavenly world, people on earth do not yet enjoy the fruits of victory but must pray for its realization.

Theological and Ethical Analysis

To live as a person of faith is to experience cognitive dissonance. One must live in the large gap between what one's faith holds and what one's experience reports. The world so often seems ruled by sinister currents and forces that are larger than any individual. Racial prejudice, the degradation of women, the exploitation of children, and the limitless cruelty of war are difficult to blame fully on particular persons or groups. It seems rather that individual racists and exploiters have tapped into an evil that was always there. A persistent evil haunts the journey of the human race through the ages. It is simply there: "For the mystery of lawlessness is already at work, but only until the one who now restrains it is removed" (2 Thess 2:7). The believer must live with this evil.

This prayer is for those times when that massive evil touches ourselves and our world. The mythology of the psalm should pose no problem. It puts in mythic terms a reality—God's governance and the persistence of evil—that is simply beyond any human words, historical or mythic. The psalm affirms that God is not indifferent to evil and that judgment on wickedness has been pronounced. It invites people to pray to the God of justice.

PSALM 83

Literary Analysis

This community lament complains that the nations are conspiring to wipe out Israel and to silence the mention of its God, Yahweh. In no one period did all the nations mentioned in the psalm threaten Israel. Moreover, the tenth nation mentioned, Assyria, was so powerful as not to need allies. The number ten in the Bible can designate completeness, as in the ten antediluvian figures of Gen 5, and the "ten times" in Gen 31:7; Num 14:22; and Job 19:3. Accordingly, many scholars rightly view the nations as symbolic of all countries and empires who wish Israel annihilated. In the psalmist's eyes, the nations' hostility is religious as well as political, for it aims to wipe out remembrance of the Lord (Ps 83:4, 12, 18). Thus the appeal to the Lord's honor: Will you let your people be destroyed so that your name will nevermore be uttered?

The logic of the poem is simple. Verse 1 is the opening plea, verses 2-8 contain the complaint (a conspiracy against Israel), and verses 9-18 are the petition that Yahweh definitively vanquish enemies (vv. 9-12) by the weapons of storm (vv. 13-17), so that once again your name may be exalted on earth (v. 18). The allusions to past victories in verses 9-12 are taken from Judg 4–8. The divine names add up to seven: "God" (vv. 1 [twice], 12, 13), "LORD" (vv. 16, 18), and "Most High" (v. 18); the opening and closing verse each contain two divine names. The careful placement of the divine name and the number of its occurrences underline the centrality of God in the poem.

Several periods have been proposed for the psalm's composition. Some suggest the psalm reflects events recorded in 1 Macc 5 (ca. 160 BCE). Others propose earlier dates in the postexilic period. The mention of the eighth-century BCE empire Assyria (v. 8), however, is a strong argument against a postexilic date, for the great hostile empire for early Second Temple Judaism was Babylon, not Assyria. If the psalm were composed in the exilic or postexilic period, one would expect Babylon to be named as the great enemy. The most likely date of composition, therefore, is the period between the entry of Assyria into the west (730s BCE) and the rise of Babylon (620s BCE).

Exegetical Analysis

Take action, Lord, for enemies attack your people and your name (vv. 1-8)

The massing enemies (vv. 2-8) and God's attack (vv. 9-18) constitute a single scene. The hostile nations in verses 6-8 are portrayed in the larger-than-life mythic language of the combat myth in which the storm-god battles hostile Sea. Examples of such mythic language are Ps 46:6-11 and Isa 17:12-14. A sense of the battle may be gained from Isa 17:12-13, which uses more heightened language than Ps 83:13 for the same scene:

> Ah, the thunder of many peoples,
> > they thunder like the thundering of the sea!
> Ah, the roar of nations,
> > they roar like the roaring of mighty waters!
> The nations roar like the roaring of many waters,
> > but he will rebuke them, and they will flee far away,
> chased like chaff on the mountains before the wind
> > and whirling dust before the storm.

The ten nations in verses 3-8 act in perfect accord. Citing the speech of conspirators (v. 4) is a common rhetorical device to highlight their arrogance as in Exod 1:10, Ps 2:3, and Prov 1:11-14. "The tents of Edom" (v. 6) refers to the inhabitants of Edom who live in tents; their territory was south of the Dead Sea on the border of Judah. The land was under Israelite control except in the late ninth and late eighth centuries BCE, after which it came under the rule of Assyria, like Moab (east of the Dead Sea, north of the Arnon) and Ammon (east of the Jordan). The Ishmaelites were nomads (Gen 37:25; 1 Chron 27:30) related to the Edomites (Gen 36). The Hagrites were a people who fought the tribes of Reuben and Manasseh and eventually submitted to Saul; their territory was east of Gilead (1 Chron 5:10, 19-20). Gebal is a region southeast of the Dead Sea in the mountains of Seir near Petra. Amalek refers to a people dispossessed by Israel in Exod 17:8-16; they disappear from the historical record after the time of David (1 Sam 15; 30:13-25). Assyria is the Neo-Assyrian Empire (935–612 BCE) that conquered the northern kingdom of Israel in 722 BCE and thereafter harassed Judah. Though the Transjordanian nations of Moab, Ammon, and Edom came under Assyrian rule in the eighth and seventh centuries BCE and were popularly associated with the great empire, the other groups were not. The listing of the nations is cumulative, like the listing of enemies in Ezek 38–39, designating all enemies of the Lord's people.

Show your enemies that you are supreme (vv. 9-18)

The historical events in verses 10-12 are mentioned in Judg 4–8. Midian was a confederation of desert tribes sometimes in alliance with Israel (Exod 2–4; 18) and other times at war with them (Num 25–31); God raised up the hero Gideon to defeat them (Judg 6–8). En-dor was about three miles from Mount Tabor. Oreb and Zeeb were renowned Midianite captains slain by Ephraimites (Judg 7:25; 8:3). Zebah and Zalmunna were kings of Midian killed by Gideon (Judg 8:4-21). The psalm takes the holy wars against Canaanites and Midianites as paradigms of what the Lord should do now. Verses 13-15 beseech the Storm God to pursue the enemies with wind and lightning to make them flee in every direction like chaff before wind. A good example of the Lord acting as Storm God is Judg 5:4-5:

> "LORD, when you went out from Seir,
>   when you marched from the region of Edom,
>   the earth trembled,

and the heavens poured,
the clouds indeed poured water.
The mountains quaked before the LORD, the One of Sinai,
before the LORD, the God of Israel."

"Whirling dust" is stirred up by the storm wind as in Isa 17:13, cited earlier. "Fire" and "flame" in verse 14 refer to lightning as a weapon as in Ps 18:12, "Out of the brightness before him / there broke through his clouds / hailstones and coals of fire" (cf. Pss 29:7; 50:3). The "shame" of the nations (vv. 16-17) is the shame of those who once boasted in their strength. Defeat will teach the nations they cannot silence the name of God. They will be forced to confess (v. 18) that the Lord is "Most High," a divine title conveying supremacy over the other "gods" (of the nations).

Theological and Ethical Analysis

The military metaphors of the psalm must be translated into modern terms. The psalmist's hostility toward the ten nations is not based merely on political considerations. The nations are bent on destroying Israel's corporate witness to the one true God (vv. 4, 12). It is important to note that the psalm leaves the defense and its timetable entirely in the hands of God. It does not lose sight of the purpose of divine intervention: that the Lord's glory be acknowledged by human beings. The poet chooses the most power-oriented image of the Lord available in the Bible: the Storm God with wind, thunder, and lightning pursuing enemies as they flee to the far corners of the earth. The result of the victory is worldwide acknowledgment that Yahweh is supreme.

Can a plea for violent intervention be Christian prayer? Yes, for basically the psalm is a prayer for the introduction of divine rule in the world, for "the reign of God." It presumes that God has chosen a specific people in the world—Israel—and that Israel is vulnerable to attacks from those who rebel against the Lord. Instead of advocating reliance on human resources, the psalmist entrusts the people's entire security to the Lord, powerful and just. Though this psalm uses the language of war to express divine power, the Bible elsewhere finds other expressions for the same purpose, for example, the wisdom and prosperity of the holy people that show forth divine favor.

PSALM 84

Literary Analysis

Psalm 84 is usually classed as a Song of Zion like Pss 46, 48, 76, and 122 on the grounds that it declares happy those who dwell in the Temple (vv. 4, 10) and speaks of the pilgrimage to Zion (vv. 5-7). It is, to be sure, about Zion, but more exactly about longing for the Temple rather than dwelling in it. Like Pss 42–43 and 63, it appears to have been sung by those away from the sacred precincts. Longing for God is underscored by the seven occurrences of the divine name "God" (*'ĕlōhîm*) and the seven occurrences of the divine name "the LORD" *(YHWH)*. The title "O LORD of hosts" begins and ends the poem (vv. 1*b*, 12*a*) with two other occurrences in between (vv. 3, 8). According to the poem, being with the Lord in the Temple is the highest good, and the journey to that place is of the greatest significance.

The dramatic movement of the poem is not entirely clear, partly because of textual uncertainties in verses 5-7. Verses 1-4 are, on formal grounds, a unit, for "O LORD of hosts" in verse 3 echoes the phrase in verse 1, and the declaration in verse 4, "happy are those," pronounced over those actually *in* the Temple, contrasts with the immediately following "happy are those" (v. 5*a*), which is pronounced over those *on the way* to the Temple. Verses 5-7 deal with the journey to the Temple. Verses 8-9 are a prayer that God bless the king, who had an important role in the liturgy. Verses 10-12 are an expression of longing for the Temple, matching in sentiment the opening verses 1-4. Though it is possible to understand the psalm as three different moments (vv. 1-4, planning the journey; vv. 5-7, the journey; vv. 8-12, the arrival), it is better perhaps to take the whole poem as an expression of longing and to view the prayer as uttered from afar as one approaches the Temple.

Exegetical Analysis

How I long for your house, O Lord (vv. 1-4)

The section expresses longing by asserting the attractiveness of the Temple, the desires of the pray-er, and the image of the bird finding a nest. "Lovely" has the meaning "beloved" as in Isa 5:1 and Deut 33:12, connoting attractiveness rather than beauty in an abstract sense. "LORD of hosts" is a traditional divine title that refers to Yahweh as undisputed lord of the inhabitants of heaven. The Hebrew word translated "soul" *(nepeš)* denotes the throat area, the moist and breathing part of the body, which gives rise to the meaning of "life" or "soul." The whole person is filled with longing, as in Ps 42:1-2*b*,

> As a deer longs for flowing streams,
>   so my soul longs for you, O God.
> My soul thirsts for God,
>   for the living God.

Birds ("sparrow" and "swallow" in v. 3) are proverbially vulnerable animals that often are forced to flee from their "place" or home, as in Isa 16:2, "Like fluttering birds, / like scattered nestlings, so are the daughters of Moab / at the fords of the Arnon" (cf. Ps 11:1; Prov 27:8). A bird fleeing its nest is a symbol of defenselessness. The phrase "where she may lay her young" (v. 3*c*) is a poetic embellishment of the images "home" and "nest"; the phrase does not mean (contrary to NRSV) that the bird makes its nest on the altar (bird nests would not be allowed on altars). Verses 3-4 are elliptical, making paraphrase necessary: as even a (homeless) bird finds a home to lay its young, so I will find my true home by your altar. "Finds" (v. 3*a*) here has the nuance of reaching a place, as in 1 Sam 23:17 and Isa 10:10. Since "altar" is a metonymy for the Temple, the meaning of the verses is that my natural place is in your Temple.

Fortunate are those whom you bring to Zion (vv. 5-7)

As if in contrast to the happy situation of those actually in the house of God, the poet declares happy all those "whose strength is in you" (v. 5*a*), which means the same as "who trust in you" (v. 12*b*). Despite the obscurity (and probable corruption) of verse 5*b* ("in whose heart are the highways to Zion"), it seems that the section describes a pilgrimage through a valley (v. 6*a*) and a journey from one place to another in order to see God in Zion (v. 7). Evidently, water is provided to the pilgrims in the dry places they pass through, as in Isa 43:20 ("I give water in the wilderness, / rivers in the desert, / to give drink to my chosen people") and Isa 44:3. "The valley of Baca" is otherwise unknown; the phrase, "go from strength to strength," is puzzling (though it has become an English idiom). It is taken by some as "from rampart to rampart," that is, the passage through the outer and inner gates of Jerusalem (NJPS). All that can safely be said is that the psalmist is part of a group making their way to one of the three major festivals, Passover, Pentecost, or Booths.

Prayer to look favorably on the king (vv. 8-9)

A petition formula occurs for the first time in the poem, and the petition is for the king. "To look on the face" means to show favor. "Shield" is a symbol for a king, as in this translation of Ps 89:18: "Surely our shield is the LORD, surely our king is the Holy One of Israel" (my translation). The king, the regent of Yahweh, was responsible for the house of his patron deity and thus was prayed for by visitors to the Temple.

Acknowledgment of the favor to be found in the house of the Lord (vv. 10-12)

Like the ardent exile of Pss 42–43, the psalmist longs for the sacred precincts, declaring in hyperbolic terms that one day there is better than a thousand anywhere else and that being on the way to the Temple is better than being inside the tent of sinners. Why? In the Temple the Lord bestows every gift to those who walk in righteousness.

Theological and Ethical Analysis

The Bible honors holy longing as well as peaceful possession. Those scholars who classify this psalm as a Song of Zion are right in their classification, but it is a Zion longed for rather than possessed. In the concrete thought of the Psalter, God dwells in Zion at the center of the universe. Only in Zion are peace and justice definitively to be found; beyond that center danger lurks. Someday, the peace of the center will reach the margins, but until it does those living away from the divine presence must express their holy desires to be in the sacred precincts. The psalmist is on the way to Zion and rejoices to be traveling with others to the center where God is. Traveling to Zion became a metaphor for the Christian life, as in John Bunyan's classic *The Pilgrim's Progress,* depicting Christian's journey from the city of destruction to the heavenly city.

PSALM 85

Literary Analysis

Community laments remember in the liturgy a particular act of God in the hope that God will renew that act in the present crisis. The ancient act remembered in Ps 85 is an act of forgiveness. As God forgave us in the past, may God do again today. Some disagreement exists concerning how to interpret the verbs in the perfect tense in verses 1-3: Do they describe past divine acts as the basis of a new intervention, or do they refer to hoped-for future events? With most scholars, this commentary takes the verbs as referring to past deeds. Though verbs in the perfect tense can be "precative" (praying that something take place in the future) or "prophetic" (announcing a future act as already having taken place), the conventions of the genre of thanksgiving strongly suggest they refer to the past.

When was the poem composed? The prayer is uttered by an exiled people, for the phrase "restore the fortunes of" is used frequently for the return of exiled people to their land (e.g., Deut 30:3; Jer 29:14; 31:23; Ezek 29:14; Amos 9:14). Hence, the psalm was composed either during the late eighth-century BCE exile in the northern kingdom (see Hos 6:11) or, more likely, during the sixth-century BCE exile of Judah.

The paragraphs reflect the dramatic logic. O God, you once acted on behalf of your beleaguered people (vv. 1-3); do the same for us now (vv. 4-7). We await your intervention (vv. 8-13). God's past intervention is named as "restoring the fortunes of Jacob" (v. 1) and forgiveness. Essentially, the two phrases mean the same thing, for to return the people from exile is to undo or "forgive" the effects of sin.

Several devices provide coherence and lend a note of urgency to the prayer. There are seven occurrences of the divine name: "LORD" (four times), "God" *('ĕlōhîm),* "God" *(hā'ēl),* and "you" (v. *6a,* independent pronoun). Other repeated words are "land," "salvation," and "righteousness." The verb *šûb,* variously rendered as "restore," "pardon," "again," and "turn," occurs five times.

Exegetical Analysis

You forgave your people in the past (vv. 1-3)

The phrase "restored the fortunes" (v. 1*b*) can refer to returning a people to its land (Jer 29:14; 30:18). More generally, it means bettering the condition of a person (Job 42:10) or a group (Lam 2:14; Ezek 39:25). The psalm focuses on God's attitude (cf. the words "favorable," "forgave," "withdrew . . . wrath," "turned from . . . anger") because it is interested in the change in

God's attitude (from anger to mercy) symbolized by the act of rescue. In the genre of community lament, the speaker asks God to renew the ancient deed. You once forgave your people in the sense of canceling the effects of their sin. Do so again.

May God end the period of wrath and revive us! (vv. 4-7)

Arguments are presented to persuade God to turn favorably to the people. Verse 5, reflecting the common view that divine anger had a predetermined time span (see commentary at Pss 39:4; 90:11-12), is a plea that it not last indefinitely. God is invoked with titles and appeals suggesting previous deliverances, "God of our salvation," "revive us again," "your steadfast love." The fixed pair "steadfast love" and "salvation" in verse 7 is the first of six such fixed pairs: "salvation" and "glory" in verse 9, "steadfast love" and "faithfulness" in verse 10a, "righteousness" and "peace" in verse 10b, "faithfulness" and "righteousness" in verse 11, "good" and "increase" in verse 12. Paired virtues are traditional for describing divine presence and activity and used to great effect in the next section. The psalm personifies virtues as engaging in actions of meeting and reconciliation: Glory dwells in a land where it did not previously; virtues meet and kiss; one virtue springs up from earth presumably to meet another looking down from heaven.

The Lord promises to bring prosperity back to the people (vv. 8-13)

"Let me hear what God the LORD will speak" (v. 8a) introduces an oracle. Numbers 9:8 is an example of such an oracle: "Moses spoke to them, 'Wait, so that I may hear what the LORD will command concerning you.'" In Ps 85:8b the oracle is favorable; God will indeed give "peace." The blessing of peace is expressed through the six word pairs in verses 9-12. The blessings will not come, however, without openness on the part of those who received them; they must be faithful (vv. 8c and 9a). Despite NRSV, it is best to take verse 9b in strict parallelism with the preceding colon: "surely his . . . glory may dwell in our land." In Exod 24:16 and 40:35, the glory of the Lord dwells in the ark of the covenant; here it dwells in the land, or better, in the earth. One should not miss the strong agricultural references: "Land" is repeated four times; in verse 11 "faithfulness" springs up (like a plant) from the ground, while "righteousness" looks down (presumably in the form of rain) from heaven; "what is good" in verse 12*a* refers to produce of the earth, as is clear from the parallelism. It is indeed possible that the promise of peace refers to the restoration of fertility rather than to military victory. Verse 10 contains a striking metaphor for the return of divine blessing: The blessings are royal courtiers meeting each other after a long absence and, with exquisite courtesy, greeting and kissing one another. Verse 3 portrays one virtue, righteousness, as a majordomo clearing the way for the procession of the Lord returning to the people.

Theological and Ethical Analysis

Community laments remember liturgically a past divine intervention so that God will renew it. This psalm does not specify the past intervention (was it the return from sixth-century BCE exile?), characterizing it only as an act of mercy that turned the tide of Jacob's fortunes: May God renew that mercy today! Alas, the current relationship is marked by "wrath," that is, divine absence leaving the land infertile and the people impoverished. Israel's survival depended on the land, and the people looked to God to make it fertile and keep it safe from usurpers. The prayer thus prays for survival, "will you not revive us again?" (v. 6*a*). Imagining God as a great potentate, the psalmist views divine outreach as heavenly courtiers sent on a mission of reconciliation.

Psalm 85 is a prayer for people numbed by adverse circumstances and habituated to loss and destruction. It enables them to imagine a better state and shows them the God who has the power to give life. Loss or destruction of the land is not what God intends. The text reveals a God who wants the people to enjoy the fruits of the land. Land, it need hardly be said, is a metaphor for life and sufficiency.

PSALM 86

Literary Analysis

This individual lament carefully establishes a relationship between the sufferer and the Lord (vv. 1-13) before giving voice to a specific request for rescue (vv. 14-17). The language of verses 1-7 is general rather than specific; it mentions no enemies and, instead of asking to be saved, asks rather to be closer to God. Verses 8-13 are equally general: You, my God, are unique and powerful (vv. 8-10); teach me your ways, I will revere you, for I have experienced your help in the past (vv. 11-13). Only on the basis of a firm relationship with God, it seems, can the psalmist make the specific request mentioned in verses 14-17.

The above analysis suggests the following structure: opening petition that the Lord become the patron of the psalmist (vv. 1-7); confession of the unique power of the Lord and the psalmist's desire to be a client (vv. 8-13); complaint and petition (vv. 14-17).

Exegetical Analysis

Opening petition that the Lord become the patron of the psalmist (vv. 1-7)

"Give ear, O LORD" and "answer me" in verses 6-7 repeat verse 1, signaling to the reader that the first section is complete. The language makes clear that the psalmist at this stage in the prayer is primarily concerned with exploring and strengthening the client-patron relationship rather than requesting a rescue. The vocabulary is general rather than specific. "Poor and needy" is a phrase for anyone in need of God's help, as in Pss 35:10; 37:14; and 40:17. "Preserve my life" (v. 2a) is a general petition, as in Pss 97:10 and 121:7. "All day long" in verse 3b means "continually." "Day of my trouble" in verse 7a is an idiom for "anytime I am in danger," as in Gen 35:3; Ps 20:1; and Jer 16:19. Most telling is the fact that no specific enemy is named. The reason for God to act is simply that the psalmist is poor (v. 1*b*), trusting (v. 3), and cries to God incessantly (v. 3). These expressions are concrete ways of saying "you are my God." The specific request for rescue will be made in verses 14-17, after the psalmist reminds God of their prior relationship.

Describing oneself as "poor and needy" (v. 1*b*) is itself a claim on God's mercy, for it is an affront to God that there are people who worship God and who are not enjoying the goods of creation. God is named twenty-two times, an indication of the intensity of the psalmist's feelings of loyalty. The listing of God's attributes in verse 5 matches the confession in verse 15. Such confessions are relatively rare in the Hebrew Bible (notable examples are Exod 33:19; 34:6; Num 14:18), which generally prefers to describe divine deeds rather than list divine attributes. Significantly, the psalmist focuses on God's mercy and readiness to forgive. The essence of the relationship to God is nicely caught in verse 7 in the paired verbs "to call" and "to answer," for the word pair expresses both tenderness and authority, as in Isa 65:12*c* (cf. Isa 65:24).

> When I called, you did not answer,
>   when I spoke, you did not listen,
> but you did what was evil in my sight,
>   and chose what I did not delight in.

Confession of the unique power of the Lord and the psalmist's desire to be a client (vv. 8-13)

Tributes and petitions (vv. 1-7) are a way of naming the Lord as patron God. Verses 8-13 show another way in which the psalmist first acknowledges the incomparability of Yahweh among the gods (vv. 8-10) and then asks to be among those who revere such a God (vv. 11-13). Biblical statements concerning the incomparability of the Lord praise great acts, such as the victory over Pharaoh's army,

"Who is like you, O LORD, among the gods?
  Who is like you, majestic in holiness,
  awesome in splendor, doing wonders?" (Exod 15:11).

Israel affirmed that Yahweh became supreme among the other members of the divine assembly by doing something no other "god" could do.

"Way" and "walk" (v. 11) are metaphors for conduct. Verse 11c is best translated: "Turn my heart to this one thing . . . to fear your name!" The form of the verb is found only here in the Bible. Support for the translation comes from the parallel verse and the root meaning of the verb, "to be one, to be the only one" (Kraus 1988–89). "I give thanks to you" (v. 12a) expresses the intent to make a thanksgiving offering for past instances of steadfast love, which are symbolized as deliverances from Sheol.

Complaint and petition (vv. 14-17)

Up to this point, the psalm has concentrated on the relationship to God. Now it turns to the psalmist's immediate problem: attacks by "the insolent" and "a band of ruffians" unmindful of God (v. 14). Verse 15 lists attributes of God (like v. 5), which function like a plea, for they set up the expectation that God will aid the psalmist who is poor and needy. Verse 16bc proposes implicit motives for God to act: "your servant" implies previous service, "the child of your serving girl" implies longtime dependence. The final petition asks for a sign that rescue will be granted. When rescue takes place, enemies will see to their shame that their plans have been foiled. Even more than rescue, the psalmist desires to be seen as a friend of the Lord.

Theological and Ethical Analysis

The psalmist desires more than anything else to enter into a relationship with the living and gracious Lord, profoundly aware that the relationship is not between equals. It is nonetheless characterized by dialogue, even if the dialogue is marked by need in the one partner and generosity in the other. Instead of using an abstract word like "relationship," the author uses pairs of verbs in which need and grace are both present, for example, "preserve my life for I am devoted to you" (v. 2*a*), "I call on you, for you will answer me" (v. 7) The poet is proud to be the servant of such a Lord. Unusual for psalms, the poet cites phrases from ancient confessions (vv. 5 and 15) to praise God's mercy and elicit divine mercy. Only when the relationship is established, and everyone knows it, does the poet ask for a specific favor to demonstrate God's intent to save. The psalmist does not try to force the divine hand, content to be known as a friend of God.

It is refreshing to find a psalm that is careful not to view God primarily in transactional terms. Prior to all specific needs is the need for God's friendship. Desire for God is built into the human heart. Saint Augustine stated the human orientation to God in the memorable opening paragraph of *The Confessions,* "you have made us and drawn us to yourself, and our heart is unquiet until it rests in you" (WSA, *The Confessions,* I/1). Psalm 86 translates that observation into prayer.

PSALM 87

Literary Analysis

Psalm 87 is a Song of Zion like Pss 46, 48, 76, 84, and 122, and is one of the psalms credited in the superscription to the Korahite guild of Temple singers. Many scholars judge it to be textually damaged. A few believe the verses are sound but in the wrong sequence.

The Hebrew text, however, is probably not corrupt, for the psalm can be read easily enough, and the Septuagint reflects the same text. The problem rather seems to be elliptical logic. The psalm seems to presuppose familiarity with ceremonies and concepts well known to its first readers but later forgotten. It is clear, however, that the psalm is a Song of Zion, which means that the conventions of the genre can help to interpret the poem.

Motifs of the Zion Songs appear in Ps 87: God's choosing Zion (v. 2, cf. Ps 78:67-69; Zech 1:17), the founding (v. 1) and establishing (v. 5) of Zion, the mentions of the nations (v. 4, cf. Pss 2, 48, 76), and life-giving waters (v. 7, cf. Ps 46:4; Ezek 47).

The placement of this Korahite psalm near the end of Book 3 of the Psalter may be intentional. As Erich Zenger (2000) has observed, Korahite Pss 42–49 open Book 2 (Pss 42–72) and Korahite Pss 84–88 close Book 3 (Pss 73–89). Books 2 and 3 begin with Korahite psalms expressing ardent longing for Zion (Pss 42–43, 84), continue with laments over the absence of God (Pss 44, 85), and conclude by celebrating Yahweh's presence in Zion (Pss 46, 48, 87). These Korahite psalms appear to be arranged according to a pattern of longing, lament, and presence. It may well be that Ps 87 was placed in its present site to complete the pattern.

Following the first two verses, which serve as introduction, Ps 87 has a concentric structure.

> A "of you" *(bāk)*, verse 3
>   B "there" *(sam)*, verse 4
>   C "in it" *(bāh)*, verse 5
>   B' "there" *(sam)*, verse 6
> A' "in you" *(bāk)*, verse 7.

Both verses 3 and 7 refer to songs and dances of praise.

The psalm states that Yahweh has chosen one place in which to dwell and encounter Israel and the world: Mount Zion. Divine choice has made the mountain an appropriate site for celebrating rituals ("Glorious things are spoken of you," verse 3*a*, "singers and dancers," v. 7). The nations acknowledge ("know," v. 4*a*) the supremacy of Yahweh among the gods and make a pilgrimage to Zion ("there," v. 4), bringing the exiles who are told they are fully children of Zion ("born there," v. 6). Singers and dancers proclaim that Zion is the center of the world and its life (v. 7).

Exegetical Analysis

The Lord has chosen Zion (vv. 1-3)

A holy site is holy because God chooses it. The verbs "he founded" (v. 1), "loves" (v. 2), and "establish" (v. 5c) express the divine choice of Zion. "Loves" here has the meaning "chooses," as in Deut 4:37; 10:15; Ps 78:68; and Isa 41:8. "To love more than all" is an idiom for choosing as in Gen 37:3, 4; 2 Chron 11:21; and Esth 2:17. "Glorious things" (v. 3) refers to the hymns of the court ceremonies that take place in the city of God, as in Pss 48:1 ("Great is the LORD and greatly to be praised / in the city of our God") and 76:1a ("In Judah God is known" = confessed and praised). The phrase "city of God" occurs in the Psalter only in Zion Songs (Pss 46:4; 48:1, 8). Verse 3 parallels verse 7, which is also about praising Zion.

Zion, city of Israel and the nations (vv. 4-6)

In verse 4, the place names have a symbolic value. "Rahab" (Egypt) to the southwest of Palestine and "Babylon" to the east represent all the powers that harassed Israel from the tenth century BCE forward. "Philistia," occupying the southern coastlands of Palestine, was a persistent enemy from the twelfth to the seventh centuries BCE. "Tyre" was one of the two important Phoenician cities. "Cush" is the name of Ethiopia far to the south. Neither Tyre nor Ethiopia were remembered as enemies in the biblical tradition.

Among the many uncertainties, the more important are: (1) how are the nations in verse 4 to be interpreted: the lands where Judahites were exiled or the nations on pilgrimage to Zion, as in Isa 2:1-4 and Zech 2:10-11? (2) what is the meaning of "was born there"? Supporting the view that they are simply the lands where many of the exiles now live is the pejorative designation for Rahab (Egypt). In mythology, Rahab is the chaos monster defeated by Yahweh (Ps 89:10; Job 9:13; 26:12; Isa 51:9); Isa 30:7 identifies it with Egypt. Calling Egypt by the name of a chaos monster suggests the psalmist has a hostile attitude to all the nations and does not envision them on pilgrimage to Zion. On the other hand, there is support for the view that the nations are on pilgrimage to Zion. The phrase "those who know me" (v. 4*a*) means those acknowledging me as their God (as in 1 Kgs 8:43; 1 Chron 28:9; Isa 43:10). The above interpretations are not mutually exclusive, however. Isaiah 40–66 (esp. chs. 60–62) depict the nations escorting the exiles back to Zion as they themselves bring gifts acknowledging their submission to the supreme Lord.

The phrase "this one was born there" occurs only in this psalm (vv. 4, 5, 6). Though the antecedent of "this one" in verse 4 is not given, one can suppose that it refers to each individual in the crowd of returnees. An uncertainty is the meaning of "here." Does it refer to a foreign land or Zion? To judge from the similar usage in verses 5 and 6 ("in it" and "there"), it refers to Zion. It is possible, however, that "there" means a particular foreign country. In the latter case, the verse denies that birth in a foreign country prevents one from calling Zion mother; every Israelite is a child of Zion. As was stated above with regard to the nations in verse 4, both meanings can be true here as well.

The metaphor of Woman Zion as mother of her children is found also in Isa 40–66. In the Babylonian destruction in the early sixth century BCE, Zion is said to lose her husband and children. When her fortunes change and restoration takes place, Woman Zion regains her husband and children:

> Sing, O barren one who did not bear. . . .
> For the children of the desolate woman will be more
>   than the children of her that is married, says the LORD. (Isa 54:1)

"For the LORD has called you / like a wife forsaken and grieved in spirit" (Isa 54:6). This psalm celebrates a kind of Deutero-Isaian restoration using the conventions of the Zion Song genre.

Singers and dancers celebrate the restoration (v. 7)

As noted already, verse 7 says the same thing as verse 3, mentioning the celebration and giving a hint of the theme of the songs.

"All my springs are in you" is a quote from a triumphal song; it refers to Jerusalem as the center of the earth's fertility. Psalm 46:4*a* is a good parallel: "There is a river whose streams make glad the city of God." Jerusalem actually had only a modest spring, the Gihon and shafts to it are still visible today. More than a geographical locale, Jerusalem, the city of God, was the source of all fertility. According to Gen 2:10-13, "a river flows out of Eden to water the garden, and from there it divides and becomes four branches. . . . The name of the second river is Gihon; it is the one that flows around the whole land of Cush." Isaiah 33:21 speaks of Zion, "there *[šām]* the LORD in majesty will be for us / a place of broad rivers and streams." In Ezekiel, "rivers" has a cosmic sense, as it does in the Ugaritic religious texts. Ezekiel 47 foresees a blissful future when waters issue from the Temple to become a mighty river that makes fertile even the bitter waters of the Dead Sea. Such is the topic of the songs sung at the rebirth of Zion and of Israel.

Theological and Ethical Analysis

Ancient readers were sufficiently familiar with Zion Songs so that poets could use allusions without explanations. Modern readers find such poems too elliptical and must turn to more complete examples of the genre to supplement the sparse statements of Ps 87. Even so, difficulties remain.

The psalm celebrates God's gracious dwelling in a particular place to offer hospitality to Israel and the nations. Zion becomes a center of restorative justice where former oppressors of the holy people learn to recognize the supremacy of Israel's God, Yahweh. Seeing evidence of that supremacy, they journey to the place where this God dwells on earth for the purpose of encountering Israel and the nations. As tokens of fealty, the nations bring the scattered children of Zion. The children hear reassuring words that their physical absence has not made them aliens; they will inherit with the native children. The psalm uses the category of spatial holiness, but it does not allow space to determine divine presence.

The psalm was written to celebrate the homecoming in the sixth century BCE and was used for further homecomings. Such homecomings were understood to complete the ingathering that undid the effects of the exile. They exemplify the great centripetal force of the holy city. Reciting the psalm will make Christians appreciate the profound attraction that the holy city continues to exert in Judaism. For Christians, Zion symbolizes the place where God's glory resides on earth—the body of Christ. The psalm can thus be understood to exalt the church as the place where the diverse peoples of the earth find a home. In a further stage in symbolism, Zion is heavenly Jerusalem, the final homeland overriding merely human boundaries:

> But you have come to Mount Zion and to the city of the living God, the heavenly Jerusalem, and to innumerable angels in festal gathering, and to the assembly of the firstborn who are enrolled in heaven, and to God the judge of all, and to the spirits of the righteous made perfect, and to Jesus, the mediator of a new covenant, and to the sprinkled blood that speaks a better word than the blood of Abel. (Heb 12:22-24)

PSALM 88

Literary Analysis

Psalm 88 is the most anguished and least hopeful lament in the Psalter. At the very brink of death, the sufferer prays to be heard (vv. 1-2, 9, 13), describing with great bitterness how it feels to die and accusing God of abandonment. The tone is bleak, as befits someone sensing life slipping away; completely lacking are the expressions of trust and hope of rescue characterizing normal laments. Another customary theme of the genre of lament is absent: personal enemies. In a sense, the enemy is God who is held responsible for all the horrors that wrack the dying individual. The poem complains against God rather than enemies: Can one trust the God who inflicts this horrible death?

There are three sections (vv. 1-9*a*, 9*b*-12, 13-18), each intro-duced by a verb of crying and mention of the Lord (vv. 1*a*, 9*b*, 13*a*). Sections 1 and 3 are parallel in theme (personal suffering) and in syntactic structure. Section 1 is introduced by verses 1-2 "O LORD . . . / I cry out. . . . / let my prayer come before you" and concluded by verse 8, "you have caused my companions to shun me." It forms a parallel to section 3, which is introduced by verse 13, "But I, O LORD, cry out. . . . / my prayer comes before you," and con-cluded by verse 18, "You have caused friend and neighbor to shun me." Between the two frames, section 2 (vv. 9*b*-12) develops its own theme (God's withdrawal) and its own rhetoric (six questions).

The argument is developed progressively in the sections. Section 1 (vv. 1-9*a*) asks only one thing: that the complaint of a dying wretch be heard. Modern readers need to keep in mind that death was regarded not just as cessation of life, but as a transference to a place of shadowy existence in the underworld. The psalmist com-plains of going to a forsaken and chaotic place, avoided by friends as a corpse that defiles (v. 8). Section 2 (vv. 9*b*-12) provides a motive for God to act: I am about to enter a place where you do no wonders and receive no praise. The implication: Rescue me now while I am in a place where you can heal and where you can hear grateful praise. Needless to say, the discussion is not theological (about God's omnipresence), but existential (about God's presence to a sufferer). Section 3 (vv. 13-18) restates section 1 with an accu-satory tone that is new. Besides the already mentioned repetition of verses 1-2 and 8 in verses 13 and 18, "my prayer" appears in verses 2 and 13; "day" appears in verses 1*b* and 17*b* (NRSV: "when," v. 1); "dark/darkness" appears in verses 6*b* and 18*b*.

As noted, the psalmist expresses no hope, a sign perhaps of stress too intense for imagining alternatives. A slight hope is implicit: Any contact with the living God is enough to keep cruel death at bay.

Exegetical Analysis

In the superscription, "Korahites" are a Temple guild; "Mahalath Leannoth" is an unknown designation, possibly referring to a melody; "Heman the Ezrahite" is a legendary wise man, according to 1 Kgs 4:31, though various individuals named Heman are mentioned as Temple musicians (1 Chron 6:33; 15:19; 25:1-8).

Lord, I am drawing near to Sheol (vv. 1-9a).

Dying is seen not so much as a physiological phenomenon as a moving toward a place, Sheol. The psalmist feels already the dread chill of the place. In verse 1, NRSV's "O LORD, God of my salvation, when," is best rendered with REB and NAB, "LORD, my God, by day I call for help [*šiwwa'tî*; MT: *yěšû'ātî*] / by night I cry aloud in your presence." The emendation results in better parallelism, and the verbs "to call out" and "to cry out" in verse 1 are also parallel in Job 19:7.

Verses 3-8 express how impending death affects the psalmist. The exact meaning of the Hebrew word *(ḥopšî)* rendered "forsaken" (v. 5a) is elusive. It means "free (from slavery)" in Exod 21:2-27, and "free" in a more general sense in its few occurrences elsewhere; in 2 Kgs 15:5, the leprous King Azariah had to live in "a separate house" *(bêt haḥopšît)*. A Ugaritic text uses the latter phrase *(bt ḥpt 'rṣ*, "house of freedom"?) for the underworld; it is parallel to "be counted among those who go down to the underworld" (CAT 1.4.viii.7-9), which is virtually the same usage as in Ps 88:4-5. The Ugaritic usage suggests the meaning here is "released" or "excluded" (from life in the community). "Your wrath" (v. 7a, echoed in v. 16) has a more impersonal meaning than in English, something like "away from your favor and blessing." As "your waves" (v. 7b) suggests, Sheol was sometimes imagined as a watery place as in 2 Sam 22:5; Ps 42:7; and Jonah 2:3. "Shun" indicates that companions are treating the sufferer almost as a corpse that defiles (see Lev 22:4; Num 5:2). "Shut in" and "my eye grows dim" (v. 8c-9a) suggest the weakening of the powers of locomotion and sight that would normally enable a sufferer to stop the descent to Sheol.

I am rapidly leaving your world (vv. 9b-12)

As in the other two sections (vv. 1-2 and 13), this one also begins with a direct prayer, "Every day I call on you, O LORD."

Though the dead in the Bible have a kind of existence, they do so beyond the ordered world where God works "wonders" and receives praise (v. 10). The striking series of six rhetorical questions in verses 10-12 conveys urgency. The psalmist reminds God that only the living can give praise, and it is in God's own interest to let the sufferer live and give praise (cf. Pss 6:5; 30:9). The pray-er wants God to act now, *before* the psalmist drifts off to a place beyond divine reach, where no acts for the righteous are done and no praise is given. The paired concepts of doing wonders and giving praise is a biblical way of describing the relationship between a divine patron and a human client.

Lord, I am drawing near to Sheol (vv. 13-18)

As is evident from the words and syntax that are repeated from section 1 (see above for details), the final stage of the argument picks up the argument of section 1. Going beyond descriptions of distress, the section details the brutal behavior of God and the horrors it has caused (vv. 15-17). Further, it asks the perennial "why" of laments (v. 14). As hopeless as the words seem, behind them is the implicit hope that even a glance from the living God ("Why do you hide your face from me," v. 14*b*) can make the brutal side of death disappear.

Theological and Ethical Analysis

Among the positive gains of recent medical practice and Christian pastoring is the recognition that death is a natural part of the human life cycle. Each person has to come to terms with death through a complex process that can involve, often cyclically, denial, anger, despair, and, finally, acceptance. At first reading, this psalm takes a completely different view of death: Death is a terrible and inexorable enemy, the termination of joy and community, a place where God is absent.

Which view is true? The answer is both. On the one hand, death is natural, for human beings are mortal, and to live is daily to approach one's death. On the other hand, human beings struggle against death as cruel and final, especially when it is premature. This psalm is a record of the struggle, showing to all a route through the bitterness. Though somber and without a statement of trust and praise, Ps 88 never abandons the hope that even a glance from the God of life (v. 14*b*) will lessen death's sting. Christian belief in the power of Jesus' resurrection might tempt one to underrate the horror of death. Death can be horrific especially when premature, violent, or attended with alienation from friends and physical suffering. This psalm guides one into the pain and dread yet does not fail to keep its gaze upon God, even though it cannot discern a face or a hand (v. 5*d*). Only someone who knows the deprivations of death can properly appreciate the resurrection victory over death.

PSALM 89

Literary Analysis

In this community lament over the defeat of the Davidic king, a speaker gives voice to the community's complaint that God has failed to honor the eternal covenant with the Davidic king. The date of composition must have been at a time when the king was a real figure in Israelite politics, that is, sometime between David in the tenth century BCE and the early postexilic period in the sixth century BCE. Though a number of scholars suppose Ps 89 is a late composite of pieces from different dates (an old creation hymn, vv. 1-2, 5-18; a lament from the fall of David's kingdom, vv. 3-4, 38-51; an oracle for David, vv. 19-37), the hypothesis is unlikely. Though old material may have been used, the components are standard for a community lament: complaint about the present distress (defeat of the king, vv. 38-51) and remembrance of the ancient deed that established the order now threatened (God's installing the king with the promise never to reject him, vv. 5-37). Stylistic features also suggest original unity: seven occurrences of the key words "steadfast love," "faithfulness," "the LORD," and "forever"; four instances of the significant words "covenant," "servant," "heavens," "establish," "hand," and "generation." Like similar laments, the psalm "remembers" how God created the world and endowed the king with the promise he would have universal sovereignty (vv. 25-27) and never be rejected (vv. 28-37). The liturgical recitation is done in the hope that God will renew the ancient act.

Modern readers need to keep in mind several points: (1) the psalm remembers not just any event of the past but the event (installation of the Davidic king) that is most appropriate for the present distress (defeat of the king); (2) laments employ both "his-. toric language" (vv. 15-37) and "mythic" or "cosmic language" (vv. 5-14) for the same event; and (3) cosmogonies sometimes included the installation of a king as representative of the deity. Examples from Mesopotamia of the association of king and creation are the following compositions: "When Anu created the heavens," the disputation *Palm and Tamarisk,* and a Neo-Babylonian text on the creation of humans and the king (Clifford 1994, 59-61, 66-71). As will be shown in the exegetical analysis, Ps 89:5-37 is the account of creation celebrated in heaven (vv. 5-14) and earth (vv. 15-37), during which the king is installed, endowed with authority (vv. 19-27), and given the promise that God will be with him forever (vv. 28-37). The psalm prays that the ancient promises to the king be reaffirmed in the present.

Exegetical Analysis

Summons to worship and divine decree (vv. 1-4)

As in Ps 77, an individual leads the community lament. "Steadfast love" *(ḥesed)* and "faithfulness" *('ĕmûnāh)* occur seven times, underscoring the divine fidelity displayed in God's creation. Implied in that creation is God's commitment to remain faithful to the created order and guide it. Nothing should be allowed to hinder that guidance. In verses 1-4, the psalmist points to the never-failing cycle of the heavens—the result of a creation decree—and associates it with the promise to David—also the result of a creation decree. The heavenly bodies and the Davidic promise will be linked again in verses 36-37. The promise to David is, to be sure, a historical event in 2 Sam 7, where Nathan delivers it to David after he has been made king. This psalm takes a different perspective on the event, tracing the installation and promise to a primordial event.

Celebration of the cosmic victory in heaven and on earth (vv. 5-18)

The combining of heavenly and earthly perspectives continues in this section celebrating the primordial victory that brought the world into being. The first section (vv. 5-14) tells how the assembly acclaimed supreme the God who defeated Sea (vv. 9-10), arranged heaven and earth (vv. 11-12), and ascended to the throne (vv. 13-14). In parallel to the heavenly celebration, the same victory is celebrated on earth by the returning warriors (vv. 15-18), as a speaker tells how one of the warriors is selected king (vv. 19-37). The selection is accompanied by a divine decree spelling out in detail under what conditions the king is anointed. God's covenant with the dynasty is eternal: If one of his descendants is unfaithful to the covenant, that king will be punished but the dynasty will not be rejected.

As in 1 Kgs 22:19-22 and Job 1–2, Yahweh is imagined as chairing the assembly of the gods ("the heavens," "the assembly of the holy ones"). As in the Mesopotamian combat myths (Lugal-e, *Ninurta*, and *Enuma Elish*) and Ugaritic combat myth (Baal cycle), the assembly confers supreme power to the warrior god returning victorious from the battle. The victorious god has no equal, because he alone established or reestablished the cosmos, demonstrating his kingship concretely. Such myths frequently picture the threat to cosmic order as vast and formless sea. Psalm 89 refers to it as "sea," "waves," and "Rahab." Rahab is a mythical chaos dragon, as in Isa 51:9 and Job 9:13. Angry Sea hurls mountains of water against the Storm God but is ineffectual. The defeat of Sea means the return of cosmic order, which is symbolized in "the heavens," "the earth," and "the world and all that is in it" (v. 11). In the Masoretic Text, "the north" and "the south" (v. 12) should be emended to "Zaphon" and "Amanus," so that there are four mountains: Zaphon, Amanus, Tabor, and Hermon. "Four" symbolizes universality, as in "the four quarters of the world." The mountains are the massive pillars upon which, according to biblical cosmology, the universe was placed. By metonymy, the mountains stand for the entire earth. Enthroned in heaven, the victorious deity is attended by virtues who are personified as courtiers (v. 14).

Heavenly events are reflected on earth. As the heavens belong to the Lord, so does the earth (v. 11). The angelic acclamation, hymn, and procession in heaven also take place among the returning warriors on earth (vv. 15-18). "Exult" means to express joy vocally. It is possible that verses 17-18 are the warriors' exultant song, for the initial Hebrew word in verse 18 *(kî),* which NRSV and most translations render "for," can introduce a quotation. The proclamation corresponds to the heavenly song in verses 5-14.

Installation of the Davidic king and the giving of the divine promise (vv. 19-37)

The scene continues. "Then" in verse 19 *('az)* marks a fresh stage in the narrative, as in other old poetic narratives (Exod 15:15; Judg 5:8, 11, 13, 22). Though most translations presume an ancient oracle is being cited (e.g., NAB and NIV: "once"; REB: "a time came when"), the poem itself makes the delivery of the oracle an event of primordial time. The promise to David is part of creation, as was implied in verses 1-4. In verse 19*b,* the Masoretic Text (lit. "I have placed a help *[ēzār]* upon the mighty man") does not make a good parallel to the following phrase. Some emend the Hebrew word to *nēzār,* "crown." Emendation is not necessary. In the Ugaritic texts *ǵzr ('zr* in Hebrew) is an epithet of heroes, meaning something like "hero, leader." Psalm 89:19*bc* is therefore: "I have set a leader over the warriors, I have exalted one chosen from the faithful" (Clifford 1980, 35-48). The Lord selects an individual from the victorious warriors and anoints him as king. The king is "the highest *[elyôn]* of the kings of the earth" (v. 27*b*). The title *'elyôn,* "Most High," is applied to Yahweh as Lord of the other heavenly beings (Gen 14:19, 20; Deut 32:8; Pss 47:2; 82:6). As Yahweh's representative, the king is given power appropriate to the vicar of the Most High God, a fact that explains the exalted royal claims of the psalm. The promises made to the king echo the divine power hymned in verses 5-18: The divine hand that defeated chaos (v. 13) is now with the chosen one in verse 21; the defeat of cosmic enemies in verses 9-10 is reflected in the chosen one's defeat of his earthly foes in verses 22-23; the steadfast love and faithfulness of the divine throne (v. 14*b*) are available to the chosen one (v. 24*a*); the "horns" (power) of both chooser (v. 17*b*) and chosen (v. 24*b*) are exalted; Sea and River, enemies now tamed (vv. 9-10), are put under the power of the Davidic king (v. 25). Just as Yahweh is acknowledged by the other members of the divine assembly as supreme because of his victory, so his lieutenant will be regarded as supreme *('elyôn)* by earthly rulers through his military success (v. 27). The representative of Yahweh in principle is the most powerful king on earth.

The covenant makes God and king extremely close. "You are my Father" (v. 26*a*) evokes Ps 2:7*bc*, "He said to me, 'You are my son; today I have begotten you.'" The promise to David receives even more emphasis in the psalm than in 2 Sam 7: It is expressly called a covenant (Ps 89:34); it will not be violated (v. 34) and is sworn by the faithful God (v. 35); dynastic permanence is as much a part of the universe as the sun and moon (vv. 36-37, cf. vv. 1-4).

The complaint: You have rejected the covenant with your servant (vv. 38-51)

The psalmist accuses God of not living up to his promises and being oblivious to the suffering of the king and the people. With unmatched vehemence, the psalmist accuses God of neglect (sixteen verbs in the second-person singular). Every defeat of the king, every breech in the walls of Jerusalem, every act of plunder means only one thing to the people: God has failed to live up to a solemn promise never to abandon them. Note the correspondence between present loss (royal defeat) and primordial promise (promise to the king). *Appropriately*, the psalmist narrates the creation of the world and Israel in order that God might "remember" the original event with its promises and redo them now.

Theological and Ethical Analysis

In the face of a military defeat of the Davidic king and destruction of Jerusalem, the psalmist could have pursued other strategies than the one recorded here. The psalmist could have reasoned that the kingship had become tarnished by kings' behavior (as attested in Samuel and Kings) and that the all-holy God simply backed away from this flawed institution. Though aware of human limit (cf. vv. 30-34), the psalmist will not be deflected from pursuing the key issue: God made a promise! The psalmist takes that promise seriously and refuses to let God off the hook. If God does not keep promises, we are all lost, for our own virtue will certainly not save us. The poet insists that God defend this fragile and all-too-human embodiment of a promise: How can you do this to us? This is the cry of a wounded lover, the demand of a relentless questioner.

Christians will be aware of two further points. New Testament texts such as Eph 1:3-4 similarly place the origin of the church at the beginning of the world: "Blessed be the God and Father of our Lord Jesus Christ, who has blessed us in Christ with every spiritual blessing in the heavenly places, just as he chose us in Christ before the foundation of the world to be holy and blameless before him in love." Also, they will see in Yahweh's promises to David a foreshadowing of God's promises to Jesus, the perfect Son of David.

Book Four (Psalms 90–106)

Psalm 90

Psalm 90 begins Book 4 (Psalms 90–106). It looks back to the last poem of Book 3 by its topics on the brevity of life (Ps 90:3-6; cf. 89:47-48) and divine wrath (Ps 90:7-10; cf. Ps 89:46) and by its question, how long? (Ps 90:13; cf. 89:46). It points forward to Ps 91:9 by the words "dwelling place" (Ps 90:1).

Literary Analysis

In this communal lament, the community prays for the restoration of divine favor lest the short life span decreed for human beings (vv. 3-6) be lived entirely under divine wrath (vv. 7-12). The distress is not specified, but its long duration suggests the sixth-century BCE exile. "Seventy years" in verse 10 may even be a reference to the exile, for Jeremiah predicted the exile would last seventy years (Jer 25:11, 12; 29:10). The poem pleads for the restoration of national life like communal laments such as Pss 44, 74, and 77.

The poem has three parts: eternal God versus short-lived humans (vv. 1-6); divine wrath without limit of time (vv. 7-12); prayer for restoration (vv. 13-17). The opening lines acknowledge that from the beginning of time God has been the secure dwelling place for the people (vv. 1-2). As God is by nature eternal, so human beings are by divine decree mortal (v. 3), a disparity underlined by the contrast of a thousand years and one day (v. 4). In comparison with God's eternity, human life flowers and fades in a single day like the grass of the field (vv. 5-6). Verses 7-10 can be paraphrased: Our lives are being spent entirely under your wrath; even if we were to reach seventy or eighty years, we still would have spent every moment under your anger.

This commentary suggests a new interpretation of the psalm (see Clifford 2000, 59-66). Verses 11-12 are the key. The poem is not, as commonly supposed, a meditation on human transience, and verses 11-12 do not pray for a deeper realization of mortality and frailty so that one may be submissive to God. Rather, the suffering community prays to know how much longer the affliction will last. Verses 11-12 can be paraphrased: "No one knows the *duration* (the full extent) of your anger . . . / Let us know how to compute accurately our days (of affliction); / let us bring that knowledge (into) our minds." Knowing the duration of the affliction helps one to bear it. Verses 13-17 contain the petition found in every lament: Change your mind, O God, become once again our dwelling place, for only when you are present are our labors fruitful (vv. 16-17).

Exegetical Analysis

The superscription attributes the psalm to Moses, presumably because he is the only individual in the Bible who dared to ask God to turn and change. Words from Moses' prayer in Exod 32:12 ("*Turn* from your fierce wrath; *change your mind* [ḥinnāhēm] and do not bring disaster on your people") are found also in Ps 90:13: "Turn, O LORD! How long? / Have compassion [ḥinnāhēm] on your servants!"

Eternal God versus short-lived humans (vv. 1-6)

The argument unfolds by contrasting divine eternity and human mortality. Verses 1-2 are best read as four lines (as in my following translation), with the first and the last line forming a chiasm (chiastic words are in italics: Lord—you—in every generation // from everlasting to everlasting—you—Lord/God).

> *Lord,* a dwelling place have *you* been for us *in every generation*
>   before the mountains were brought forth;
> (before) you formed earth and world
> *from everlasting to everlasting you* are *God.*

"Dwelling place" can refer to God's dwelling in the heavens (Deut 26:15) and in the Temple (Pss 26:8; 68:5; 76:2). Figuratively, it can mean God as "abode" in the sense of a refuge for the people (as in Ps 91:9), and this is the sense here. "Dwelling place" here may allude to the Temple as the symbol of divine presence, for words in verse 14 (rescue in the "morning," "steadfast love") and verse 16 ("let your work be manifest," "glorious power") occur elsewhere in Temple contexts. "Brought forth" and "formed" (lit. "born") in verse 2 are metaphors for creation, though creation as birth is rare in the Bible (though see Job 38:8; Prov 8:25). By asserting at the outset God's benevolent intentions toward the people, the psalm makes the character of God the basis for the restoration.

God's decree that humans are mortal is important in the argument. In verse 3, "You turn us [*ādām,* lit. "humankind"] back to dust, / and say," NRSV "say" refers to this decree. More aptly, NJPS translates, "you decreed." Other divine decrees of mortality for human beings are found in Gen 2:17; 6:3, and the Mesopotamian epic poems Atrahasis and Gilgamesh. The related theme of the brevity of human life prepares for verses 9-10, where the argument is made that though we accept spending some of our days under your anger, we cannot accept spending all of them. Though verse 5a is corrupt (lit. "you poured out sleep"), the rest of verses 5-6 is clear enough: Human beings, like plants, flourish in the morning and die by evening; they are creatures of a day in contrast to God's uncounted years. Psalm 103:15-16 is like our passage in comparing the brevity of human life to the brevity of plant life ("for the wind passes over [the grass], and it is gone") without attributing mortality to divine anger. It is important to distinguish divine anger, which is the theme of Ps 90:7-12 from mortality, which is the theme of verses 1-6. The two are distinct themes. Though NRSV "for" (v. 7a) seems to connect the brevity of human life to divine wrath, the Hebrew word *kî* here has an intensive meaning, "yea, surely, certainly."

Divine wrath without limit (vv. 7-12)

The topic of divine wrath is introduced in verse 7 and becomes a major theme for the rest of the poem. Divine wrath can be portrayed impersonally, a symbol of the divine withdrawal that leaves human beings without vitality or fulfillment. The psalmist tells God there is one sure way to mollify the divine anger: Do not hold our iniquities before your eyes (v. 8)! Verses 9-10 are the core of the psalmist's argument: The entire life span of the people in your community ("all our days"; "our years") has been spent under divine wrath. Even the oldest among us have never known a time when you drew near to bless them.

The pair "seventy" and "eighty" in verse 10 is an instance of parallel numbers, like the numbers "three" and "four" in Amos 1–2, and "six" and "seven" in Job 5:19 and Prov 6:16-19. To judge from comparable modern societies, average life expectancy at that time was probably forty or fifty years, though a fortunate few reached seventy or eighty years. The psalmist argues that even the oldest members of the community have never experienced anything but divine wrath. As already noted, "seventy years" may also be a reference to the length of the exile predicted by Jeremiah (Jer 25:11, 12; 29:10). A long life, which is ordinarily a sign of blessing, is not so here, for it is full of trouble from God's absence or wrath (v. 10cd). Verse 10, though often taken as a statement about the human condition, is a statement about Israel enduring a period of divine absence.

Verses 11-12 conclude the complaint section. The usual interpretation of the verses—the psalmist is asking for a deeper sense of the transience of life so that the community can face its tribulations with equanimity and faithfulness—runs into major linguistic and logical problems. The verses require close analysis. NRSV "who considers?" means simply "Who knows?" in the sense of "nobody knows," as in 2 Sam 12:22; Prov 24:22; and Eccl 3:21. But how can the psalmist say that no one knows the "power of your anger" when, according to verses 7-10, the psalm has made it clear that the community has felt God's anger? The only satisfactory answer is that the community has not yet experienced the complete extent, that is, the full duration of the divine anger, and nobody knows how much longer it will last. People of the time believed there were predetermined periods of affliction such as the seventy years of exile in Jer 25:11, 12; 29:10; and the different time periods in the offer to David in 2 Sam 24:13. Moreover, it was believed that the gods might reveal the terms of the periods through oracles or omens, which is suggested by Ps 74:9c, "there is no one among us who knows how long." Psalm 39:4 is an example of a request to know the term of an affliction. Set periods of affliction also occur in Ugaritic and Mesopotamian literature. Psalm 90:12 is a request to know how long the affliction will last. Similarly, Isa 40:2 is an example of an oracle declaring the period of wrath to be over, "[Israel] has served her term, / that her penalty is paid." Verses 11-12 ask a specific question: "Who knows the full extent of your anger, / . . . Let [us] know how to compute accurately our days [of affliction], / let us bring that knowledge [into] our minds" (my translation).

The prayer for restoration (vv. 13-17)

The plea to turn your face toward your people in kindness is similar to the prayers in Exod 32:12; Pss 6:4; and 80:14. "How long?" is a genuine question, continuing verses 11-12, that is, how much longer will the affliction last? The question expresses both impatience and hope (Pss 13:2; 74:9, 10; 80:4; 89:46). The vocabulary of verses 14-15 is more specific than appears at first sight. The verbs "satisfy," "rejoice," "be/make glad" are associated with worship in the Jerusalem Temple in several psalms: Ps 16:11bc (related words are in italics): "In your presence there is *fullness* of *joy*; / in your right hand are *pleasures* [favor, v. 17] forevermore"; Ps 65:4cd, "We *shall be satisfied* with the goodness of your house, / your holy temple"; Ps 91:16, "With long life *I will satisfy* them, and *show* them my salvation." The psalmist seems to make the restoration of the Temple and its worship a symbol of the restoration of the entire people. The Temple was, after all, the Lord's house, and Israel's well-being depended on the presence of the Lord.

Verses 16-17 expand verses 13-15. "Your work" in verse 16 refers to the Lord's activity on behalf of Israel, as in Hab 3:2 and Ps 77:12. "Glorious power" can refer to the glory of nature (Isa 35:2), of human beings (Ps 8:6; Isa 53:2), and of God, as here. Verse 17 acknowledges implicitly that human activity done without God's support has no permanence, "Unless the LORD builds the house, / those who build it labor in vain" (Ps 127:1). Verse 17, "the favor of the Lord" *(nōʿam ʾădōnāy)* reverses the order of words and even the consonants of a phrase in verse 1, "Lord . . . dwelling place" *(ʾădōnāy māʿôn)*. This inclusio brings the poem to a close and implies that restoration can only come from God.

Theological and Ethical Analysis

Thoughts of one's mortality and the transience of one's community can easily lead to melancholy and depression, especially when people have long endured political and social disorder and feel forgotten by God. Such a situation has the opposite effect on this psalmist who confronts God with boldness and hope. Building on a firm belief in the God who has ever been Lord of Israel, the psalmist asks: How can you, who have made our life span so short, sit idly by as each of us sees our lives passing away under your wrath? How can you not bring our acts to completion?

This psalm is a model of prayer for people who have waited long and patiently for God to bring prosperity to the community. The prayer stays focused on God who has always been a "home" for Israel, but who has not lived up to that wonderful title for a long time. Few psalms are so eloquent on the topic of human beings lacking divine blessing. The brevity and frustration of their lives weigh them down. The hope and the despair are made into an unforgettable prayer that God turn to bless the suffering community.

PSALM 91

In its context in the Psalter, Ps 91 responds to the anguished prayer of Ps 90:17, "Let the favor of the Lord our God be upon us!" God is a "dwelling place" in Pss 90:1 and 91:9. It is linked to the following psalm by the title "Most High" (Pss 91:1, 9; 92:1) and the act of looking triumphantly upon one's foes (Pss 91:8; 92:11).

Literary Analysis

This poem is a song of trust with a special concern to teach that trust to others; hence it has a didactic tone. The poem contains three promises of assistance, each of progressively decreasing length: verses 1-8; verses 9-13; and verses 14-16. The third statement is climactic not only by its third position but also by its speaker, for it is divine speech in the first person. The metaphors for God's protection in the first two parts are noteworthy. In part 1, God is a mother eagle carrying its threatened chicks to safety, and, in part 2, God is the one who sends angels to lead the frightened individual through the perils of life. Both metaphors come from the exodus tradition: the protective eagle in Exod 19:4 and Deut 32:10-12, and the guardian angel in Exod 23:20, 23 and 32:34.

Exegetical Analysis

Taking shelter in the Most High assures true security (vv. 1-8)

The psalm assures one who seeks divine protection that such protection enables one to say truthfully of the Lord "my refuge and my fortress." "Shadow" is a metaphor for divine protection in Ps 63:7; Isa 49:2; and 51:16. "Shelter" is a metaphor for protection in Pss 27:5; 31:20; and 61:4. A person who makes a conscious decision to rely on God alone must forswear other sources of protection. In antiquity, one rejected other gods and revered Yahweh alone as patron. In modern times, one rejects all absolutes except God for life and protection. "To live, to sit" *(yōšēb)* implies continuing or abiding as in Ps 107:10, "Some sat in darkness and in gloom, / prisoners in misery and in irons."

Verses 3-8 give the grounds for the assurance: God protects poor and endangered clients by bringing them to a safe place. Though many commentators assume that "pinions" and "wings" (v. 4) refer to the winged cherubim guarding the holy of holies in the Temple (Exod 25:20; 1 Kgs 6:23-28, 32; 2 Chron 3:10-13; Ezek 1:4-9), the reference is more likely to a protecting bird. In Egyptian iconography, a god's wings overshadow and protect the king. Biblical tradition has its own portrayal of a protecting bird, however, which is the likely source of the metaphor in this psalm. The Lord is an eagle in two venerable passages: "You have seen what I did to the Egyptians, and how I bore you on eagles' wings and brought you to myself" (Exod 19:4) and

> [God] sustained [Israel] in a desert land,
>   in a howling wilderness waste;
> he shielded him, cared for him,
>   guarded him as the apple of his eye.
> As an eagle stirs up its nest,
>   and hovers over its young;
> as it spreads its wings, takes them up,
>   and bears them aloft on its pinions,
> the LORD alone guided him;
>   no foreign god was with him. (Deut 32:10-12)

Though eagles do not actually fly with their young upon their wings, people of the time apparently assumed that they did. The metaphor of a bird bearing its young away from danger would explain several phrases in Ps 91:3-8: "the snare of the fowler"

(v. 3), "his pinions," and "under his wings" (v. 4). It also would explain the assurance that the pestilence "will not come near you" (v. 7), for the endangered chick would have been snatched away. In verses 5-6, the word pairs "night" // "day" and "darkness" // "noonday" mention two times of the twenty-four-hour day to assert that protection extends to all times.

Verses 7-8 offer a truly memorable description of an individual wondrously protected as fellow warriors fall on either side. The verses bring to mind the battle at the Red Sea, where the Lord fought, and the people had only to watch: "But Moses said to the people, 'Do not be afraid, stand firm, and see the deliverance that the LORD will accomplish for you today; for the Egyptians whom you see today you shall never see again. The LORD will fight for you, and you have only to keep still'" (Exod 14:13).

An angel is sent to those who made God their refuge (vv. 9-13)

Part 2 is parallel to part 1, restating it with variations. Verse 9a quotes verse 2a ("the LORD," "my refuge"). As was the case in verses 3-8, verses 9-13 give an assurance of divine protection. The metaphor for protection is angels. They are sent by the Lord to guard the journey, carrying the traveler in their hands and making possible safe progress through the haunts of dangerous beasts. Like the eagle in part 1, the angels in part 2 are also from the exodus traditions. Verse 11 evokes the messenger who accompanied Israel to Canaan: "I am going to send an angel in front of you, to guard you on the way and to bring you to the place that I have prepared" (Exod 23:20).

By using metaphors from the exodus—a bird carrying its chicks to safety and the angelic guide—the psalm relates God's protection in the present to the founding moment of Israel. Psalm 23 similarly correlates daily guidance and the guidance out of Egypt.

I will rescue and bless the one who trusts in me (vv. 14-16)

Like the preceding two parts, part 3 begins with an assurance of divine protection. Though the shortest section, it is the climax of the poem because of its third position and the dignity of its speaker (God). Seven verbs (counting the implied verb in the nominal sentence in v. 15b) depict God's acts of kindness toward the loyal and trusting person. The accumulation of verbs intensifies the divine kindness and generosity. The blessings—protection; readiness to respond to prayer; willingness to rescue; the granting of honor, long life, and prosperity ("salvation")—respond to the prayerful statement of verse 2.

Theological and Ethical Analysis

Only someone who, in danger, trusted God and was rescued could have uttered this bold and challenging instruction. Without hesitation or doubt, the psalmist declares that God comes to the aid of those who stay in the sheltering arms of God. Just as Israel was protected in their wilderness journey to Zion, so will those who love God be protected in their journey through life.

The psalm enables a modern pray-er to hear assurances of the Lord's protection in the depressing and dangerous moments of life. It invites people to put aside false or self-constructed refuges in order to focus on the one unfailing source of protection. The New Testament transposes abiding in God to abiding in Jesus: "Abide in me as I abide in you. Just as the branch cannot bear fruit by itself unless it abides in the vine, neither can you unless you abide in me" (John 15:4).

PSALM 92

This poem is linked to the preceding one by the title "Most High" (v. 1, cf. Ps 91:1, 9) and the gesture of looking down upon one's defeated enemies (Ps 92:11, cf. Ps 91:9). It points forward to the enthronement psalms (93, 96–99) by portraying the Lord defeating the wicked from on high (Ps 92:9).

Literary Analysis

Psalm 92 is predominantly a hymn, though the praise is firmly rooted in a rescue from danger (vv. 10-11). The thanksgiving song has developed into a hymn because the rescue has stirred the singer deeply (vv. 1-5). Only a dullard could be unaware of God's governance that effected the rescue and now grants the prosperity that is symbolized by the sacred trees in the Temple orchards (vv. 6-15).

The singer invites praise for "your work / . . . the works of your hands" (v. 4). To what divine act or acts does the speaker refer? Elsewhere in the Psalter, "work" and "works" (singular or plural) refer to the great events of sacred history such as the exodus and guidance in the wilderness to the promised land (as in Pss 44:1-2; 77:14; 95:9; 111:2-3; 143:5). The general meaning here is that God's work takes the form of punishing the wicked and saving the righteous. The "dullard" (v. 6a), who deliberately rejects wisdom, is unaware of the course of divine justice (vv. 6-9). The middle line of the poem (v. 8) expresses the triumph of justice: "you, O LORD, are on high forever." In contrast to the dullard, the psalmist is righteous in wholeheartedly embracing God's governance. In verses 4-5, the psalmist rejoiced in God's work. God not only rescues the righteous but also constantly blesses their lives (vv. 12-15). In a word, the psalmist invites the community to proclaim the faithfulness and justice of God toward the saints. The divine name Yahweh ("the LORD") occurs seven times.

Exegetical Analysis

Invitation to praise God (vv. 1-5)

The phrase "it is good to give thanks," taken together with the infinitive functions like a verb in the imperative mood, "come, let us" (cf. Ps 147:1). The three verbs in verses 1-2—"give thanks," "sing praises," and "declare your steadfast love"—are synonymous, meaning to publicize an act of God that otherwise would remain hidden. To give thanks in the Bible means to declare what one's benefactor has done so that others might acknowledge it. "In the morning" and "by night" means at all times. NRSV "thoughts" in verse 5 is more accurately "plans, designs" (as in Job 5:12; 21:22; Ps 33:10, so NJPS and NAB); "deep" means buried and, hence, needing to be revealed (as in Job 12:21; Prov 20:5). The psalmist will bring what is hidden to light for all to recognize. What has been hidden up to now is God's just governance of the world, which includes a particular act: rescue of the psalmist.

God's act of judgment (vv. 6-11)

Dullards and the stupid cannot recognize the hidden action of God and, hence, are unaware of the triumph of God's governance. The actual judgment is expressed in an indirect and reverential manner, "you, O LORD, are on high forever" (v. 8). So effortless is the act that it need not be described; one need only assert the Lord is on high. This phrase (v. 8) occupies the exact center of the poem. The judgment consists in the doom of the wicked (vv. 7, 9) and the exaltation of the righteous (vv. 10-11).

The blessings that come upon the righteous person (vv. 12-15)

The righteous person is compared to a tree, as in Pss 1:3; 52:8; and Jer 17:8. This tree is special, however, for it grows in the garden of God within the Jerusalem Temple. Ancient temples had sacred orchards that symbolized the fertility found in the divine dwelling. Declared righteous by the Lord, the rescued psalmist and other righteous people are in a sense already near the Lord, sharing the life found in the Temple. Their vigor proves God's ability to grant prosperity to loyal clients.

Theological and Ethical Analysis

Though the psalmists often complain of justice denied or delayed, they do on occasion sing a serene song such as this one, which acknowledges that God has frustrated the plans of the wicked and upheld the designs of the loyal. Such an experience of salvation brings intense joy (v. 4) and inspires the psalmist to make a declaration to the community. The poem does not tell what the particular act of justice was. If the speaker was the king, as some scholars suppose, then the act would by its nature be national and beneficial to all. If it affected only an individual, it is still understandable why the rescued person would want to show public appreciation, for the act favored a member of the community. At any rate, it is good to have psalms that affirm God is at work in the world and that invite all voices to recognize that happy fact.

Though God's work often is hidden, it is sometimes plain to see. This psalm provides a text for discovering God's just and merciful activity in one's life and rejoicing in the deed with others.

PSALM 93

This poem, like Pss 24, 29, 47, and 95–99, celebrates the accession of Yahweh to preeminent kingship among the heavenly beings, a position that demands worship by all beings on earth. This, the shortest of the enthronement psalms, introduces a cluster of psalms on the topic. The immediately following Ps 94 depicts universal judgment by the newly installed king.

Literary Analysis

Regarding this and other enthronement psalms, three points must be kept in mind. First, kingship was understood concretely as resulting from a specific victory, in this case a victory that established the world. Second, the kingship is depicted by means of the narrative of the combat myth. Third, the enthronement was celebrated liturgically. In fact, the psalm seems to be derived from such a celebration. The most likely situation was the New Year festival, which was celebrated at the Feast of Ingathering. It was also called the Feast of Tabernacles or simply the Feast. In pre-exilic times, the feast commemorated the New Year. Fall was the time when the rains returned and the dry season ended. It was an apt time for celebrating Yahweh's coming as the Storm God and bestowing life upon a parched earth and people. Later, under Babylonian influence, the New Year festival apparently was shifted to the spring. For further details, see the Introduction, "The Genres and Rhetoric of the Psalms," no. 5, in *Psalms 1–72*.

A single narrative gives unity to the poem. Psalm 93 proclaims that Yahweh has become king ("The LORD is king") and put on the splendid garments befitting a conqueror and king (v. 1). Yahweh exercises royal dominion over the newly pacified world. As the earth is eternal, so also is Yahweh's kingship (v. 2). Verses 3-4 describe the cosmic battle and victory of Yahweh. Though Sea ("floods," v. 3) lifted high its mighty waves in attack, Yahweh, the Storm God, decisively beat it back. The imagery seems inspired by a storm at the seashore. Rain, thunder, and lightning seem to drive back Sea, which advances toward the land. Sea is finally contained at the shore. Having contained Sea from encroaching upon the land and engulfing it, Yahweh takes his throne and from his palace utters decrees that shape the new world (v. 5). The poem first describes the Lord enthroned as king (vv. 1-2) and then the victory that led to the kingship (vv. 3-4).

Exegetical Analysis

The enthronement and vesting of Yahweh as king over the world (vv. 1-2)

The exact translation of the first two Hebrew words in verse 1, *YHWH mālak,* is disputed. On the basis of grammar alone, one can translate "Yahweh is king" or "Yahweh has become king." The same Hebrew verb occurs in Pss 47:8; 96:10; 97:1; and 99:1. First Kings 15:33 exemplifies both meanings of *mālak* (my translation): "In the third year of King Asa of Judah, Baasha son of Ahijah *became king* over all Israel at Tirzah; he *was king* twenty-four years." Another undisputed instance of the verb in the sense of enthronement is 2 Kgs 9:14 (my translation): "and they blew the trumpet, and proclaimed, 'Jehu has become king.'" In Ps 93, the context makes certain the rendering "Yahweh has become king," for the psalm narrates how Yahweh achieved kingship by defeating Sea. The singer recognizes the triumph of the deity and ascribes "majesty" and "strength" symbolized by his garments.

The cosmic battle between the Lord and Sea (vv. 3-4)

With great economy of language, the poet describes the battle and victory in two tricola. The poetic device of the tricolon imparts exceptional emphasis to the third colon. The last line, "majestic on high is the LORD," is the delayed and grandly effective climax of the battle between Sea and the Lord. Widely attested at the time, the battle between Sea and the storm-god had cosmic significance, for the defeat of Sea removed the threat to cosmic order. After the victory, the world "shall never be moved."

The decree that determines the destinies of the world (v. 5)

Comparable cosmogonies tell how the newly triumphant god created or restored the universe. In the Mesopotamian creation poem *Enuma Elish* (tablet VII), the storm-god Marduk, after defeating the monster Tiamat and separating heaven and earth, creates the human race and builds the great temple in Esagila in Babylon. In the new protocol for honoring gods, Marduk is proclaimed the first of the deities. Psalm 93:5 declares that the Lord's world-determining decrees will indeed prevail. In some cosmogonies, the Creator God assigns to every entity the "destiny" that characterizes it. Another feature of creation accounts was the building of a palace for the victorious deity. The phrase, "holiness befits your house," means that the Lord's unique position makes his dwelling special, unlike any other. It is set apart, holy.

Theological and Ethical Analysis

The psalm realistically acknowledges the enormity of evil in the world and symbolizes it in an impressive way. Evil at one time threatened to destroy the entire world. It has been confined, however, by Yahweh, the king of heaven and earth, who now determines the course of nature and history.

The psalm celebrates the great act of God that established beauty, order, and peace and maintains them. Though evil is still present, it has been, in principle, defeated. One can commemorate the Lord's great victory and hope for its total triumph in the future. When one celebrates the creation victory of the Lord, one celebrates at the same time a blessed future. Christians will see in the resurrection of Jesus, the conquest of evil, and the creation of a new world.

PSALM 94

This psalm is linked to nearby poems by its theme of the Lord as king defeating evil; divine kingship is celebrated in Pss 93 and 95–99. God as rock in verse 22 occurs also in 92:15 and 95:1; the word pair "dullest" // "fools" (v. 8) occurs in Ps 92:6 ("the dullard" // "the stupid").

Literary Analysis

Psalm 94 is a lament complaining about the prosperity of the wicked. It has a petition (vv. 1-2), a complaint (vv. 3-7), questioning of God (vv. 3, 20), challenges to the wicked (vv. 9-10, 16), and statements of trust (vv. 17-18, 22). It goes somewhat beyond the lament genre, however, by its vivid portrayal of the psalmist as a model of confidence in God (vv. 17-18). Despite the complaints of God's absence, the psalmist trusts God's effective governance, which (the psalm asserts) is carried out in a hidden way and not according to a human timetable (vv. 8-19).

The main stanza divisions are introduced by questions (vv. 3, 16, 20), commands (v. 8), and beatitudes ("happy are those," v. 12). Five stanzas follow the opening petition (vv. 1-2), each with approximately the same number of words: verses 1-2; verses 3-7; verses 8-11; verses 12-15; verses 16-19; and verses 20-23. Stanzas 3 and 4 are closely related, for stanza 4 declares happy the individual (plural in NRSV: "those") who accepts God's guidance and teaching (v. 12) in contrast to the wicked (plural) who reject that guidance (stanza 3). The end of the poem is signaled by the reprise in verse 23 of elements from verse 1: "the LORD" and the Hebrew verb *šûb* ("give . . . what they deserve" and "repay them").

The progress of thought is easy to follow: O Lord, avenge the poor by putting down their oppressors who boast that you do not see them (vv. 1-7); O fools, understand that the God who chastises the nations will also chastise you (vv. 8-11); happy the one who accepts God's discipline (vv. 12-15); I know that God sustains me (vv. 16-19); the Just One will never ally with evildoers, no matter how high-ranking, but will avenge evil (vv. 20-23).

Though a few commentators identify the wicked in the poem as the nations, the oppressed group is not Israel but the "widow," "stranger," and "orphan" *within* Israel. The entire people is diminished whenever one part is attacked. The psalmist cries out against the injustice that some members of the community inflict upon others.

Exegetical Analysis

Rise up and repay evildoers (vv. 1-2)

In order to move God to act, the psalm uses divine titles that imply God is a just ruler. The wicked are described as claiming God does not see them. "God of vengeance" is a Hebrew expression for "God who characteristically avenges injustice." "Avenging God" (NAB) or "God of retribution" (NJPS) are perhaps more accurate renderings of the divine title. The psalmist does not doubt that God has the capacity to put down evil but is frustrated by God's inactivity. Hence, the psalmist pleads "shine forth," which is used of God's appearance in a storm theophany as in Deut 32:2; Job 37:4; and Ps 50:2. "Judge" (v. 2) is a broader term than legal officer; it is a ruler responsible for ensuring divine justice and order (though the tasks involve overseeing and administering the legal system). The vocabulary used later in the poem—"justice" (v. 15), "wicked rulers" (v. 20; lit. "throne of injustice") and "statute" (v. 20)—suggests that the judicial system has broken down and is not protecting the poor.

The wicked attack the weak and boast that God does not see them (vv. 3-7)

The pray-er complains about the *words* of the wicked; "exult," "words," "boast," and "they say" imply verbal expression. In the Wisdom literature, one's words reveal one's true feelings and plans. The wicked do not deny that God exists (such "theoretical atheism" was unknown), but deny rather that God is able or willing to rule justly. By citing the malefactors' words, the psalmist appeals to God's honor: Will you allow them to say you are weak and indifferent toward evil?

As noted, verse 5 does not imply that foreigners are persecuting Israel, for no nations are named. Rather, it is the wicked within Israel who are harming God's people by attacking its vulnerable members. Widows, resident aliens, and the fatherless are outside the family system that protects others. The complaint echoes such prophetic indictments as Isa 1:17, 23; 10:2; and Jer 5:28.

A warning to fools (vv. 8-11)

This stanza and the next (vv. 12-15) use the language of Wisdom literature. Wisdom literature employs types (often contrasted) to describe human behavior. One such contrast is between the wicked (usually plural) and the righteous person (usually singular); another is between fools (who reject wisdom) and the wise person. This contrast is found in stanza 3, which depicts the foolish (plural), and in stanza 4, which depicts the wise person (singular, NRSV plural). There is other "wisdom" vocabulary in the verses, for example, "teach," "chastise," "be wise," and "knowledge."

Verses 9-10 refute the fools' claim, made in verse 7, that God does not see or perceive what is happening on earth. The refutation of the claim is made by *a fortiori* argumentation (lit. "from the stronger [argument]"): the more self-evident (stronger) argument is stated first so that the conclusion will not be disputed. You admit that God created the ear, so you must admit that God can hear perfectly. Verse 10 continues the *a fortiori* argumentation: You admit (as any Israelite would) that the Lord guides or disciplines the nations, so you must admit that God guides every individual within a nation. Therefore you will be disciplined, that is, punished by God. Wisdom literature presupposed that God teaches by a sometimes rough tutelage, punishing and rewarding human behavior in a vigorous this-worldly process.

The wise individual as an example to the people (vv. 12-15)

In contrast to the fools (plural) who refuse divine discipline (v. 10) and teaching (v. 10), the psalm declares happy the individual who is open to God's guidance (v. 12). "Law" (*tôrāh*, v. 12) is better rendered "teaching," for the word refers to inspired counsel rather than judicial pronouncements. To the receptive individual God gives the serenity and poise of the wise (as in Job 4:5; 6:2), whereas a pit is dug for the wicked (as in Prov 26:27; 28:10, 18). The psalmist's hope is specifically Israelite: the Lord's unconditional commitment to Israel (v. 14). "People" and "heritage" in verse 14 are repeated for emphasis from verse 5. Justice will again be done to the righteous. The individual declared happy in verse 12 will be identified with the psalmist in the next two stanzas.

The Lord has come to my aid (vv. 16-19)

The questions in verse 16 are rhetorical, and the implied answer is "No one but God!" Verse 4 had declared that "evildoers" directed arrogant words against God; verse 16 states that

God "stands up for me against evildoers." In fact, God has kept the psalmist from death in "the land of silence" (as in Ps 115:17) and supplied bold words (vv. 8-11) to counter the boasts of the wicked (vv. 3-7). The discouragement that weighs down the just is assuaged by God (v. 19). Throughout, God is a bringer of consolation and delight to the psalmist (vv. 12-13, 18-19, 22). A strong bond of affection and loyalty unites human client and divine patron.

I know my God has nothing to do with the wicked (vv. 20-23)

Like the previous section, this one begins with a rhetorical question (v. 20). The implied answer is, "No, God has nothing to do with such wickedness!" The threat of "wicked rulers" (lit. "throne of injustice") is indeed daunting, but the pray-er is nonetheless able to express bold confidence in God. The metaphors for God express safety from violence: "stronghold" (2 Sam 22:3; Pss 9:9; 46:11) and "rock of my refuge" (Ps 62:7). As the psalm began with the psalmist's petition that God "give *(hāšēb 'al)* to the proud what they deserve" (v. 2), so it ends in verse 23 with the firm hope that God will "repay them" *(wayyāšeb 'al)*. As the expression "God of vengeance" was repeated twice in the opening line, so "wipe them out" is repeated twice in the closing line.

Theological and Ethical Analysis

Praying to a "God of vengeance" (v. 1) is distasteful to most people, for vengeance is a trait of unforgiving people who refuse others a second chance. When applied to God, however, vengeance means something quite different: redressing wrongs when ordinary means fail. The psalmist prays for this kind of vengeance, that God stop evildoers from preying on those who cannot defend themselves. On their behalf, the psalmist appeals to the divine honor: How can you, the just God who protects me so well, fail to stop criminals who destroy your people and ridicule you?

One can appreciate the achievement of this psalm only when one realizes how easy it is to be defeated by systemic evil. The psalmist is certainly not defeated by such evil. Though aware how evil has corrupted the institutions of justice, the psalmist never loses sight of the presence of divine justice in the world. From where does such a conviction come? Three sources: the nature of God revealed in the title "God of vengeance" (v. 1), God's enduring commitment to Israel (vv. 5, 14), and a profound personal experience of a God who protects (vv. 17-18) and consoles (vv. 19, 22). Instead of retreating into that happy relationship with God, however, the psalmist bravely steps into the public arena and speaks up for the voiceless: O God, help the aggrieved poor! In so doing, the psalmist becomes a true servant of God in the style of Moses, Jeremiah, and the servant of Isaiah 40–55. The prayer transforms one's relationship with God into action and care for others.

PSALM 95

Psalm 95 invites people to worship the Lord, king over all the beings of heaven, and shepherd of the flock Israel. Its distinctiveness lies in its exhortation to the Lord's flock to manifest absolute loyalty to their Lord.

Literary Analysis

Beginning as a hymn (vv. 1-7c), the psalm turns into an exhortation to fidelity to the creator (vv. 7d-11). It has three sections (vv. 1-5, 6-7c, 7d-11). Each of its two invitation verses (vv. 1-2, 6), which are introduced by "for" (kî, vv. 3a, 7a), mentions a motive to give praise. The third section is an exhortation to obedience with the implied threat that disobedience will exclude the worshipers from God's presence.

The first section (vv. 1-5) invites the worshipers four times to give praise. The motive is that Yahweh stands above all gods and holds the disk of earth and the surrounding sea. God's hands (vv. 4, 5, 7) are a symbol of care for the world. The poem presupposes a narrative, the combat myth. See the Introduction, "The Genres and Rhetoric of the Psalms," no. 5, in *Psalms 1–72*. According to the myth, a warrior god is commissioned by the divine assembly to combat a threat to the universe posed by a chaos monster. What is threatened is cosmic order, "the world as we know it." The warrior kills the monster, and returns victorious to the divine assembly which proclaims him the Great King. Though viewing the sovereignty of Yahweh in mythic language, it adapts the originally polytheistic background to fit Israelite monotheism. The myth explains the absolute supremacy of the Lord over heaven and earth and grounds Israel's praise and song.

The second invitation verse (v. 6) invites the joyous throng to enter the courtyard gate, commanding obeisance expressed in bodily movement (bowing down and kneeling) and spiritual resolve (vv. 7d-11). Since ancient creation accounts typically ended with a *peopled* universe, it is not surprising that Israel acknowledges Yahweh as their "Maker" (v. 6b), creating them as "he made" the sea (v. 5a). The psalm assumes the people are elected as special to the Lord in the creation. The poem conveys the election by the phrases "people of his pasture" and "sheep of his hand" (v. 7).

The third section, the exhortation (vv. 7d-11), draws out the implications of the election mentioned in the second section. Recalling the people's origins in the exodus, the singer focuses on only one part, the journey to the Holy Land. The singer reminds the congregation that the original generation did not enter "my rest." "Rest" is the goal of the exodus journey to Canaan (as in Deut 12:9; 1 Kgs 8:56). It has another, related, meaning as well—the place where God rests, that is, the Temple (as in 1 Chron 28:2; Ps 132:14; Isa 66:1). The psalm plays on the two meanings, promised land and Temple. The officiant invites Israel to enter (v. 6a) the Temple precincts and now warns them that their disobedient ancestors did not "enter my rest" (v. 11b). The meaning is unmistakable: Israel cannot truly enter God's rest, the Temple and the land, unless they are obedient to God. Using liturgical language, the singer delivers the same message as the prophets: If you want to remain on the land, be faithful.

Exegetical Analysis

First invitation verse: Sing to the Lord (vv. 1-5)

Each of the four cola of verses 1-2 command music and song; "thanksgiving" means a song of thanks as in Pss 26:7 and 42:4. The noun "rock" is a common metaphor for God, occurring thirty-three times in the Old Testament. Here it means a massive cliff or mesa offering a secure place of refuge. "Rock of our salvation" is a Hebrew expression for the Rock who rescues. "A great king" is more accurately rendered the Great King as in 2 Kgs 18:19 (so NAB and NJPS), for it was an actual title of ancient kings. As already noted, the acclamation comes out of the combat myth, where the victorious deity returned to the assembly and was acclaimed supreme over the other gods. Verses 4-5 describe creation by listing the cosmic pairs that emerge from God's creative acts, as in Pss 74:15-17 and 89:11-12: "earth" // "mountains," "sea" // "dry land." According to biblical cosmology, the disk of earth floats upon the cosmic waters, securely anchored by mountains sunk deep into the waters. That the Lord made the world is mentioned no fewer than five times.

Second invitation verse: Bow down before the Lord (vv. 6-7c)

Whereas the first invitation invited song, this one invites worshipful gestures. The phrase "sheep of his hand" (v. 7c) connotes special love like the similar idiom in Ezek 27:21, "favored dealers," which means "merchants of your hand." Ezekiel 34:10 similarly shows the Lord personally replacing predatory shepherds: "I am against the shepherds; and I will demand my sheep at their hand, and put a stop to their feeding the sheep; no longer shall the shepherds feed themselves. I will rescue my sheep from their mouths."

Exhortation to obey the Lord with a whole heart (vv. 7d-11)

The exhortation follows logically from the statement that the congregation is the Lord's flock. Similar warnings are in Pss 50 and 81:8-9. The place name "Meribah" is related by folk-etymology to "place of strife," and the place name "Massah" to "place of testing." For the background of the rebellion of Israel in those places, see Exod 17:1-7; Num 21:1-9; Pss 78:18-20; 81:7; and 106:32. In the Pentateuch, the Lord tests Israel. Here, abnormally, it is Israel who tests the Lord. God's refusal to allow the first generation to enter the promised land is told in Num 14; Deut 1:34–2:15; Pss 78; 105; and 106. Verse 10 plays on the language of journey: The original generation did not find their way to Canaan because they did not attend to God's ways. "Forty years" is regarded as the duration of a generation.

Theological and Ethical Analysis

Psalm 95 allows the community to meet God in a special way. As the community worships the God of gods, an authoritative voice commands them to bow down. The voice announces to them a message that is at once consoling and challenging: You are the Lord's own people, your care will never be delegated to another. Thus there can be no other God in your lives except the Lord Yahweh. The voice warns that your ancestors were unable to learn it and so never entered the land of Canaan. You must recognize what it means to enter God's rest.

The psalm enables the community to learn from history and avoid the mistakes of the first generation. The psalm insists that "today" the community learn how to enter God's rest and imitate what their ancestors did "on the day at Massah." In churches with an official tradition of morning and evening prayer, Ps 95 is the favorite opening prayer. It is easy to see why, for it makes the praying community aware of the ethical demands of their worship. At the same time, despite its serious tone, the psalm appeals to the people's freedom to enter into God's place. The shepherd imagery evokes that found in the New Testament, especially in John 10.

PSALM 96

The hymn is an enthronement psalm (like Pss 47, 93, 95, 97–99) inviting Israel and the entire world to acknowledge Yahweh as sole king of the universe. For the background of these psalms, see the Introduction, "The Genres and Rhetoric of the Psalms," no. 5, in *Psalms 1–72*.

Literary Analysis

Part 1 (vv. 1-6) begins with the thrice-repeated invitation "sing to the LORD." Part 2 (vv. 7-10) begins with the thrice-repeated invitation "ascribe to the LORD." Part 1 (vv. 1-6) invites the whole world to sing, part 2 (vv. 7-10) invites the family of nations, and part 3 (vv. 11-13) heaven, earth, and sea. The different aspects make up the entire universe. Parts 2 and 3 both end with the announcement that the Lord rules the world with justice.

Like other hymns of enthronement, this one presumes readers know the combat myth, how Yahweh, the Lord of Israel, became king. With the world threatened by chaos, the frightened assembly of gods pick one god and give him supreme power. Returning victorious to the assembly, his supreme kingship is acknowledged by the gods, and he establishes a new world order. Psalm 96 is derived from the traditional story.

Psalm 96 adapts the combat myth with considerable freedom. It invites all the people of the world ("all the earth," v. 1) to proclaim the Lord's victory ("salvation," v. 2) and "marvelous works" (v. 3). Yahweh's supremacy is indicated by the phrase "revered above all gods" (v. 4). Verse 5 draws a distinctively biblical conclusion to the narrative: Since Yahweh is alone victorious, the other gods are powerless, and their images are worthless. The Lord's victory has dethroned them. In verse 6, paired attributes ("honor // majesty," "strength // beauty"), like court attendants, stand in attendance upon the Lord. Part 2 (vv. 7-10) shifts the focus from heaven to earth as it invites the nations to come to the Temple and acknowledge the Lord's rule. Part 3 invites the non-human world to offer homage and similarly ends with the declaration that the Lord will come to judge the earth.

Exegetical Analysis

Let all on earth declare the great deed of the Lord (vv. 1-6)

"New song" occurs seven times in the Hebrew Bible. See the remarks on the phrase at Ps 40. Typically, the new song contains an invitation to behold the wondrous actions of Yahweh and respond with worship (cf. Ps 40:3cd). The phrase "new song" does not mean, as it would in English, an original melody and words. It is rather a response to a new divine act; "new" refers to the act it celebrates. Further, the act is not "brand new" and unprecedented but a renewing or reviving of an act of the past. An example of a new song is Deutero-Isaiah's proclamation in the sixth century BCE that the journey of the exiles through the desert to Zion is a renewal of the journey of the Israelites through the sea to Canaan (Isa 42:10-12; 43:16-21). In Ps 96, the new song tells the story of Yahweh's creation victory over chaos. The proper response to a divine deed is praise, for praise gives what the Lord does not yet possess: full recognition on earth. God's faithful ones are thus exhorted to declare the Lord's glory, that is, preeminence in the heavenly world, to those who do not yet know and acknowledge it.

Worship given to Yahweh alone is done at the expense of other gods, according to verse 4. Such gods are nothing more than their statues ("idols"). In contrast, Yahweh created the vast heavens. In verse 6, Yahweh is surrounded by symbols of divinity—brilliant light ("honor and majesty") and the splendor of the sanctuary.

Let the nations praise the Lord (vv. 7-10)

Attention now shifts to the earth and to the nations who once worshiped the gods dethroned by the Lord's victory. At one stage in the development of biblical monotheism, the Bible conceded that each nation of the world had its own god, though it affirmed Yahweh, the Lord, was the Most High over all of them (Deut 32:8). Psalm 96, however, like Pss 58 and 82 and Isa 40–55, dismisses other heavenly beings as utterly powerless and no longer deities. They have been exposed as nonentities by Yahweh's effortless victory. Instead of revering their no-gods, the nations should enter the Lord's house with their tribute, chanting "The LORD has become king!" (v. 10, my translation). For the translation, see Ps 93:1 and the Introduction, "The Genres and Rhetoric of the Psalms," no. 5, in *Psalms 1–72*.

As verse 10 makes clear, the proclamation of the Lord as king implies that the victory established the world ("the world is firmly established"); the Lord "will judge" (i.e., rule) the world in virtue of the kingship won by that victory.

Let heaven and earth rejoice before the Lord (vv. 11-13)

"Heaven and earth" is the biblical idiom for the universe. The universe rejoices as the Lord restores its harmony and fertility. Something more may be intended by the nature imagery, however. The New Year festival was, in preexilic times, held in the fall at the return of the winter rains bringing fertility to field and forest. The exultant rejoicing of nature is a metaphor for its blooming and fruitfulness. "He is coming" in verse 13 is taken by some scholars as referring exclusively to a future event on the grounds that the kingdom of God is purely eschatological and only realized in a far-off future. The phrase, however, refers to a present reality that will be fully realized in the future.

Theological and Ethical Analysis

The absolute claims of the sole deity of the Lord made by this psalm can conflict with the instincts of modern Christians and

Jews to respect and accord worth to other religions. There is no easy reconciliation of biblical claims for the sole deity and modern viewpoints. One must respect the uniqueness of this psalm, its intense focus and its liturgical character. One can even say that the highest possible worship is to leave in the one God's hands the tremendous diversity and richness of human religious response.

The psalm expresses, positively, belief in the one Creator and, negatively, rejects everything else that poses as God. It credits the Lord with the beauty and diversity of the universe and leaves in the divine hands the varieties of human response. It celebrates a God who rules justly and wishes to be known and worshiped by the entire universe. In the famous first line of his *Confessions,* Saint Augustine quotes verse 4, "Great are you, O Lord, and exceedingly worthy of praise," continuing (even more famously), "you have made us and drawn us to yourself, and our heart is unquiet until it rests in you" (WSA, *The Confessions,* I/1:39).

PSALM 97

Literary Analysis

Psalm 97 is an enthronement psalm along with Pss 47, 93, and 95–99. It celebrates the supremacy of Yahweh over the peoples of the earth ("most high over all the earth," v. 9a) and over the denizens of heaven ("exalted far above all gods," v. 9b). The triumph of Yahweh the Storm God, manifested in earth-shattering thunder and lightning, renews the world and dethrones deities, bringing joy to Yahweh's own people. As noted in the Introduction, "The Genres and Rhetoric of the Psalms," no. 5, in *Psalms 1–72,* the storm symbolizes kingship based on cosmic victory.

The traditions of kingship used in this psalm derive ultimately from the combat myth, according to which one deity becomes supreme over the others by vanquishing chaotic forces threatening the world. The focus in the poem is on the battle victory, the embarrassment of other gods' clients, and the joy of Yahweh's clients.

The narrative shapes the structure. A singer proclaims that Yahweh has become king ("The LORD is king!" v. 1*a*) as the victorious God appears in a storm (vv. 2-6). Verse 6*b* ("all the peoples behold his glory") is the transition to part 2, which shows people reacting in diverse ways to the victory (vv. 7-9). "Worshipers of images," that is worshipers of the deities dethroned by Yahweh's victory, are put to shame (v. 7), whereas Yahweh's own people rejoice (vv. 8-9). Part 3 celebrates the happy state of those who are the clients of the Lord (vv. 10-11). The divine name occurs seven times (YHWH six times and "Most High" once).

Exegetical Analysis

The Lord has become king and the earth rejoices (v. 1)

For the translation "The LORD has become king!" instead of the customary "The LORD is king!" see under Ps 93:1 and the Introduction, "The Genres and Rhetoric of the Psalms," no. 5, in *Psalms 1–72*. English readers need occasional reminding that the Lord, a title, is the ancient Jewish and Christian translation of "Yahweh," a proper name. This commentary on occasion uses "Yahweh" in order to emphasize the particular deity named Yahweh in contrast to other deities. "Coastlands" can mean the shore of the mainland (e.g., Isa 23:2), an island (e.g., Jer 2:10), or faraway nations (e.g., Isa 40–66). The latter is the meaning here, for the whole world sees the storm theophany. Intense rejoicing is the natural response to victory.

The battle and victory of the Lord of the storm (vv. 2-7)

The storm symbolizes at once the tumult of battle and the grandeur of victory, for verse 7 shows victory achieved. The landscape pounded by lightning and thunder is portrayed with bold metaphors, for example, the earth seeing and trembling (v. 4*b*; cf.

Hab 3:10; Ps 77:16; Jer 51:29), mountains melting like wax (Ps 97:5*a*; cf. Ps 22:14; Mic 1:4). Some of the vocabulary is drawn from stock descriptions of God appearing in the storm: "clouds and thick darkness" (cf. Deut 4:11; 5:22; Ezek 34:12); "fire goes before him" (cf. Ps 50:3), and "lightnings." In the storm clouds, God marches across the sky, which is suggested by the phrase "goes before [the LORD]" in verses 3 and 5. "The heavens proclaim" means that the thunder and lightning announce victory.

Who is the enemy defeated by Yahweh? In the traditional combat myth (reflecting a polytheistic worldview), the enemy was a force that threatened cosmic order. Though the enemy is not named here, it seems to be the other gods, for the human clients of the gods are shamed by the victory of Yahweh (v. 7). The emphasis, however, is on the Lord's victory rather than on the vanquished.

Zion joyously receives its victorious Lord who bestows gifts and protection (vv. 8-12)

"Zion hears" the thundering and lightning-filled heavens and reacts with joy to the news of victory. The shift from third to second person within a single verse (v. 8) is a poetic device that underlines the new intimacy of people and the Lord. "Your judgments" (v. 8) refers to the result of the divine intervention or "judgment." Verse 9 is the acclamation of supremacy that one expects after such a grand victory. In the combat myth *Enuma Elish,* "The great gods assembled / And made Marduk's destiny highest; they themselves did obeisance. . . . Thus they granted that he should exercise the kingship of the gods / And confirmed for him the gods of heaven and earth" (Dalley, VI.95-96, p. 264). In Ps 97, Zion rather than the divine assembly makes the proclamation. Verses 10-11 tell of the rewarding of the Lord's people. Similarly, in *Enuma Elish,* tablet VI, Marduk follows up his victory over Tiamat by holding a trial and condemnation of Tiamat's allies, building a palace, and honoring the gods who supported him. In Ps 97:10*a*, the literal rendering, "You who love the LORD, reject evil!" is preferable (so NJPS and NIV). NRSV and NAB emend the text. "Love," here and in similar usages in Deuteronomy (e.g., Deut 6:5; 30:16), connotes affectionate choice and exclusive loyalty to a particular god. To the faithful people God offers protection (v. 10bc) and well-being (v. 11). "Light" in verse 11 is divine favor as in Isa 58:8, 10. "Joy" probably means "radiance" (so NJPS); two similar Hebrew roots, "light" and "rejoice," were collapsed into one verb over the course of time. Verse 11 therefore exhorts the people to adopt the proper response to God's great victory. Verse 12 similarly exhorts the people to shout with joy and praise the name of Yahweh, which presents the deity to worshipers on earth.

Theological and Ethical Analysis

The psalm celebrates the moment when Yahweh, the Lord, became king over heaven and earth. That primordial moment, celebrated in the liturgy, serves as a paradigm of what will finally be: a future time when the Lord's sovereignty will be perfectly realized. Celebrating the Lord's sovereignty dethrones the powers and principalities that demand people's total allegiance. Ancient peoples imagined those powers as deities. Today, one might imagine the deities as honor, power, or money. To love God exposes these deities as false. The poem invites an unselfish rejoicing in the great work of the Lord, the creation and the governance of the beautiful universe and the people within it. It also forms the hope that the moment of victory will prevail; the wicked will be defeated and light will dawn for the righteous.

PSALM 98

Literary Analysis

Psalm 98 is an enthronement hymn, like Pss 47, 93, and 95–99. It urges Israel and the whole world, animate and inanimate, to respond in glad song to the Lord's victory on behalf of Israel. Like other such psalms, it draws on the combat myth, the narrative of how one god won a victory and ascended to first place in the pantheon. This psalm concentrates on the worldwide response to the divine victory. See the Introduction, "The Genres and Rhetoric of the Psalms," no. 5, in *Psalms 1–72*.

The dramatic logic of the poem is easy to follow. Verses 1-3 invite Israel to sing praise, "for" the Lord "has done marvelous things" (v. 1*b*). Verses 1*c*-3*a* elaborate the Lord's act in verse 1*b*. Verses 4-6 invite the inhabitants of the earth to join in the same song, and verses 7-9 invite the inanimate elements of the world as well. The conjunction "for" in verses 1*b* and 9*a* balance each other. "For" in verse 1*b* introduces the victory, and "for" in verse 9*a* introduces the judgment of the world produced by the victory. Essentially, the psalm summons the world to welcome and accept their new Lord. It begins by announcing the Lord has won a great victory and ends by introducing the Lord to his new subjects. "To judge the earth" does not primarily refer to judgment at the end of time but rather to the Lord taking up rule now as befits the king of the universe

Exegetical Analysis

Sing, O Israel, to the triumphant Lord (vv. 1-3)

The group addressed by the plural imperative "sing" is not specified, but the references to God's promises to Israel in verse 3 indicate that it is Israel. Israel fits nicely in the sequence of addressees—Israel (vv. 1-3), the nations (vv. 4-6), and inanimate nature (vv. 7-9). The "new song" responds to the wondrous act of Yahweh. "New" does not mean original words and lyrics, but a new divine act. The act is new in the sense of renewing or "repowering" an ancient act. A good example of such renewal is Second Isaiah's interpretation of the sixth-century return of the Babylonian exiles as renewing the ancient passage of Israel through the Red Sea (e.g., Isa 42:10-12; 43:16-21).

What is the divine deed that is "repowered"? One can infer its nature from its worldwide effect—the universe welcomes the

Lord as its sole ruler. The deed, therefore, created and renewed the world. The psalm elicits a response to the divine deed. All people, not just Israel, should recognize and praise what the Lord has done. God has made the victory public (v. 2), presumably by means of the traditional storm-god theophany of thunder and lightning. Israel must only acknowledge the benefits received from being the Lord's own people.

Let the nations of the world welcome their new Lord (vv. 4-6)

As a result of the victory, the nations of the world are Yahweh's subjects. The nations are now invited to welcome their new divine Lord with jubilant song and musical accompaniment. The verses describe the ceremony that welcomes the deity. "Lyre" *(kinnôr)* is often associated with singing (Gen 31:27; 2 Sam 6:5). The "horn" *(šôpār,* lit. "ram's horn") was used both in war and worship; it was also used in the coronation of a king (1 Kgs 1:34, 39, 41; 2 Kgs 9:13).

Let the nonhuman world welcome its new Lord (vv. 7-9)

The distinction between Nature and human beings is not so sharp in the Bible as in modern Western thinking. Endowed with human traits, Nature welcomes the victorious Lord who exercises the role of king. The sea "roars" thunderously, the rivers "clap their hands" like human beings (cf. Ps 47:1). "Rivers" is a better translation than NRSV "floods," which wrongly suggests a hostile sea. Rather, the world is fully and beautifully organized in paired constitutive elements—"sea" and dry land (NRSV: "world"), rivers and mountains (holding up the great disk of earth).

"At the presence of the LORD" in verse 9a has the nuance of "at Yahweh's approach" (NJB). One can imagine the Lord proceeding solemnly to the palace. People and Nature applaud as the Lord approaches to take up rule. The Lord will rule with "righteousness" and "equity" *(mîšārîm).* The two nouns are a word pair found with slight variation also in Isa 11:4; 33:15; 45:19; Pss 9:8; and 58:1. The words describe the just rule that assures the flourishing of human beings and nature and protects the vulnerable from oppression. Kings in Mesopotamia sometimes proclaimed a *misharum* decree on their accession. Second Samuel 8:15 describes King David: "So David became king over all Israel; and David administered justice and equity to all his people" (my translation). "To judge" in Ps 98:9 is thus much broader than issuing judicial decrees. No wonder the nations are to welcome it with joy!

Theological and Ethical Analysis

At first reading, all of the enthronement psalms seem to be saying the same thing. Closer reading reveals different emphases. This poem is intent on preparing the nations for accepting their new Lord. This Lord has acted out of special fidelity to Israel and now is revealed as the sole sovereign of the nations. The Lord issues divine decrees that make the world a just and hospitable place for the entire human race.

The insistence on the universal rule of Yahweh, the God of Israel, might seem to denigrate other religions. The poem certainly presumes there is one deity to the exclusion of all others and that the deity has chosen Israel as special. Worshiping the Lord with absolute devotion, however, means entrusting the same Lord with ruling other peoples with their ways and allegiances. By its nature, a hymn does not reflect on the validity of other religions but invites worship of one God. This psalm proclaims that the Lord has generously created the world and invites all peoples without exception to enjoy it. It invites all and condemns none.

PSALM 99

Literary Analysis

Psalm 99 is the last in the series of enthronement hymns (Pss 47, 93, 95–98) that celebrate the Lord's victory, ascent to the throne, and decrees that determine the course of the world.

Vestiges of the combat myth are discernible, in particular the enthronement (v. 1), the universal acknowledgment of the Lord's supremacy, the issuing of decrees, and the grant of benefits to the Lord's own people. Like other enthronement psalms, this one presumes readers know the full story and focuses on aspects of the story. See the Introduction, "The Genres and Rhetoric of the Psalms," no. 5, in *Psalms 1–72.*

Recurrent phrases guide the reader through the poem. The exclamation "Holy is he!" in verses 3 and 5 rises to a climax at the end of verse 9 where the emphatic pronoun "he" is replaced by "the LORD our God." The invitation "extol the LORD our God" concludes both the first section (vv. 1-5, 42 Hebrew words) and the second section (vv. 6-9, 41 Hebrew words). The divine name "LORD" *(YHWH)* occurs seven times. Formal markers suggest the following structure: summons to the nations to recognize Yahweh who establishes justice in the world (vv. 1-5); mediation of justice by Israel's traditions (vv. 6-9).

Exegetical Analysis

Summons to the nations to recognize Yahweh who establishes justice in the world (vv. 1-5)

The poem depicts the moment of the Lord's appearance as victor over chaos and proclaimer of decrees. "Sits enthroned" reflects the traditional understanding of the verb as a participle. The word can, with equal appositeness, be interpreted as the perfect tense of the verb, that is, "has taken his throne," which would be parallel to "he has become king." The two verbs in verse 1 are parallel in 1 Kgs 1:13, 17, 24, 30; and 16:11. The "cherubim" are the large composite animals (e.g., human face, lion flanks, eagle wings) that appear in ancient Near Eastern art as guardians of royal thrones. "Exalted over" in the context means recognized by the nations as supreme. "Mighty King" in verse 4 is an uncertain translation of an unusual Hebrew phrase. The same verse describes an important aspect of creation: the establishing of justice in the universe by the newly enthroned king. In the combat myth, the victorious deity arranged the good order (justice) of the universe. See the notes for Ps 97 regarding the storm-god, Marduk, establishing justice in the epic poem *Enuma Elish*. The god not only created the physical universe but also regulated how the universe functioned ("justice"). The Lord issues these "decrees" in Jacob. As Zion is the place where the Lord is enthroned and issues such decrees, the nations must come there to worship and learn.

Mediation of justice by Israel's traditions (vv. 6-9)

The sudden appearance of Moses, Aaron, and Samuel in verse 6 has puzzled commentators. Some suggest they are mentioned to show God communicated with the great ancestors indirectly (through a cloud), suggesting that divine communication is indirect. More common is the suggestion that the three speakers are intercessors for a sinful people, suggesting that Israel, privileged as they may be, are still sinners. The text, however, emphasizes that ancestral leaders conversed with God and heard "his decrees" and "statutes." Though the verbs "cried" and "answered" can mean crying out and being rescued (cf. Ps 22:5), they designate here ordinary converse between a divine patron and human clients, as in Isa 65:12, 24. The interpretation proposed in this commentary is that the great ancestors and founders—Moses, Aaron, and Samuel— heard God's just decrees and mediated them to Israel. "Priests" were teachers in Israel. Moses and Aaron work closely together in Exod 4–5, and Moses hears God speaking from the pillar of cloud in Num 12:1-9 and Deut 31:15. Samuel also taught the people; his association with the word of God is memorably stated in 1 Sam 3:10*b*, "Speak, for your servant is listening." In short, the three are named because Israel's traditions enshrined the decrees by which the world operates. James Moffatt's free translation suggests that the worship and teaching system continues the work of the founders:

His priests have still a Moses and an Aaron,
   his worshippers have still a Samuel;
and the Eternal answers when they call to him,
   still through a cloudy pillar speaks to them.
(*A New Translation of the Bible: Containing the Old and
New Testaments* [New York, Harper & Brothers, 1935]).

The conclusion is that the nations should go to Zion for the authoritative teaching of the Lord. Indeed, Isa 2:3 (cf. Mic 4:2) is explicit on the topic:

Many peoples shall come and say,
"Come, let us go up to the mountain of the LORD,
   to the house of the God of Jacob;
that he may teach us his ways
   and that we may walk in his paths."
For out of Zion shall go forth instruction,
   and the word of the LORD from Jerusalem.

The Zion songs exalt the holy city as the place of the Lord's presence and revelation (Pss 46, 48, 76, 84, 87, 122).

Theological and Ethical Analysis

One of the paradoxes of the Old Testament is that the God of the entire world chooses a particular nation and a particular city. According to this psalm, the justice with which God wishes to endow creation has been revealed in Zion and is to be found in the authoritative traditions of Israel. The nations are to realize that the Lord meets them in a particular place and that the Lord's decrees are somehow available to them in the traditions of a particular people.

The dangers of being the group elected are, of course, obvious. They can be smug; they can turn away from their God-given task of mediating the Lord's presence and words to the nations; their evil conduct can make it difficult for the nations to see God in them. This psalm, being a hymn, does not dwell on the dangers. It simply states the divine choice of Zion and the divine decrees uttered to Israel's leaders and invites all to marvel and obey. It shows a loving God who wishes to enter into a relationship with all human beings and a just God who wishes the world to be founded on divine righteousness.

PSALM 100

Literary Analysis

Though not usually classed as an enthronement psalm, this short hymn is a fitting conclusion to the series. It invites the nations to come to the Jerusalem Temple and acknowledge Israel as the Lord's special people, so that they too will benefit from the Lord's bounty and fidelity.

The poem is structured by its seven verbs in the imperative mood—"make a joyful noise," "worship," "come," "know," "enter," "give thanks," and "bless." All express an aspect of worship. There are two occurrences of the Hebrew conjunction *kî* ("that" in v. 3*a* and "for" in v. 5*a*), which in a hymn gives the motive for praise. The verb "know" (v. 3*a*) occupies a central place. The parts of the poem, verses 1-3 and 4-5, are signaled by imperative verbs plus Hebrew *kî*. The two parts are parallel, making essentially the same statement. The theme of the psalm, the pilgrimage of the nations to the holy mountain Zion, is also the theme of Pss 48:1-2; 78:68-69; Isa 2:1-4, 60-62; 66:18-23; Ezek 40:2; and Zech 14:10.

Exegetical Analysis

Come into the Temple and recognize the Lord's own people (vv. 1-3)

Like the preceding hymns, this one begins with a verb in the imperative mood commanding the nations to worship the Lord. "Gladness" and "singing" characterized Israelite worship; it was noisy and joyous. Though the Old Testament does not have many descriptions of popular worship, hints such as these suggest grand processions into the Temple courts accompanied by musical instruments and choirs.

The nations are to confess that Yahweh is *the* God (such is the force of the emphatic pronoun *hû* in v. 3*a*, left untranslated in NRSV). The speaker asserts that this God created us and hence we belong to him. The Hebrew text tradition has handed down two interpretations of verse 3*b* as NRSV notes in a footnote. One tradition, called "ketib" ("written"), has *lō'*, "not," which yields "and not we ourselves." The other tradition, called "qere" ("spoken"), has *lô*, "to, of him," which yields "we are his." The second tradition is correctly chosen by NRSV and most translators, for it alone is idiomatic Hebrew.

"Sheep of his pasture" is a Hebrew idiom meaning sheep that the Lord personally pastures, not delegating to anyone else (as in Pss 74:1; 79:13; 95:7; Jer 23:1; Ezek 34:31). Every other flock is shepherded by its own divine patron, whereas Israel is shepherded by the Most High. According to Deut 32:8-9,

> When the Most High apportioned the nations,
>   when he divided humankind,
> he fixed the boundaries of the peoples
>   according to the number of the gods;
> the LORD's own portion was his people,
>   Jacob his allotted share.

The people believe they are the Lord's own; their prosperity advertises to the world the power of their Lord. The Lord's universal power and lordship is visible in a particular place and people.

Enter the Temple of the Lord who is a model of love and fidelity! (vv. 4-5)

The second part of the psalm parallels the first, repeating the invitation and the motive. Verse 4 makes it clear that the nations enter the Temple in Jerusalem by specifying "his gates" and "his courts." The phrase "for the LORD is good" means reliable toward us, trustworthy. "Steadfast love" *(ḥesed)* and "faithfulness" *('ĕmûnāh)* are a common word pair (e.g., Pss 36:5; 88:11; 89:2), expressing the absolute fidelity of God toward Israel. Israel is a showcase of the Lord's goodness. The nations should take note and, the poem implies, consider honoring the Lord as God.

Theological and Ethical Analysis

Israel's awareness of the Lord's universal sovereignty and pride in being his special people shine through the poem. All nations are invited to come to Jerusalem, enter the Temple, and worship the Lord. They will see there a people created (v. 3) and sustained (v. 5) by the Lord. The text shapes the prayer of the community who believe they in some way represent to the world the blessings that God wishes all nations to have. Israel cannot take inordinate pride in their vocation, for it is a pure gift of God. Their task is to open their gates and let in the nations. The psalm holds out the possibility that all the nations will join Israel in prayer before the Lord.

PSALM 101

The previous psalm invited the nations to "enter his gates with thanksgiving, / and his courts with praise" (100:4). In Ps 101, the Israelite king tells how he will conduct himself as the Lord's ruler of the place to which the nations are invited to come.

Literary Analysis

Though unique in the Psalter, this poem contains clues to its purpose and the identity of its speaker. The speaker ("I") is in charge of a great "house" (v. 7), has the authority to destroy the wicked in his territory (v. 8), and lives in "the city of the LORD" (v. 8). The speaker is therefore the Davidic king, and the psalm is most likely his public proclamation at his enthronement or its annual commemoration. As he begins to reign, the king assures his divine patron, Yahweh, of his loyalty and willingness to carry out divine justice. Modern readers might assume from the prophetic books that the Israelite king was subject to constant critique, but the king in the ancient Near East (including Israel) was generally regarded as a pillar of the universe and essential instrument of divine governance. Even the prophets' criticism presumes a lofty ideal of kingship. A random selection of proverbs gives the view of the king's role that is presupposed in Psalm 101: "Loyalty and faithfulness preserve the king, / and his throne is upheld by righteousness" (Prov 20:28); "take away the wicked from the presence of the king, / and his throne will be established in righteousness" (Prov 25:5). The psalm is a king's inaugural statement of purpose before his divine patron and his people.

The poem opens with the king's acknowledgment of the divine initiative ("loyalty and justice") that brought him to his throne (v. 1) and a prayer that the same divine strength uphold him in his royal duties (v. 2ab). There follow twelve promises (in the first person) to be faithful in attitude and intention (vv. 2c-4), to prohibit abuses of power by members of the court (v. 5), to appoint only God-fearing administrators (v. 6), to expel the wicked (v. 7), and to administer a fair judicial system (v. 8). The vows express a profound desire to be a good servant of the Lord and thus an ideal ruler.

Exegetical Analysis

I praise the divine favor that brought me here and plead for continued help (vv. 1-2b)

The poem begins with thanks and petition. The opening phrase means "I will sing of *your* loyalty and justice," that is, I acknowledge God's mercy that placed me on the throne. In Ps 89:1-2, the king begins a lament in just this way: "I will sing of your steadfast love, O LORD, forever; / with my mouth I will proclaim your faithfulness to all generations." In Ps 101, the declaration of loyalty to God, the king first acknowledges God's prior loyalty to him. The question "When shall I attain it?" expresses longing for the virtues necessary to be a good king for God.

Promises of fidelity to the Lord (vv. 2c-8)

Some biblical expressions call for comment. The Hebrew verb "to walk" (v. 2c) is a biblical metaphor for "conduct oneself." "Heart" (v. 2c) in biblical anthropology is the center of intelligence and judgment rather than of feeling; the king promises to make honest judgments as he rules. "House" (v. 2c) here means royal palace as in 2 Sam 11:2; 1 Kgs 3:1; and 14:26. In the language of biblical "psychology," what the "eyes" (v. 3a) take in is stored in the heart. The king promises never to take the wicked as role models. Hebrew "to hate" (v. 3c) refers to action rather than attitude, hence actively to thwart. Verses 4-5 describe his conduct toward wicked people. "Perverseness of heart" (v. 4a) is an inner attitude that cannot always be discerned by outsiders; the king expresses his intent that such people never enter his inner circle. "Evil" (v. 4b) is an instance of the figure abstract (evil) for concrete (evil people). In verse 5a, "secretly" has the nuance "when the other person is absent"; slander would be common among ambitious courtiers. "Haughty" and "arrogant" (v. 5cd) are common attitudes of royalty. Such attitudes interfere with the king's administration of (divine) justice, which has as an essential element of respect and care for the poor.

Though the first promise in verse 2c was couched in positive terms, the next seven (vv. 3-5) are cast in negative terms. The king returns to positive formulations in verse 6, promising, like the head of a family, "to take care of" those who are loyal to him. Such loyalists will make up the pool of talent for royal service. The king's criteria for appointments prize loyalty to the Lord and virtues especially suitable for administering a kingdom: honesty, respect for others, and truthfulness.

Verses 7-8 return to negative formulations. They are all concerned with the administration of justice in the land. "Deceit" and "lies" suggest perjury and abuse of the judicial system. To judge by the numerous exhortations to judge impartially in the prophets and in the law codes, judicial bias must have been rife. "Morning by morning" means "each morning." Second Samuel 15:2 and Jer 21:12 are sometimes adduced as evidence that royal judgment was exercised in the morning, but neither supports such a conclusion. Night may simply be a metaphor for the time of sin, with justice coming with the morning sun as in Job 38:12-13:

> "Have you commanded the morning since your days began,
>   and caused the dawn to know its place,
> so that it might take hold of the skirts of the earth,
>   and the wicked be shaken out of it?"

In comparable religions, the sun was a god or goddess of justice. Psalm 19 associates the all-seeing sun and the law.

Theological and Ethical Analysis

The Davidic king solemnly accepts his office and its responsibilities, acknowledging his divine patron and praying for further help. He promises to be faithful even in his inmost heart. All the promises are related to his royal office and are concerned with the roots rather than the particulars of royal behaviors. It is significant that the Israelite king does not, for example, promise to expand the boundaries of the land by leading military expeditions or to build monuments and temples to his divine patron. Rather, he promises his own loyal conduct and that of his court officials. The ideal qualities in his courtiers is not loyalty and obedience to himself but loyalty and obedience to God.

The great figures of the Bible—kings, prophets, priests, servants—were great because they were loyal servants of God. Moses was the great servant, and his model of service influenced other servants such as Gideon, Samuel, Jeremiah, and the unnamed servant in Isa 40–55. David too was a model servant, though the Bible does not hide or disguise his faults. The poem, a "mirror of the king," is a model prayer for anyone aspiring to serve in a responsible position. It supports courageous and magnanimous service to the community.

PSALM 102

Literary Analysis

This lament is one of the traditional seven penitential psalms (Pss 6, 32, 38, 51, 102, 130, 143). They were so designated in the Christian liturgy from early times. Its anguish contrasts with the confident tone of the surrounding psalms. Operating from the ancient assumption that the world is made by the gods for themselves, the psalmist seeks to demonstrate that it is to the Lord's advantage to grant healing. By so doing, the Lord will gain the praise and recognition of the nations (vv. 15, 18-22) and ensure a new generation of Israelite worshipers (v. 28). The psalmist's sufferings affect the people, for recovery of health in Jerusalem advertises to the nations the Lord's protection of the sacred city of Israel (vv. 18-22). The blending of private perspective (esp. in vv. 1-11) and corporate perspective (esp. in vv. 12-23, 25-27) puzzles some commentators, leading them to suggest that an individual lament was supplemented with national elements. There is no need to suppose additions, however. Private and national concerns can appear in a single psalm, for example Ps 77 and Lamentations. It is possible that a public figure like the king speaks for himself and for the people. Concern with the sorry state of Zion suggests a date of composition in the sixth century BCE.

The sufferer assumes that it is in the Lord's interest to ensure a sufficiency of human worshipers: I, a member of your own people, have had my days cut short (vv. 3-11, 23-24). I have not lived the days allotted to human beings and not had my allotment of children. May God not "take me away at the mid-point of my life" (v. 24a), before I can give birth to a new generation who will worship you (v. 28). Moreover, healing me in the Temple will cause the nations to acknowledge the power of your name in this place (vv. 15-17, 21-22). To make the argument, the psalmist emphasizes the contrast between afflicted and mortal human beings (vv. 3-11, 23-24b) and the eternal and powerful Lord (vv. 12-22, 24c-27).

The argument is made in three parallel sections: hear me, for my days pass away (vv. 1-11); you receive honor in your Temple in Zion (vv. 12-22); do not cut short my life, O Eternal One; let our children praise you (vv. 23-28). "LORD" (v. 1a) and "day" (vv. 2d) are significant in the poem, for each word occurs seven times.

Exegetical Analysis

Hear me, for my days pass away (vv. 1-11)

The superscription borrows the key word "prayer" from verses 1 and 17 to characterize the psalm. Verses 12-22 (esp. v. 17) make clear that verses 1-2 are uttered in the Temple. The psalmist asks to be heard in a particular place (the Temple) and time, "the day of my distress" (v. 2). Psalm 18:6, which uses almost identical language to verses 1-2, is explicit about the Temple as the locale:

> In my distress I called upon the LORD;
> to my God I cried for help.
> From his temple he heard my voice,
> and my cry to him reached his ears.

Five times in two verses the sufferer asks God to pay attention.

Verses 3-11 are a subsection defined by several inclusions: "my days" in verses 3 and 11; "withered like grass" in verses 4 and 11; "eat bread" in verses 4 and 9. The list of the psalmist's physical and social suffering comes to a climax in verse 10 with the statement of its cause: divine anger. "Indignation and anger" in verse 10 is a conventional way of stating divine absence.

The psalmist's self-description uses memorable images of fragility and lifelessness—smoke disappearing (v. 3), a body so desiccated from weeping that its bones are visible (vv. 4-5), living apart from others (v. 6; see Isa 34:11; Zeph 2:14), living outside one's home (v. 7), loss of reputation and social standing (v. 8), taking part in a mourning ritual (v. 9; see Isa 61:3). Important for verse 4 is Hos 9:16 (identical verbs are in italics),

> Ephraim is *stricken*,
>   their root is *dried up*,
>   they shall bear no fruit.
> Even though they give birth,
>   I will kill the cherished offspring of their womb.

Generative power is destroyed both by desiccation and premature death. A "lonely bird" (v. 7) is a symbol of vulnerability, as in Ps 11:1; Prov 27:8; and Hos 9:11. Verse 10 holds God directly responsible; it does not consider "secondary causality."

You receive honor in your Temple in Zion (vv. 12-22)

Verse 12 signals a new section by its change of grammatical person from third to second and its new topic, God's eternity and residence in Zion. It is in God's interest to grant the request to live out the full course of life, for the nations will see the Lord's glory in the Temple, and there will be future generations to give praise.

The Lord lives "forever," "to all generations" (v. 12), but human beings are short-lived, especially when they are afflicted and cut off before their time. The eternal Lord must therefore see to it that there be a sufficient number of worshipers. Verses 13-17 assume that the healing will take place in the Temple, for Israel holds it dear (v. 14); the Lord built it (v. 16); and it is the ordinary place of hearing of prayer (cf. 1 Kgs 8).

Verses 18-22 continue the argument: Your rescue of me will be recorded for those not yet born (v. 18) as an instance of your care for needy clients (vv. 19-20) and will motivate nations and kingdoms to praise you (vv. 21-22). Verse 22 envisions a time when the nations of the world will come to Jerusalem to acknowledge the power of the Lord. God's mercy is reckoned as an act of power bringing the nations to praise.

Do not cut short my life, O Eternal One; let our children praise you (vv. 23-28)

Because the contrast between mortality and eternity has been so clearly drawn up to this point, the psalm needs only to mention the points of contrast. The prayer that the psalmist not be taken away "at the mid-point of my life" means dying before living out the allotted life span and providing children for the next generation. The argument is similar to that made in verses 12-22 with one difference: The "place" the Lord has built is not the Temple in Zion but the entire universe. Even the seemingly ageless universe is not ageless when compared to the divine being. Heaven and earth wear out like clothing, but the Lord endures. The concluding prayer flows from the argument: If you want future worshipers, help our dying selves. Give us children that you might always have worshipers; let the nations see your saving activity. Verses 25-27 are quoted in Heb 1:10-12.

Theological and Ethical Analysis

Few psalms accept so unquestioningly the view that the world was made for God and that one must therefore persuade God to act by appealing to God's interest. The afflictions in verses 3-11 are portrayed as those of someone about to die prematurely (vv. 3, 11, 23-24) without leaving children to carry on the divine service. The motives presented for God to act are all God-centered: The nations of the world will see your rescue of me in Zion as a proof that your dwelling is a place of healing and will acknowledge its holiness; allowing me to live the full measure of my days will ensure future worshipers of you (vv. 18, 28). The concerns go beyond a private healing. The pray-er has in view the universal acknowledgment of the Lord's sovereignty and the future of Israel. Healing the sufferer is equivalent to having compassion on Zion (vv. 13-14).

One's initial reaction to the psalm can be negative. The strategy can seem excessively political: It's in your interest to help us. Would it not be more appropriate to mention as motive God's love and respect for human beings, which is asserted many times in biblical covenants and assurances? It is true that the poet's strategy of persuading God is calculating; it is also true that it is unselfish and reverent. The psalmist behaves as a guest in the world, keenly aware that nothing is owed, all is grace. Debilitating sufferings have not stifled awareness of God's grandeur and eternity. The psalmist's own mortality brings thoughts of God, eternal and unchanging, and of the place, Zion, where this God meets mortals. In the psalm, God is at once distant and near, transcendent yet found in a particular place. Oneself is not the starting point of conversation with God. Rather, divine eternity and grandeur, at first sight perhaps off-putting, turn out to be an entry into a new relationship with God.

Psalm 103

Literary Analysis

As the preceding lament (Ps 102) blended personal and national complaint into a single lament, so this hymn blends personal and national benefits into unified praise. Indeed, some form critics are so struck by the presence of personal and national elements that they posit a "mixed genre" of late date, when, it is supposed, traditional genres began to be shaped in new combinations. Such a conclusion is possible but not necessary, for a singer with a keen national consciousness, such as the king, would see communal issues reflected in personal experience.

There are twenty-two verses, the number of consonants in the Hebrew alphabet, making it an acrostic even though the verses do not begin with successive letters of the alphabet. The poem has a clear argument. There are two basic contrasts: (1) God as healer of an individual (vv. 1-5) and the nation (vv. 6-14); (2) earthly beings (vv. 15-18) and heavenly beings (vv. 19-22). Fragile earthly beings and robust heavenly beings are alike summoned to give praise to the Lord. In terms of formal structure, opening verses (1-5) match closing verses (19-22), both in the number of Hebrew words in each section (thirty-five) and in the opening verb "Bless."

Exegetical Analysis

Bless the Lord, O my soul, for all that he has done for you (vv. 1-5)

The opening verb in the imperative mood, "bless" (singular) addresses the psalmist's own "soul" or self. The community is invited to join its voices in praise. "Name" (v. 1) presents the deity to the worshiper; "holy" (v. 1) qualifies the name as discontinuous with everyday reality, utterly transcendent. To bless God is to tell others of the benefits one has received so that others might acknowledge them, thus increasing the clients of the Lord. "All his benefits" (v. 2b) are not enumerated. Instead, the psalmist describes the Lord acting (using the participle form of the verb characteristic of hymns), literally, the one "who forgives all your iniquity, / who heals all your diseases" (v. 3).

The six blessings mentioned in verses 3-5 boil down to one: healing life-threatening disease. Linking sin and disease, mentioned in verse 3, is common in the Bible. Verses 3b, 4a, and 5b explicitly refer to recovery from life-threatening illness. The fixed pair "steadfast love" and "mercy" refers to God's favor that restores health. Renewing of youth in verse 5b means the restoration of health, like the renewed vigor that seems to come with the annual molting of the eagle. Verses 3-5 are crucial to the argument: The bold proclamation of the Lord who overcomes death prepares for the next section, which proclaims that the Lord will heal the people (vv. 6-14).

The Lord deals with Israel with the compassion of a father toward his children (vv. 6-14)

The psalmist interprets the Lord's care for the people as compassion and forgiveness. The hymnic participle "who works vindication" in verse 6*a* continues the syntax of the preceding verses. Verses 6-7 describe one divine action: the revelation to Moses and the liberation from Pharaoh. The following verses (vv. 8-14) seem to echo Exod 33–34, which describe the forgiveness of Israel after their apostasy. The psalm regards the exodus as the forgiveness of Israel rather than the defeat of Egypt. Verse 7*a*, "He made known his ways to Moses," refers to Exod 33:13, "Now if I have found favor in your sight, show me your ways, so that I may know you and find favor in your sight." Verse 8 explicitly quotes Exod 34:6,

> "The LORD, the LORD,
> a God merciful and gracious,
> slow to anger,
> and abounding in steadfast love and faithfulness."

Similarly, verses 9-18 use the language of Exod 34:7,

> "keeping steadfast love for the thousandth generation,
> forgiving iniquity and transgression and sin,
> yet by no means clearing the guilty,
> but visiting the iniquity of the parents
> upon the children
> and the children's children,
> to the third and the fourth generation."

This section is a beloved passage in the Psalter, for it describes the relationship between Israel and God as entirely one of mercy and compassion.

The Lord and earthly beings (vv. 15-18)

Part 2 contrasts earthly and heavenly beings. Verse 14 already hinted at the theme: "he remembers that we are dust." The language of human transience is traditional, being found, for example, in Job 20:8; Pss 37:2; 90:5; and Isa 40:6-8. Counterbalancing the fragility and mortality of human beings is the eternal God whose "steadfast love" and "righteousness" (v. 7) uphold fading human life, bringing it back from the edge of the grave. The psalmist knows this from personal experience (vv. 1-5).

The Lord and heavenly beings (vv. 19-22)

The four-times repeated verb in the imperative mood, "Bless," reprises the same verb in verses 1-2 and signals the conclusion of the poem. The scene shifts decisively from earth to heaven. Unlike humans on earth, heavenly servants are not mortal and sinful but eternal and obedient, offering unfailing and perfect service to their King. The text underlines the full obedience of the heavenly servants: "do his bidding," "obedient to his spoken word," and "do his will." Here God's rule is universal and unhindered, unlike the earth where sickness and sin drag humans down to Sheol (vv. 3-4), and Israel is oppressed (v. 6), sinful (vv. 8-14), and transitory as grass (vv. 15-18).

The phrase "in the heavens" (v. 19) reveals the underlying idea: God understands compassionately that "those who fear him" (vv. 11, 13, 17) on earth are *not* like the angels. God's servants on earth are subject to sin and sickness, oppression, infidelity, and mortality, and their creator knows their limits (v. 14). How can the people not have confidence that God takes human nature into consideration?

Theological and Ethical Analysis

Modern believers may find it disconcerting that ancient people sometimes considered life-threatening illness as an instance of sin. It is true, however, that when unexplained misfortune struck, an ancient was wont to ask, "What have I done wrong?" Mere mortals, it was thought, hardly had an inkling of divine standards and were, moreover, creatures of a day. To be healed of a major disease, therefore, could be interpreted as forgiveness of sin, for it restored one to the land of the living and to God. The psalm reflects such ideas. The pray-er has an extraordinary sense of God as healer. Instinctively and without hesitation, the pray-er knows that the healer is the God of Israel and interprets the founding moment of Israel as an act of compassion. God entered into a relationship with the nation in the time of the exodus fully aware of Israel's needy and sinful condition. God already had grand servants in heaven, magnificently ready, to proclaim and implement universal rule. Such servants offer unhesitating obedience and powerful service. Israel on earth is not like them, and God accepts the difference, ready to forgive and adapt.

Though the psalm might appear to make excuses for failure, it enables one to relate to an infinite God who is not put off by the failings of Israel, who remains utterly faithful to promises made and love offered.

PSALM 104

Psalm 104 is linked to the preceding poem by its opening, "Bless the LORD, O my soul" (which repeats the first and last line of Ps 103), by the theme of God's cosmic rule at the end of Ps 103 and the beginning of Ps 104, and by several shared words ("angels/messengers" and "ministers" in Pss 103:20-21 and 104:4; "renew" in Pss 103:5 and 104:30; and "dust" in Pss 103:14 and 104:29). As many scholars have suggested, it is quite possible that a single author wrote both poems, for both portray a responsive and compassionate God delighting in a variegated and harmonious world.

Literary Analysis

Psalm 104 is a hymn eliciting praise through a series of vignettes (vv. 1-9, 10-12, 13-18, 19-23, 24-26) and offering a reflection (vv. 27-30) and a prayer (vv. 31-35). God, luminous and triumphant (vv. 1-4), organizes primordial waters (vv. 5-18, 24-

26) and darkness (vv. 19-23) into a beautiful whole (vv. 27-35). The depiction of God owes much to the mythology of neighboring cultures—the Canaanite storm-god who vanquishes Sea (vv. 1-18) and the Egyptian sun-disk Aten whose rays illuminate the world (vv. 19-30).

Exegetical Analysis

Yahweh, the creator, defeats Sea (vv. 1-9)

Though most scholars distinguish verses 1-4 as the salute to God and verses 5-9 as the victory of God over the forces of evil, the verses depict a single scene. The singer reverses the expected chronology of events, first describing the Lord enjoying the fruits of victory (vv. 1-4) and then describing the victory itself (vv. 5-9). Formal elements also suggest unity. The two opening verbs ("you are very great" and "you are clothed," v. 1) and the two closing verbs ("you appointed" and "you set a boundary," vv. 8b-9a), both in the second-person singular, have God as their subject. Between these verbs, Yahweh's activity is described in seven participles characteristic of hymns. (NRSV and other translations smooth over the differences between the four verbs in the perfect tense and the seven participles by rendering all with "you.")

Verses 1-9 depict Yahweh as the Storm God who defeats Sea and creates the cosmos. Though Ugaritic texts narrate how the Storm God defeated Sea and bestowed fertility to the earth through his rain, they do not interpret the defeat of chaos as creation as do the biblical texts. The best biblical parallel to verses 3b-4 is Ps 18:7-15 (= 2 Sam 22:8-16), in which the storm-god rescues the king: "He rode on a cherub, and flew; / he came swiftly upon the wings of the wind" (v. 10). In the Ugaritic texts, the storm-god travels with his allies clouds, winds, and rain (CAT 1.5.vi.6-11), as in Ps 104:4. Verses 6-9 tell how the waters covered even the tops of mountains and how God's "rebuke" (v. 7), that is, thunder, threw them into a panic (cf. Job 26:11; Pss 18:15; 76:6). Like panic-stricken soldiers, the waters retreat pell-mell up mountains and down valleys until they arrive at the seashore, their new boundary. Never again will they cover the earth. Earth, freed of encompassing water, can support life. The world is created.

Fertility for the universe: water from below the earth (vv. 10-12)

The theme of fertility dominates this section and the next as the Creator supplies water to the world. The underground water rises to the surface of earth and flows through riverbeds. "Valleys" can mean both perennial rivers and wadis that only occasionally run with water. Wild animals and birds, beyond the range of human beings, find strength and refreshment from the water. The animals add color, sound, and movement to the world.

Fertility for the universe: water from above the earth (vv. 13-18)

From the palace built over the waters in heaven (v. 3), God sends rain for domestic animals and crops, human beings, and the birds and animals of the forest (vv. 16-17). The trio "wine," "bread," and "oil" is found also in Eccl 9:7-8: "Go, eat your *bread* with enjoyment, and drink your *wine* with a merry heart; . . . do not let *oil* be lacking on your head." In the Ugaritic epic Kirta (CAT 1.16.3.7-8, 13-16), drought is described as the absence of the trio bread, wine, and oil, and the storm-god's rain is declared to be "good for the earth." This vignette ends like the preceding one (v. 12) with trees and birds nesting in them (vv. 16-17).

Enlivening light for the universe (vv. 19-23)

At this point, the psalm seems to draw on the mythology surrounding Aten, the divinized sun-disk in Egyptian religion, especially on the "Great Hymn to Aten" of the mid-fifteenth century BCE. Though some scholars deny any influence, the hymn is strikingly similar to the psalm: "When you set in western lightland, / earth is in darkness as if in death. . . . Every lion comes from its den" (*ll.* 13-14, 20, cf. Ps 104:20-21); "When you have dawned, they live, / When you set, they die" (*ll.* 121-22; cf. Ps 104:22, 27-

30). The Egyptian material has been thoroughly reworked in Psalm 104: in verses 19-23, the sun, with the moon, is the marker of day-night rhythm; in verses 27-30 the enlivening sun in Egyptian religion is combined with the divine breath.

Awe and wonder before such divine generosity and power (vv. 24-26)

"How manifold!" is the almost inevitable human response to such an articulated and fertile world. The section completes the picture of the universe by mentioning "the sea" (v. 25), full of life (even human life onboard ships). "Leviathan," who elsewhere is a deadly monster (e.g., Job 3:8; 41:1; Ps 74:14; Isa 27:1), is here a large fish for God's amusement!

The Lord on whom all things depend for life (vv. 27-30)

The verses bring together the themes of fertility associated with the storm-god and of light associated with the Egyptian god Aten. All creatures of land and sea depend directly on God for sustenance. "Breath" and "spirit" translate one Hebrew word, *rûaḥ* ("air in motion"). When God takes it away, people die. When God breathes upon them, they live. The absolute need of God's breath is also emphasized in Gen 2:7 and Ezek 37:10.

A threefold wish: for God (vv. 31-32), the poet (vv. 33-34), and a just universe (v. 35)

The "glory of the LORD" refers back to the brilliance of the victorious deity (vv. 1-2). So total is divine dominion over "earth" and "mountains" that God's mere glance or touch shakes mountains and stirs up volcanoes (v. 32). The poet's response will continue as long as life breath exists (v. 33a). The poem functions like a sacrifice to God—may it be found pleasing (v. 34)! In Hebrew, "meditation" can mean utterance, and "rejoice" can refer to vocal expression. Taken together, the two words refer to joyous performance of the poem.

The wish that sinners be destroyed (v. 35) may strike modern readers as breaking the joyous and positive tone of the poem. It is not an expression of meanness or vengeance, however, but a (negatively expressed) desire that all on earth accept the Lord's dominion. Sinners refuse to acknowledge God as the source of the wonderful world. Justice demands their removal. It should be noted that the psalmist puts their removal in God's hands. The poem ends by reprising the opening line.

Theological and Ethical Analysis

"Joyfully, the psalmist raises a goblet to his lips and rejoices in the gift of the good God," wrote the great Psalms scholar Hermann Gunkel in 1929.

To be sure, lions roar in the night, but the poet finds it completely right. . . . Leviathan rages but God reins him in. Volcanoes smoke, but even these reveal God's splendor. Death is abroad on earth but God is the one who imparts life breath. The poet does not avert his eyes from corruption in the world, but transcends it because he views it with the eyes of God. There is only one thing that the poet does not embrace—sinners, but they will be destroyed. (my translation)

The joy of the psalm arises from viewing the world from God's perspective. God made the world harmonious and capable of supporting every form of life, of which human beings are only one variety. Order and fertility is a precious divine gift (disorder once reigned), and it is God alone whose warming rays and fertilizing waters make the world come alive. God rejoices in this and so should human beings. In fact, their joyous appreciation is as acceptable as a sacrificial offering. Liturgically, the psalm is perfect for Pentecost when God sends the Spirit to enliven and warm the human race through the church (John 20; Acts 2).

PSALM 105

Literary Analysis

After the celebration of the Lord's creation and sustaining of the world in Ps 104, this hymn praises God's wonderful actions in the history of Israel. Similar historical recitals are found in Pss 78, 106, 135, and 136. The aim of Ps 105 is to strengthen the people's faith in God who remained faithful to his promise of land even in times when the people did not actually possess it. In each section of the psalm (from v. 7 forward), the promise of land spoken by a servant of God drives the action forward.

The structure is as follows. Invitation: O offspring of Abraham and Jacob, praise and seek the Lord (vv. 1-6); the Lord remembers the covenant with the ancestors (vv. 7-11); the ancestors in the land of Canaan (vv. 12-15); Joseph in the land of Egypt (vv. 16-22); Israel in Egypt (vv. 23-38); and Israel in the desert (vv. 39-45).

In each section after the invitation, a form of the key words "word/promise," "land," and "servant" (named) appear. The promise of land is realized differently in each period, depending on where Israel is and who the servant is. Thus the promise of land is shown to be effective at all times and in all places. The word "land" occurs ten times; Abraham, Isaac, Jacob, and Joseph occur eight times; synonyms of "word" or "promise" are numerous, for example, "covenant," "sworn promise," "what he had said," "word of promise." A likely date of composition is when Israel was keenly aware of not possessing the land, that is, the early days of the exilic period. Literature of the period displays great interest in the patriarchal period (e.g., Ezek 33:24; Isa 51:1-3). The Chronicler quotes Ps 105:1-15 in 1 Chron 16:8-22, mentioning only the ancestors "few in number" and "of little account," and omitting references to the exodus and conquest.

Exegetical Analysis

Invitation: O offspring of Abraham and Jacob, praise and seek the Lord (vv. 1-6)

In this unusually long invitation, the exact center is verse 3*b*, "let the hearts of those who seek the LORD rejoice." The Hebrew verb "seek" in the Bible usually means to visit the Lord's shrine. The invitation holds off identifying the invited group until the very last line when it names Israel as "offspring" of Abraham and "children" of Jacob. Why is Abraham named three times in this psalm (vv. 6, 9, 42) when elsewhere the Psalter has only one mention of him (Ps 47:9)? The answer seems to be that the psalm is an exploration of God's promise of land to the patriarchs, and Israel is addressed as the seed of Abraham to whom that promise was given.

The Lord remembers the covenant with the ancestors (vv. 7-11)

In verse 7, the singer points to the God whom the people are praising and seeking, employing the emphatic third-person singular pronoun "he" as in Deut 10:17. Here is the Lord our God, whose decisions affect all lands (v. 7*b*), whose legal agreements with beloved clients do not expire (vv. 8-10), including the promise made to the ancestors of old (v. 11). The key words are promise, land (v. 11), and servants (Abraham, Isaac, and Jacob, vv. 9-10).

The ancestors in the land of Canaan (vv. 12-15)

In verses 12-15, the ancestors own no land, being defenseless sojourners in a land ruled by hostile or indifferent kings. Yet they are protected by the divine promise "Do not touch my anointed ones" (v. 15). Genesis 20:6-7 uses "touch" and "prophet" of Abraham, but did not portray him as "anointed." "Strangers" in the Bible are those outside the majority social group, like Abraham among the Hittites at Hebron (Gen 23:4) and Moses among the Midianites (Exod 2:22).

Joseph in the land of Egypt (vv. 16-22)

The complex story found in Genesis is here reduced to three actors: God, the king/Egyptians, and Joseph endowed with the word of the promise. The same actors will appear in the next episode (vv. 23-38) except that Joseph is replaced by Moses and Aaron. What gives power to Joseph exiled from his own land is the word of the Lord entrusted to him (v. 19). (Parallelism suggests the translation of verse 19b should be "until the word of the Lord proved him true," as correctly recognized by REB and NAB.) That word is the reason he is released from prison and ascends to a lofty position in Egypt. The three key words appear: the divine "word" to the "servant" Joseph that enabled him to live safely in the "land" of Egypt.

Israel in Egypt (vv. 23-38)

Two subtle literary devices link this scene with the preceding. First, the verbs that open verses 17, 20, 21, "sent," "sent," and "made" (šāmô) are also the opening verbs in verses 26-28, "sent," "performed" (šāmô), and "sent." Second, the sequence of words spoken in Egypt, "[God] spoke, and there came [wayyābō'] swarms of flies" (v. 31) and "[God] spoke, and the locusts [wayyābō'] came" (v. 34), are in contrast with the sequence of words spoken in the wilderness, "[Israel] asked, and there came [Septuagint, v. 40: wayyābō'; NRSV: "he brought"] quails." The contrast underlines the fact that God prevented the Egyptians from eating the food of their rich land while giving Israel rich food in the desert.

Divine providence is underscored in the story of Israel in Egypt. God not only foresaw Egypt's hostility but actually caused it so that Israel would leave the devastated land with its silver and gold (v. 17). The psalm does not see the desert as a place of rebellion (contrast Num 13-14; 16; 20:1-13; Ps 78:17-33, 56-66) but as a place of miraculous nurture and feeding (vv. 39-45).

Psalm 105 departs from the Pentateuch in making darkness the first plague rather than the ninth (v. 28). Why the change? Presumably, it was done to contrast the land of Egypt with the desert: God's first act for Israel in the wilderness is to light their darkness with fire (v. 39), whereas God's first act against Egypt is to turn their light into darkness. Verse 42 gives the reason for God's leading out of the people from Egypt. The three key words occur in the section: the holy "word" ("promise," v. 42), the "servant" (v. 42), and "the lands" (v. 44).

Israel in the desert (vv. 39-45)

The psalm ends with Israel outside of the land in the desert, yet the people sing joyously (v. 43). Why? They see God's word as a promise. Their future is bright; they have a land according to the promise of God. Note that the psalm does not regard the promise as privilege. It holds up the purpose of election squarely before the eyes of the people: God is speaking the "promise," choosing "servants," and granting a "land" in order that Israel "might keep his statutes and observe his laws" (v. 45). This last phrase reminds us that God's word is not only promise but also law; it demands as well as assures.

Theological and Ethical Analysis

The psalm looks upon God's history with Israel as open-ended and capable of revealing new things. In a time of exile (when the psalm was evidently composed), Israel would be tempted to regard God's promise of the land to Abraham as a thing of the past, annulled by the facts of history. This hymn joyously praises the God who fulfilled the ancient promise of land in different ways. The promise protected the sojourning ancestors, Joseph in Egypt, and Israel in the desert. So too, for Israel now in "the wilderness of the peoples" (Ezek 20:35), God's promise of land is not just for the future; it protects them now and assures them a happy future.

Christians often do not consider God's promise of land, made to Abraham, Isaac, and Jacob, for Christians no longer regard Palestine as their land. In the New Testament, the Acts of the Apostles ends when Paul reaches Rome, the capital of the Gentile world. This psalm, however, does not view God's promise of the land as having only one meaning. The psalmist shows how the promise of land applies also to a landless people. The promise operates differently according to circumstances—protecting (Abraham and Isaac), liberating (Joseph), nurturing in an infertile realm (Israel in the desert). It is impossible that God be unfaithful. It is, alas, possible for the people to sell God short, to interpret promises too literally. Precisely for this reason, the psalm helps us to remember God's wonders in a new way.

PSALM 106

Literary Analysis

Book 4 of the Psalter ends with this lament, which names seven occasions of grace, sin, and forgiveness. Like other historical psalms (78, 105, 135, 136), it selects details with rhetorical mastery. It begins by acknowledging the goodness of God (vv. 1-2) who performed a gracious deed, punished the people when they spurned it, and then forgave them. Verses 1-5 create a template of divine-human encounters. Evidently living in a period of divine anger, the psalmist asks to be there when God's favor returns to the people (vv. 4-5); the assumption is that divine punishment lasts for a predetermined period (see the comments at Pss 39:4; 90:11-12). When the period of wrath comes to its end, God "remembers" and again shows favor (v. 4).

The recital of history in verses 6-46 demonstrates God's initiatives and readiness to start anew when the people rebelled: rebellion and rescue *at the Red Sea* (vv. 7-12); testing God *in the desert* (vv. 13-15); rebellion against Moses and Aaron *in the camp* (vv. 16-18); the calf *at Horeb* and Moses' intercession (vv. 19-23); refusal to attack from the south and divine threat, the sin with Baal *of Peor*, and Phinehas's intercession (vv. 24-31); sin *at the waters of Meribah* (vv. 32-33); the people sacrifice their children *in Canaan*, alternately experiencing God's anger and forgiveness (vv. 34-46). There are seven episodes, each identified by a place name (shown in italics). The fourth and fifth episodes have a complex structure. In the fourth, Moses' intervention turns away the divine wrath (v. 23) that in the other episodes was unleashed against the people. The fifth episode takes up themes from the fourth: As God's angry oath looms unappeased over the people (vv. 26-27), they sin, astonishingly, a second time (vv. 28-29). A plague ensues and only Phinehas's grand intervention saves them (vv. 30-31). The seventh and climactic episode (vv. 34-46) is also complex, for the sin is a typical rather than a single act: the sacrifice of infants (vv. 34-39) that represents the people's adoption of corrupt, native ways. The punishment is also typical, a series of punishments (v. 41) and mercies ("many times he delivered them," v. 43a). The psalm ends with a petition.

Exegetical Analysis

Place me with your people when you again show them favor (vv. 1-6)

The opening invitation, "Praise the LORD!" is also the final word of the preceding psalm. Verse 1 states the theme: God's goodness and steadfast love are everlasting. Though one generation may reject that love, God always offers it to the next. Verse 3 answers verse 2, "Who can utter the mighty doings of the LORD?" The loyal best declare God's praise. Verses 4-5 are crucial: The pray-er knows from history that God's favor will return to the people and so begs to be alive when it happens. What could be greater than living amid a favored and prospering people!

First event: rebellion and rescue at the Red Sea (vv. 7-12)

Verse 6 is transitional, associating the psalmist and community with the ancestors' sins and also with inevitable forgiveness. According to Exod 14:10-31, the advancing Egyptian army provoked the terrified Israelites to complain, "Was it because there were no graves in Egypt that you have taken us away to die in the wilderness? What have you done to us, bringing us out of Egypt?" (Exod 14:11). Despite the people's unbelief, God acts and Israel responds in praise. The pattern presented in the opening verses is verified in the particular incident.

Second event: testing God in the desert (vv. 13-15)

Numbers 11:18-24a, 31-34 tell of the people's desire, "If only we had meat to eat! Surely it was better for us in Egypt" (Num 11:18). Though the Lord indeed provided meat (quails), the gift was a punishment, for the quails carried the plague. Psalm 106 assumes it took place before the arrival at Sinai, probably on the basis of the truncated narrative in Exod 16:13. God's response to the sin in this episode and the next is immediate punishment.

Third event: rebellion against Moses and Aaron in the camp (vv. 16-18)

According to Num 16, Dathan and Abiram led a rebellion against Moses, motivated by jealousy of Moses' privileged position. The sin is punished immediately by the death of the rebels.

Fourth event: the calf at Horeb and Moses' intercession (vv. 19-23)

The making of the golden calf, God's cancellation of the covenant, and Moses' successful intercession is told in Exod 32–34. "To stand in the breach" means to plug up a gap in a defense wall with one's body, as in Ezek 22:30. In Exod 32–34, Moses succeeded in turning away God's wrath by arguing that destroying the people would make it appear that God had failed. Unlike the two previous episodes, God does not inflict punishment. Prayer can assuage divine wrath. The history of Israel does not follow a rigid and unchanging pattern.

Fifth event: refusal to attack from the south and divine threat,
the sin with Baal of Peor, and Phinehas's intercession (vv. 24-31)

Numbers 13–14 (cf. Deut 1:19-45) is the ancient account of the people's refusal to enter Canaan from the south. After initially refusing to go, the people attacked on their own and were defeated. They were compelled to remain in the wilderness forty years until the disobedient generation died out. "Pleasant land" designates Palestine, as in Jer 3:19 and Zech 7:14. This section builds on the preceding by mentioning the divine curse (vv. 26-27). While the curse still looms over them, the people do the unthinkable: They commit another impiety by worshiping Baal of Peor (Num 25). A second apostasy is added to the first. To atone for such apostasy seems impossible. Only someone of Phinehas's stature could succeed in stopping the plague and annulling the oath. Significantly, the fate that the people are saved from (being dispersed among the nations, v. 27) is the very same fate the final prayer has in view (v. 47).

Sixth event: sin at the waters of Meribah (vv. 32-33)

The rebellion at the waters of Meribah is told in the Pentateuch at the beginning of the wilderness journey (Exod 17:1-7) and also at the end (Num 20:2-13). Moses' sin (Num 20:12) is here blamed squarely on the people; their stubbornness forced Moses into it. The people's sin comes close to destroying the very means of attaining forgiveness.

Seventh event: The people sacrifice their children in Canaan,
alternately experiencing God's anger and forgiveness (vv. 34-46)

From the very beginning, Israel was forbidden to mingle with the inhabitants of the land (Exod 23:23-24; 34:10-16), but they disobeyed. The psalm singles out one sin as typical of the people's unfaithful acculturation: the sacrifice of infants to gods. It was thought that the god owned the firstborn, which had to be given back to the god either directly or through an animal substitute. Infant sacrifice was practiced in the ancient Near East and sometimes even in Israel (e.g., 2 Kgs 16:13; Jer 19:5). No sin could be greater, for it violated the first commandment. The Hebrew word rendered "demons" (*šēdîm*, v. 37*b*) occurs in parallelism with "gods" in an eighth-century BCE inscription found at Deir Alla in Transjordan, and so should be translated "gods" here.

God's response to this typical sin differs from earlier divine responses to specific sins. This latter sin was repeated. The punishment was to fall into the hands of their enemies (vv. 40-42), after which God attends to the defeated people's pleas (vv. 43-46). The celebrated Deuteronomistic passage in Judg 2:6–3:6 describes this very same pattern: apostasy, falling into the hands of enemies, anguished prayers that move God to rescue, a period of favor, then a new round of apostasy, defeat, and so on.

Save your people and gather them from the nations (v. 47)

The poet prays at the beginning (vv. 4-5) and the end (v. 47) to experience the return of God's favor. The nations have acted out their role as the instruments of God's wrath, invading the land and exiling the people. Exile is implied by the prayer, "gather us from among the nations." "Save" is an important verb in the poem, occurring previously in verses 8, 10, and 21 in reference to God saving the people. Verse 48 is the doxology that ends Book 4; it is not part of this psalm.

Theological and Ethical Analysis

The history of Israel can be read purely as a history of sin, which would serve to remind the people that they have no claim on God's mercy. Though the psalm is a record of the people's failure, it is not primarily about them but about their God. And their God refuses to let go of them. Though just in punishing sin, God's steadfast love prevails over justice. God will not walk away even when they worship other gods. The people's sorry record is presented undisguised but subordinated to the portrait of their faithful God. The somber threads of the narrative finally reveal a glowing tapestry portrait of a passionate and faithful God. The picture inspires the psalmist to wait with eager longing for the return of divine favor (vv. 4-5, 47).

One can read history, whether it be of biblical Israel or the church or even one's own life, as a history of woes. Horrible infidelities have been perpetrated by members of the holy community. Disguising them by triumphalistic history is dishonorable. It is possible, however, to read history as this psalm does, as a story of a persistent and loving God who will not abandon the people. The history then becomes dialectical, the story of the Lord and the people and their rhythms of "wrath" and "favor," that is, their relationship. This is how Ps 106 reads the history, and it invites the holy community to read its story in the same way.

BOOK FIVE
(PSALMS 107–150)

PSALM 107

The final psalm of Book 4, Ps 106, is concerned with Israel's failures in the journey from Egypt to Canaan (though it ends with God turning to the people in mercy). Psalm 107, which opens Book 5, alludes to a new exodus (vv. 2-3, 35-38), suggesting that something new and hopeful will be the theme of the final book of the Psalter. The last poem of Book 4 and the first of Book 5 are related by the words "desert/wilderness," which occur three times in each psalm (106:9, 14, 26; 107:4, 33, 35). Moreover, Pss 105–7 form a triptych showing dramatic progression. Psalm 105 tells of God's deeds of kindness, Ps 106 tells of Israel's rebellion, and Ps 107 tells of the praise due the acts of love that culminate in the deliverance from exile. All three psalms share the vocabulary and outlook of Isa 40–55.

Literary Analysis

The poem is a community thanksgiving that invites the people (v. 3) to praise God for their return from Babylonian exile. The Bible reports three deportations of Judahites in the sixth century BCE: one in 597 (2 Kgs 24:10-16), another at the destruction of

Jerusalem and the Temple in 586 (2 Kgs 25:11), and a third in 582 (Jer 52:28-30). Though evidence is sparse, it appears that the first generations of exiles in Babylon were forced to perform state labor under harsh conditions. Rescue from such conditions and return to the homeland were events to be celebrated with great joy. Psalm 107 invites the exiles to praise God not only for their own return but also "for his wonderful works to humankind" (vv. 8b, 15b, 21b, 31b). Most probably, the psalm was written at the end of the exile, sometime in the late sixth or early fifth century BCE.

The structure of the poem is clearly marked. After an invitation (vv. 1-3), there are four similarly framed panels of divine deliverance (vv. 4-9, 10-16, 17-22, 23-32), followed by a final scenario (vv. 33-43) that transposes the theme of deliverance in verses 4-32 into the theme of daily governance of the land. Because the panels describing the various acts of deliverance are not perfectly symmetrical (the longest has 56 Hebrew words and the shortest 31), some scholars claim that certain sections were added to an original core. Ancient Hebrew literature, however, was not ruled by modern ideas of symmetry; diversity in style is no indication of diverse authorship. In fact, the section of the psalm most often judged to be an addition (vv. 33-43) deliberately uses vocabulary from previous sections (e.g., "desert," "hungry," "a town to live in" [vv. 33-36, reprising vv. 4, 5, 9, 32]) to show that deliverance in extraordinary cases is not different in kind from governance in ordinary ones.

Those called to give thanks are "the redeemed of the LORD" (v. 2), a phrase that in its one other biblical use refers to the inhabitants of restored Zion (Isa 62:12). They are summoned to "give thanks to the LORD [hôdû]," a verb that the four rescued groups also use (Ps 107:8, 15, 21, 31). The reference to the four directions here suggests totality, as in the phrase "from the four corners of the earth" (Isa 11:12d; cf. Gen 2:10; 13:14; Jer 49:36). In the psalm, the people come from the four directions (v. 3).

The structure of each panel is similar: a danger occurs (vv. 4-5, 10-12, 17-18, 23-27); the afflicted cry out to the Lord (vv. 6, 13, 19, 28) who rescues them (vv. 6b-7, 13b-14, 19b-20, 28b-30), prompting them to respond with thanksgiving (vv. 8-9, 15-16, 21-22, 31-32). Verse 33 signals a new section by breaking the pattern through its initial verb ("he turns") with the Lord as its subject (repeated in v. 35). The final verse (v. 43) reprises "the LORD" and "steadfast love" from verse 1 to signal the end of the poem.

The structure can be outlined:

> invitation to the returned exiles to give praise (vv. 1-3)
> four rescued groups (vv. 4-32)
> > those hungering and thirsting in the wilderness (vv. 4-9)
> > prisoners (vv. 10-16)
> > the sick (vv. 17-22)
> > those caught in an ocean storm (vv. 23-32)
> the Lord's rescue and governance of Israel (vv. 33-43)

Exegetical Analysis

Invitation to the returned exiles to give praise (vv. 1-3)

"Steadfast love" and "the LORD" (v. 1) will be repeated in the final verse, showing that the Lord's love has brought matters to their proper conclusion. In the Bible, "to give thanks" tells others what God has done, enabling them to join the rescued person in giving honor to God. In this case, God's deed consists in bringing back the exiles (vv. 2-30) and making it possible for them to resume their national life (vv. 41-43). Scholars today debate the extent and seriousness of the exile. A few estimate that at least 75 percent of the population remained in the land. Others, impressed by archaeological evidence of large numbers of sites destroyed in the sixth century BCE, emphasize widespread poverty and the breakdown of government. They concede, however, some demographic continuity (perhaps 40 percent). The horrors cannot be minimized. A large portion of the population of Judah was killed in the destruction of Jerusalem and the surrounding villages. What happened to the exiles? In an inscription, Nebuchadnezzar II (605–562 BCE) says he put deported people to forced labor. An archaeological survey of the central floodplain in Babylonia shows a rapid growth in settlements of the period, suggesting large numbers of people were forced to work on state projects. References in exilic literature to bonds and fetters (e.g., Ps 107:10-12; Isa 52:2) and to hunger and thirst (Ps 107:4-5; Isa 49:10) are evidently to be taken literally. Judahites were rounded up and deported. Deliverance from such misery was indeed an occasion for giving thanks.

The phrase "redeemed of the LORD" (v. 2) shows that Yahweh has performed the duty of kinsman to Israel, redeeming them from captivity. The people acknowledged Yahweh as the patrimonial authority over the children of Israel, who were bound to him by covenant as his kindred or kindred-in-law. By effectively performing this kinship duty, Yahweh wins praise as "good" (v. 1a) and as acting from "steadfast love" (v. 1b).

First rescued group: those hungering and thirsting in the wilderness (vv. 4-9)

The first group experiences deliverance from the hunger and thirst that result from being lost ("wandered") in the desert. The text does not mention any fault that might have caused the distress. Verse 6a, "then they cried to the LORD in their trouble," is transitional. Rescue is carried out through God leading the people to an inhabited town. The response is to give thanks *(hôdû)* for "his wonderful works to humankind," in this case feeding the thirsty and hungry. The psalm obviously has in mind God's actions for the nations ("humankind") as well as for Israel. Despite its general reference, there are echoes of Israel's own journey through the wilderness to Canaan.

Second rescued group: prisoners (vv. 10-16)

The second group has landed in prison for rebelling against the word of God. There is perhaps an allusion to Israel's situation in the exile. Exilic literature speaks of bonds and chains (Isa 52:2; 58:6; Lam 3:7), the unhappy symbols of the exile.

Third rescued group: the sick (vv. 17-22)

The traditional Hebrew text of verse 17a is "fools" *('ĕwilîm)*, which NRSV, REB, and NAB emend to *ḥôlîm*, "sick," on the basis of the parallel verse. NJPS and NIV retain the traditional text on the grounds that a biblical fool chooses to do evil, which brings serious sickness. Loathing food (v. 18*a*) is a sign of mortal illness. The sick are not so foolish, however, as to remain silent before the healing God. They cry out, and God's word cures them. The victims in the first and last panels are not said to have sinned, whereas the victims in panels two and three are said to have sinned. Verse 22 asks the rescued to offer sacrifices, as well as giving thanks.

Fourth rescued group: those caught in an ocean storm (vv. 23-32)

Verses 23-27 is one of the fine poetic passages in the Bible, memorably describing sailors' work and the terrors of a storm. It is considerably longer than the other sections. Some suggest that since the topic of the sea is so different from the previous dangers and foreign to Israel as an agricultural society, it must be an addition. The panel, however, is necessary to bring the number of dangers to four. The storm is directly from God. The rocking of the boat affects the sailors like alcohol, making them sick and dizzy (cf. Prov 23:29-35; Jonah 1:5-6). Their fervent prayer leads God to calm the roiling sea and bring the sailors to port (Ps 107:30), just as God brought the lost ones in the desert to an inhabited city. The last detail is another link between the first and the fourth panel, for both feature cosmic elements.

The Lord's gift of the land to Israel (vv. 33-43)

Though many scholars consider the final section to be a post-exilic addition, the psalm—describing four typical stories of deliverance—is incomplete without it. The psalm after all is an Israelite poem, and one expects the Lord to save Israel also.

This section particularly uses material from the first panel (vv. 4-9) and applies it to Israel's history, making that history conform to the divine activity in all the panels. Verses 33-34 show God transforming fertile land into desert, drawing on traditions of the destruction of wicked cities (e.g., Gen 18–19) to depict the defeat of the Canaanite in the conquest. God's mastery over land operates with equal ease in a positive sense by transforming desert into fertile land (v. 35) so that people flourish in towns and in fertile fields (vv. 36-38). When affliction comes (v. 39), as it came in the preceding four panels, God acts by exiling the people's enemies ("princes") to the desert (v. 40) and aiding Israel (v. 41). The rescue prompts praise (v. 42), as it did for the distressed folk in the four panels. The wise will know that the reason for deliverance of the nations and of Israel is the steadfast love of the Lord.

Theological and Ethical Analysis

It is difficult for a community to give thanks. For one thing, the words "thank you" fall short; one hardly knows how to fill out the silence that ensues after one utters the words. One's tendency after experiencing deliverance from a life-threatening danger is to breathe a sigh of relief and count oneself lucky. This psalm teaches the holy community how to recognize that their rescue is only one instance of the Lord's saving work in the world. The expansive recitals help the people see how the Lord heals and reconciles in a variety of dangerous situations. Divine governance is interpreted as rescue from life-threatening situations and as healing. The Lord is committed to the safety and prosperity of the nations as well as of Israel.

PSALM 108

Psalm 107 ends with Israel giving thanks for deliverance in Canaan. Psalm 108 continues the thanksgiving (vv. 1-4) and prays that God will defend the land against its hostile neighbors (vv. 5-13). Its vehement petitions foreshadow the anguished pleas of Ps 109.

Literary Analysis

Major segments of the poem appear in other psalms virtually unchanged. Verses 1-5 come from Ps 57:7-11 and verses 6-13 come from Ps 60:5-12. Though the material contained in Ps 108:1-5 seems to fit better as a thanksgiving in Ps 57, it is difficult to say which context is more original. Evidently, the sections were set pieces capable of being used in variety of contexts. Liturgical prayer is, after all, highly conventional. For detailed treatment of each section, the reader is referred to the commentary on Pss 57 and 60.

Though sharing sections with the other psalms, Ps 108 makes its own statement as a community lament. Verses 1-5 show boldness from the very start; verses 6-13 give reasons for the boldness. The psalm has three parts: I will wake the dawn with praise of your love and faithfulness (vv. 1-6); the oracle (vv. 7-9); complaint and petition (vv. 10-13).

Exegetical Analysis

I will wake the dawn with praise of your love and faithfulness (vv. 1-6)

The poem opens with a robust and confident cry, "My heart is steadfast," that is, my resolve is holding steady, not weakened by fear and lack of commitment. In Hebrew psychology, the heart is the storehouse of sense impressions, the organ of decision making, and the source of words and actions. The words that come from this steady heart are songs of thanks and praise (vv. 1*b*-3), proclaiming that God's "steadfast love" and "faithfulness" fill the universe (v. 4) and praying that they may become even more visible to human beings. "Steadfast love" and "faithfulness" here describe the relationship of two covenanted parties. By their free agreement, each vows to maintain deep and affectionate loyalty to the other. On God's side, loyalty means protecting and nurturing "the children of Israel," that is, all those belonging to the Lord's family through covenanted kinship. On the people's side, loyalty means giving praise and trusting in being God's kin by adoption. The psalmist expresses the wish that God's glory be seen and that God's sovereignty (in the form of victory) be established (vv. 5-6).

Verse 6 with its mention of rescue is the first indication that there is a crisis.

The oracle (vv. 7-9)

Having expressed confidence in God's covenant loyalty and stated the desire that the divine glory be seen by all, the psalmist prays for the victory that will make that glory visible. The confident assertions of the opening lines may have disguised the fact that a crisis looms over the community: Attacks by nations have compromised the boundaries of the Holy Land. The psalmist speaks for a community in danger.

Community laments typically cited an ancient divine act or word in virtue of which they ask God to act now. The warrant for divine interventions in most laments is the primordial deed that establishes the present order. In this case the "deed" is a promise of victory God made "in the sanctuary" (v. 7a). The word "exultation" suggests the promise was originally spoken at a moment of military triumph, for the word "exultation" in 2 Sam 1:20 and Ps 149:5 is part of a victory celebration. The oracle affirms the Lord's ownership of the land and the right to distribute it, as the phrases "I will divide up" and "portion out" in verse 7 suggest. The place names evoke the Davidic Empire of the tenth century. On the eastern and southeastern borders, David subjected Moab and Edom. In the southwest he defeated the Philistines. Shechem is a city forty-one miles north of Jerusalem located in the key pass between Mount Ebal and Mount Gerizim. It was important in the old tribal confederacy and in the later northern kingdom (Josh 24; Judg 9:22-25; 1 Kgs 12:1). Though the precise location of the Vale of Succoth is unknown, it seems to have been in middle or northern Transjordan in the tribal holdings of Gilead and Manasseh. Ephraim and Judah represent respectively the northern and southern kingdoms. Moab is a country west of the Dead Sea, between the Arnon and Zered Rivers, and Edom lies south of it on the eastern side of the Arabah. Philistia, homeland of the Philistines, is a swath of land extending from Joppa south toward Egypt. The oracle captures the moment when the victorious Divine Warrior apportioned conquered territory to loyal troops (v. 6). The expression "hurl my shoe" may refer to the legal gesture of claiming ownership attested in Ruth 4:7, "Now this was the custom in former times in Israel concerning redeeming and exchanging: to confirm a transaction, the one took off a sandal and gave it to the other." Given, however, the contemptuous tone of the claim of Moab in the immediately preceding phrase, "hurl my shoe" may be a boast rather than a legal gesture.

Complaint and petition (vv. 10-13)

"Who will bring me" (v. 10) is equivalent to, "O that I might be led!" The speaker of the psalm may well be the king who, as commander of the army, would naturally express the wish that Yahweh lead the army to conquer "the fortified city," which represents all the armed might arrayed against Israel. "Lead" (v. 10) refers to the Lord leading the people in war as in Ps 77:20 and Jer 31:9. The question in verse 11, "Have you not rejected us?" implies the people are currently undergoing a period of "wrath," that is, withdrawal of blessings. God does not go out with the army. The last two verses make clear Israel has learned an important lesson through bitter experience: Human help is worthless. The final petition is a conclusion from that experience and returns to the spirit of boldness that opened the psalm.

Theological and Ethical Analysis

Many community laments reveal a struggle involving feelings of fear, confusion, and depression as they ask God to intervene. Not this lament, however, for it is defiant from the opening verse. The reason perhaps is that the psalmist's vision is unwaveringly God-centered. The heart of the singer (perhaps the king) holds steady, is not disturbed by fear and confusion, and becomes the source of song to the glory of the Lord (vv. 1-3). The psalmist is awed by God's glory and wants it to be visible to everyone (vv. 4-5). The next section (vv. 6-9) gives the reason for the confidence: God has sworn (v. 7*a*) to give the land to the children of Israel and defeat those who wish to take it for themselves: Moab, Edom, and Philistia. The victory has not yet been brought to its full conclusion, however. Prayer is necessary, prayer that is founded on God's promise rather than on human strength.

This psalm describes the kingdom of God in concrete terms as the boundaries of the Holy Land. That kingdom suffers assault from its enemies. Its "citizens" are in danger. The reign of God on earth can take various shapes in the course of human history. In a broad sense, it is the sovereignty of the Lord over human history. In this psalm, the contours of the kingdom are those of a particular historical period. In the New Testament, Jesus announces the kingdom of God and embodies it. The church offers a glimpse of it as it seeks to proclaim and live it in the world. Its full expression lies in God's future, however. This psalm allows the holy community to proclaim the kingdom boldly and to base their hope of its full coming in God's own promise.

Psalm 109

A major theme of Ps 109, "kindness, steadfast love" (vv. 12, 16, 21, 26), is also important in Ps 107 (vv. 1, 8, 15, 21, 31, 43) and occurs as well in Ps 108:3. Psalm 109 points ahead to Ps 110 with its hope that God "stands at the right hand of the needy" to save them (109:31*a*) and with its reference to David in the superscription. In Ps 110:1, the Lord says to the Davidic king, "Sit at my right hand / until I make your enemies your footstool." Not a random collection like a modern hymnbook, the Psalter's arrangement encourages readers to connect God's exaltation of the poor (Ps 109) with the exaltation of the king.

Literary Analysis

Psalm 109 has the unenviable reputation as the most vehement of the cursing psalms. In the traditional understanding, the sufferer, pushed to the limit, unleashes in verses 6-20 a series of horrifying curses against enemies. There are no less than thirteen pairs of curses. This psalm has had an unhappy reception in the Christian church. Acts 1:20 applies Ps 109:8*b* ("May another seize his position") to the betrayer of Christ, Judas Iscariot, and the psalm was called the "Iscariot Psalm" by some church fathers. It was recited in pogroms (ethnically or religiously motivated attacks) against Jews in the Middle Ages. In 1971, Pope Paul VI removed it from the psalms recited in the restored Liturgy of the Hours.

Modern scholars are, however, divided on whether it genuinely is a cursing psalm. To many, it is a conventional individual lament and verses 6-19 quote the accusers' intentions rather than express the psalmist's curses hurled at them. NRSV, NAB, and REB follow this relatively recent interpretation. NRSV adds "They [the enemies] say" before verse 6 and encloses verses 6-19 with quotation marks to show that the psalmist is quoting the accusers, not cursing. One objection against this interpretation is that the psalmist would never risk quoting in such detail a curse against himself because such words might become actualized. There are, however, good arguments in favor of the quotation theory: (1) in most laments (and in the aphorisms of Proverbs), the righteous person is normally in the singular number (as in vv. 6-19) and contrasted with the wicked who are in the plural number; (2) the quotation theory fits the formal structure of the individual lament in that the vehement curse illustrates the extreme malice of the enemies.

The outline of the psalm is as follows: address and first plea (v. 1); complaint regarding the enemies' intentions (vv. 2-20); address and second plea (v. 21*ab*); complaint regarding the psalmist's condition (vv. 21*c*-24); plea for the psalmist (vv. 25-27); plea for the enemies (vv. 28-29); promise of praise (vv. 30-31). Dramatic logic and word repetition support the outline. Verses 1-4 and 29-31 form an inclusio, the latter repeating in reverse order from verses 1-4: "praise," "mouth(s)," and "accuse(rs)." Verses 7-14 are united by chiastic word repetition: "guilty" in verse 7 and "sin" in verse 14 (both *ḥaṭāʾāh* in Hebrew), "another" in verse 8 and "second" in verse 13 (both *'aḥēr* in Hebrew), and "orphans/orphaned" in verses 6 and 12. The divine name "the LORD" occurs seven times in the latter part of the poem (vv. 14-30), as the pray-er turns more and more to God. In the latter part of the poem the emphatic Hebrew personal pronouns "you" (v. 21), "I" (v. 25), and "they/them" (v. 28) establish a dramatic setting where the actors are God, the sufferer, and the accusers.

Can the psalmist and the setting be identified? As in other laments, the trouble is described in general terms so the poem can be used by other sufferers; lament is not biography. Some specificity, however, is provided by the charge that he "pursued the poor and needy / and the brokenhearted to their death" (v. 16*bc*). Traditional ancient Near Eastern terminology is invoked to accuse the sufferer of the ultimate act of injustice: killing the vulnerable who stand under the special protection of God and king. Ancient law codes protected weaker members of society, and kings boasted of protecting the widow and orphan. If the psalmist were found guilty of the heinous charge, the terrible chastisements listed in verses 7-19 would be unleashed. Against this serious charge (which is not further specified), the psalmist launches a spirited defense, including the counterassertion "*I* am poor and needy, / and my heart is pierced within me" (v. 22). Far from persecuting the innocent poor, the psalmist is in their ranks, deserving therefore of divine protection.

Exegetical Analysis

Address and first plea (v. 1)

Words are important in the poem: the psalmist's words of praise and petition to God, the enemies' accusing words and bitter hopes, and the expected saving word of God. The plea in verse 1 is itself a motive for God to intervene: "O God whose praise I sing, do not be silent" (my translation; NRSV: "O God of my praise"), that is, I have never been silent when your honor is at stake. Do not be silent when my safety is at stake.

Complaint regarding the enemies' intentions (vv. 2-20)

In a lament, the complaint lays out the suffering before God in order to prepare for the plea for help. The extraordinary length of the complaint shows how deep a wound the enemies' hateful words have left. Verse 4*b* ("even while I make prayer for them") is best rendered "I can only plead for mercy." It will be answered in verse 7*b*, "his plea for mercy has failed" (my translation; NRSV: "let his prayers be counted as sin"). Hebrew *ḥaṭāʾāh* can mean "falling short, failure" as well as "sin."

Verse 6 begins the quotation of the accusers' malicious intentions, which continues to verse 19. NRSV (and NAB and REB) adds an explanatory phrase, "they [the enemies] say," to make the point clear. The enemies conspire against the psalmist who has been summoned into court. They want a guilty verdict with no mercy shown (v. 7) and they hope for the disintegration of the psalmist's household and family (vv. 8-15). Verse 8*b*, "May another seize his position," seems to suggest the psalmist occupies a high position. Seeing that divine justice triumphed was a special obligation of the upper classes in antiquity. It is even possible that the speaker is the king, who had a special responsibility for justice. The king would undoubtedly have enemies trying to unseat him.

Verses 16-17 give the reason for the accusers' vehement intentions. In their view, the psalmist "pursued the poor and needy." It is only appropriate that curses come on the head of the one who hurled curses at the poor (vv. 18-19). Verse 20 is transitional. The psalmist wishes to turn back their malicious desires on the head of the accusers and begin a new phase of the prayer. The first colon harks back to verse 4*a* ("they accuse me") and the second colon harks back to verse 2*b* ("speaking against me").

Address and second plea (v. 21ab)

The verse reaffirms the plea of verse 1. It begins with the emphatic pronoun "you," which is the first of four occurrences of the emphatic pronouns. "I" appears in verse 25*a*, and "them" and "you" in verse 28*a*.

Complaint regarding the psalmist's condition (vv. 21c-24)

This complaint is about the psalmist, not about the enemies. The psalmist is defenseless ("poor and needy," v. 22*a*), sick ("heart is pierced," v. 22*b*), "shaken off like a locust" that attaches to one's clothes (v. 23*b*), pale and unsteady in gait (v. 24).

Plea for the psalmist (vv. 25-27)

As the previous section began with "you" (God, v. 21*a*) and the following section begins with "them" (the accusers, v. 28*a*), so this section begins with the emphatic pronoun "I." Verse 25, which is concerned with shame, is the transition from the imme-diately preceding description of physical ailments. In the eyes of the accusers, the sufferer's life and commitments are worthless; all hopes are seen to be mistaken. The psalmist is shamed. "Shame" in the ancient Near East was more "objective" than in the mod-ern world where it describes inner feelings rather than a public situation. Because of the shame, the psalmist prays in verse 27 that God "let them know that this is your hand; / you, O LORD, have done it." Only through an act of healing that comes from God will people realize the psalmist is innocent. The act will be seen as a divine judgment that proves false the malicious accusa-tions of verses 2-20.

Plea for the enemies (vv. 28-29)

The prayer is that God's blessing override the curses of the ene-mies. Verse 28 is best translated: "Though they curse, may you bless. Though they rise up, they will be shamed and your servant will rejoice." Verse 29 continues the reversal of fortune. The accusers' plans will fail, not the psalmist's. They will be shamed, not the psalmist.

Promise of praise (vv. 30-31)

In laments, the sufferer promises praise when deliverance is given. Instead of the accusers' malicious words in verses 2-3, the psalmist's mouth will be filled with the Lord's praise (v. 30).

Instead of the lying witness the accusers tried to place at the right hand of the psalmist (v. 6), God will be at the right hand of the needy (v. 31).

Theological and Ethical Analysis

A detailed quote of the accusers' real intent was necessary in order to show just how needy and poor the psalmist really is. Though the accusers make the psalmist out to be the ultimate unjust person, that is, one who tries to kill the poor (vv. 16-17), the truth is just the opposite: The psalmist is the most vulnerable of all. If the false accusation stands up in court, all will be ruined—household, spouse, and children. The plea cannot go unheard.

When properly understood, the psalm that seems so full of curses, turns out to be a powerful and poignant expression of misery and hope. Powerful and systematic accusers press down on the psalmist. They have reflected carefully about what they plan to do: strip the psalmist of occupation, house, reputation, spouse, children, and life. The psalmist fights back with equal care, trusting the just God to attend to every detail. Accused of a serious crime—persecution of the poor—the psalmist has no alternative but to turn to God and make this eloquent and moving plea. The terrifying experience distilled into this psalm can be a model for others struggling to integrate great suffering into a life of faith.

PSALM 110

Literary Analysis

Psalm 109 opened with a wicked accuser standing at the right hand of an innocent person (v. 6) and concluded with the hope that God "stands at the right hand of the needy" (v. 31). Psalm 110 continues the picture by its oracle "sit at my right hand" (v. 1*b*), which is repeated in verse 5.

Psalm 110 is a royal psalm, consisting largely of oracles delivered to the king presumably at a ceremony of installation or an anniversary of it. There is an implied narrative and its plot can be supplied from the royal Pss 2 and 89 and the Songs of Zion 46, 48, and 76. Davidic kingship was rooted in the kingship of Yahweh, the patron of the dynasty. Kingship was understood as leadership over the creatures of heaven and earth achieved by victory over malicious forces. The narrative, called the combat myth by modern scholars (see the Introduction, "Implied Narratives" in *Psalms 1–72*), begins with a threat to cosmic order by a monstrous force. One god alone is able to defeat the threat and is acclaimed king by the other gods. The new king builds a palace and institutes human kingship to implement justice on earth. The king represents the god, extending the rule of his divine patron; his enemies are the enemies of the god. This myth was adapted by Israelite poets to celebrate Davidic kingship. Israel had liturgical ceremonies where poems such as Ps 110 would have been used. It is a string of oracles assuring the king of the royal patron's favor and help.

Other psalms similarly celebrated the royal office. Psalm 2 tells how the Lord defeated enemy kings:

> Then he will speak to them in his wrath,
>   and terrify them in his fury, saying,
> "I have set my king on Zion, my holy hill."
> I [the king] will tell of the decree of the LORD:
> He said to me, "You are my son;
>   today I have begotten you.
> Ask of me, and I will make the nations your heritage,
>   and the ends of the earth your possession." (Ps 2:5-8)

Psalm 89:5-37 tells of the creation of the world through the defeat of Sea and the installation of the Davidic king accompanied by oracles of assurance: "I have found my servant David; / with my holy oil I have anointed him" (v. 20); "I will crush his foes before him / and strike down those who hate him" (v. 23);

> He shall cry to me, "You are my Father,
>   my God, and the Rock of my salvation!"

I will make him the firstborn,
  the highest of the kings of the earth.
Forever I will keep my steadfast love for him,
  and my covenant with him will stand firm.
I will establish his line forever,
  and his throne as long as the heavens endure. (vv. 26-29)

These psalms fill out the narrative in Ps 110: the divine victory that includes defeat of earthly kings (v. 1), authorization to wage war (vv. 2-3), legitimacy without limit of time ("forever," v. 4), and the king as the instrument of divine rule (vv. 5-7). The speaker of Ps 110 is probably a court official, perhaps a poet whose duties included producing texts for royal ceremonies (cf. Ps 45:1).

Psalm 110 is constituted as a series of oracles. The words "say" and "has sworn" in verses 1-4 each introduce two oracles in grammatical second person (vv. 1 and 4). NRSV marks them as oracles by quotation marks. The first is developed in verses 2-3, and the second in verses 5-7. The two parts of the poem, verses 1-3 and 4-7, are approximately equal in length. Word repetition unites the poem. The divine name occurs four times, symbolizing universality; "LORD" *(YHWH)* occurs three times and "Lord" *('ădōnāy)* occurs once. "Your enemies" occurs twice; "shatter" twice; "head(s)" twice; "on the day of" twice. Shift of grammatical person from second (v. 1) to third (vv. 2-3) is common in Hebrew style and is not necessarily a sign of later expansion.

Exegetical Analysis

Be seated on the throne while the Lord gives you victory (vv. 1-3)

In verse 1 the singer quotes an oracle of "the LORD" *(YHWH)* "to my lord [the king]." Though the phrase "the LORD says" *(ne'um YHWH)* is used frequently in the Bible in divine oaths (e.g., Num 14:28; 1 Sam 2:30; Isa 1:24), it occurs only here in the Psalter. It forms a parallel to verse 4a, "The LORD has sworn," dividing the poem into two parts. "Sit" means sit enthroned as in Pss 2:4; 22:3; and 61:7. As in Ps 2, the Lord gives vent to anger against the kings of the nations while the Davidic king watches. ("Until" [*ad*] in verse 1 is best rendered "while.") "Footstool" occurs in contexts of the worship of the Lord (Ps 99:5; Isa 66:1). The gesture here is one of military triumph; the king plants his foot on the necks of his defeated enemies as in Josh 10:24, "Come near, put your feet on the necks of these kings."

In virtue of the victory, the Lord in Ps 110:2 holds aloft the king's scepter and commands him to rule. Though the poem focuses on Yahweh's actions rather than the king's, its theme is the divine sovereignty exercised by the Davidic king. Verse 3*a*, "your people will offer themselves willingly" (*'ammĕkā nĕdābōt*), expresses the readiness of the army to fight the battles of the Lord just as in Judg 5:2*b*: "when the people offer themselves willingly" (*hitnaddĕb 'ām*). Hebrew *'ām* can mean "army" as well as "people" (e.g., Num 31:32). The remainder of verse 3 (from "on the holy mountains" to "come to you") is corrupt or obscure, forcing translators to rely on traditional renderings that do not make much sense. A few suggestions can be made, however. "Dew" (v. 3*e*) may have links to the royal Ps 72:6, "May [the king] be like rain that falls on the mown grass, / like showers that water the earth." The phrase "your youth" (v. 3*e*, Hebrew consonants *yldty*) may refer to adoptive sonship as in Ps 2:7, "[The LORD] said to me, 'You are my son; today I have begotten you [*yldty*].'"

You are ordained as priest while the Lord wins victory over kings (vv. 4-7)

The second part of the poem begins with a phrase "the LORD has sworn" (v. 4*a*) that echoes verse 1, "The LORD says." He "will not change his mind" (v. 4*a*) is equivalent to other assertions of permanent rule such as those in Ps 89 ("always," v. 21; "forever," vv. 28, 29; "endure . . . like the sun," "forever like the moon," vv. 36-37). Though priesthood (v. 4*b*) is a separate office from kingship in the Hebrew Bible, David and Solomon occasionally exercised the role of priest (2 Sam 6:17; 8:18; 1 Kgs 3:4). The king had the responsibility of seeing to the proper functioning of the Temple, the earthly palace of his heavenly patron. Moreover, Melchizedek was a priest as well as king according to Gen 14:18: "And King Melchizedek of Salem brought out bread and wine; he was priest of God Most High." Verse 4*b* of Ps 110, "according to the order of Melchizedek," is the standard Christian rendering and is as old as the Septuagint. Linguistically, it is possible to translate "Melchizedek" as "a rightful king by My decree" (so NJPS), though "priest" and "king" are nowhere else placed in parallel.

Verses 5-7 expand the oracle of verse 4. The king is at the right hand of the Lord (v. 1). As in the first oracle, though the actions are ascribed to the Lord, the king will also carry them out in the course of his duties. The king's battles are the Lord's; such is the ideology of holy war. Why is divine rule depicted in violent terms such as shattering the heads of kings over the wide earth? One reason is the mythic background of Davidic kingship in which the king rises to sovereign rank by defeating chaotic forces. Another reason is that the king is charged with furthering divine justice in the world, which, in biblical terms, means putting down the wicked and raising up the aggrieved innocent. To effect justice implies the use of force, at least occasionally. Finally, a basic function of government is protecting its citizens from criminals within and foreign armies without. It is important to understand that the ultimate goal of the king is to extend the reign of God. The defeat of enemies means the defeat of *evil* enemies in the pursuit of a positive final goal: the realization of the just and peaceful world that the Lord intends.

The images require comment. The phrase "wide earth" (*'ereṣ rabbāh*) in verse 6 seems to mean the entire earth as in Jer 28:8. It may also be an imitation of "the great deep" (*tĕhōm rabbāh*, Gen 7:11; Ps 36:6; Isa 51:10; Amos 7:4). Verse 7 has long puzzled interpreters. Some suggest it refers to a ritual of drinking from the spring of Gihon in Jerusalem (cf. 1 Kgs 1:33). Others propose it refers to a warrior pursuing enemies to their hideout, which means living off the land and drinking water "on the road" until the mission is completed. Or it may refer to the Lord giving a victorious drink to the king and lifting up his head. The latter gesture is a gesture of comfort (Ps 3:4) and of victory (Ps 27:6).

Theological and Ethical Analysis

Royal psalms are concerned with the kingdom of God, for the king was the institutional means to further the divine reign. God chose a particular people to embody and display the divine glory in the world, and kingship was Israel's system of governance from the tenth to the sixth centuries BCE and, so, was important in their witnessing task. After the sixth-century BCE exile, kingship became a symbol for God's future reign. The New Testament presents Jesus as the royal Son of David (Matt 2:6; 21:9; Luke 3:31; 18:38-39), who will reign forever.

For Christians, the psalm celebrates God's reign over the whole world and the human means chosen to effect it. God chose Israel and the Davidic king to bring about peace and justice in the world. Christians can pray this poem to express their appreciation for the kingdom of God and for the means of achieving it, Christ, Son of David and high priest.

PSALM 111

Psalm 111 begins a trio of Hallelujah Psalms, for each opens with *halĕlû yāh* ("Praise the LORD!"). Psalms 111 and 112 are both twenty-two line acrostic poems in which each line begins with a successive letter of the Hebrew alphabet. Psalm 111 celebrates the righteousness of the Lord, and Ps 112 celebrates the righteousness of a person living in accord with divine righteousness. Psalm 113 praises the name of God.

Literary Analysis

Though acrostic poems normally rely on the successive letters of the alphabet for their structure, they often, like Ps 111, have an inherent logic as well. "The works" celebrated in the poem (vv. 2*a*, 6*a*, 7*a*) are all aspects or consequences of the exodus: the liberation from Egypt (vv. 2-4), the feeding in the wilderness and the covenant at Sinai (vv. 5, 7b-8, 9b), the conquest of Canaan (v. 6), and the governance of the people in Canaan (v. 9a). Though the phrase "works of the LORD" can refer to divine acts of a general kind (as in Pss 104:24; 107:24), it frequently refers to the foundation of Israel, as in Exod 34:10; Deut 11:7; and Josh 24:31. The particular sequence of the "works of the LORD" in Ps 111—liberation, guidance in the wilderness, and governance in the land—is found also in Pss 105 and 106. This hymn links narrative and ethics in a striking way. Among the mighty acts narrated in the poem are the covenant that binds God and people (vv. 5, 9) and precepts that enable that people to respond and become wise (vv. 7b, 10a).

Exegetical Analysis

The praise is public and liturgical. "Praise Yahweh" invites others to join the praising action of the narrator. "I will give thanks" is a standard response to an act of God (e.g., Pss 7:17; 9:1; 109:30). Verse 1c, "in the company of the upright, in the congregation," is a hendiadys (one concept expressed through two nouns), meaning the assembled congregation of the upright. "His work" is "full of honor and majesty" (v. 3a) because it reveals the divine majesty on earth. "His righteousness" (v. 3b) is a divine attribute, referring perhaps to God's intentions that will always prevail ("endures forever").

One verse requires close examination. Verse 2b, "studied by all who delight in them," is a traditional rendering of a puzzling phrase that reads, literally, "sought by all who have pleasure in them." Though the verb *dāraš* means basically "to seek, to resort to," it can mean "to seek with application, to study, to practice," which is the meaning here, hence "studied." Psalm 119:45 is helpful in understanding the precise meaning of the phrase, for it contains two words of the phrase in one verse (italicized here): "I shall walk at liberty, / for I have *sought* [cf. Ps 111:2b] your *precepts* [cf. Ps 111:7b]." The parallel in Ps 119:45 suggests that "studied" in Ps 111:2b means respond to the divine deeds mentioned in verse 2a. One can paraphrase verse 2b: "the ethical demands of God's works are put into practice by all who delight in them."

Verse 4b, "the LORD is gracious and merciful," turns the hymn in a slightly different direction: to God's care of humans (specifically Israel) and interaction with them. God feeds the people in the wilderness, dealing with them in accord with the covenant that both parties have entered into (v. 5). Verse 5 regards the conquest (v. 6) chiefly as a demonstration of God's power and love for Israel. The Hebrew reads, literally, "he showed his powerful deeds to his people, giving them the inheritance [i.e., land] of the nations." "Works" is repeated for the third and last time in verse 7 and given an ethical slant. The works are "faithful and just," that is, they should be considered as acts of faithfulness and the standard of what is right. Verse 7b implies that the works include the ethical teachings of the covenant, for it declares "all his precepts" trustworthy and everlasting (v. 8). Verse 8b says the same thing as verse 2b, that is, God's deeds invite an ethical response. Verse 9 likewise blends ethics and narrative, implying that redemption includes Israel's response to the covenant.

"Holy and awesome is his name" (v. 9c) is the second adjectival description of God in the psalm, the other being verse 4b. It sums up what has gone before: God is holy ("Totally Other") by doing "works" that no other god can perform, and thus is feared ("awesome"), that is, worshiped and obeyed. "Awesome" (v. 9c) is etymologically related to "fear" in the immediately following phrase, "fear of the LORD." Such fear is the beginning of wisdom, for wisdom is given only to those who revere the Lord (v. 10b). "Forever" is the fifth statement of limitless time in the poem. Such statements occur in verses 3, 5, 8, 9, and 10 in an ABABA order: lā'ad, lĕôlām, lā'ad lĕôlām, lā'ad. God's work will always prevail.

Theological and Ethical Analysis

Psalm 111 is a distinctively Israelite hymn, for it praises the great foundational work of God, the exodus, in terms general enough to apply to subsequent divine interventions. The psalm allows one to incorporate thanks for a particular benefit into the thanks of all Israel for God's founding the people. The poem fits personal prayer into national prayer.

God's works invite not only wonder but also participation and response. The act that brings the people into being also invites them to respond with praise. Among the works of God are the covenant and its precepts. The works of the Lord make possible communication between people and God. No wonder the psalmist invites everyone to join in praise!

PSALM 112

Even a cursory reading reveals that Pss 111 and 112 are paired hymns. Both are acrostic poems. Psalm 111 praises God for the actions and teachings that founded Israel. Psalm 112 describes an individual who fears the Lord, that is, who honors and obeys the Lord. The two poems share several words and phrases: "fear of the LORD," "the upright," "delight (in commandments)," "righteousness," "forever," and "gracious and merciful."

Literary Analysis

Though the opening command, "Praise the LORD!" might indicate the genre is that of a hymn, the immediately following formula, "happy are those," suggests something different. "Happy are those" is a beatitude (or macarism; cf. Matt 5:3-12) declaring someone fortunate because of a quality possessed or a choice made. (NRSV makes the subject plural to be inclusive.) Five such beatitudes occur in Job and Proverbs and twenty-five in the Psalter (e.g., Pss 1:1; 32:1, 2; 33:12; 40:4; 41:1; 119:1, 2). The beatitude is normally followed by a nominal or verbal sentence stating the reason for the happiness. The closest parallel to Ps 112:1 is Ps 1:1-2, which declares that observing the commandments is the source of true happiness: "Happy are those / who do not follow the advice of the wicked, . . . / but their delight is in the law of the LORD." Psalm 1 similarly contrasts the "happy" individual (Pss 1:1-2; 112:1-9) with the wicked (plural; Pss 1:4-6; 112:10). Psalm 112 differs from Ps 1, however, in its extended treatment of the blessings of the righteous and its brief treatment of the misfortunes of the wicked. The blessings of the righteous are portrayed in the language found in the Wisdom literature, for example, those who give to the poor suffer no loss of wealth (cf. Prov 14:21), the descendants of the righteous are blessed (cf. Prov 13:22), the righteous will never be moved (cf. Prov 10:30), and their light will always shine (cf. Prov 12:9). The sheer number of the blessings in Ps 112:2-9 serves to intensify their richness and diversity. The portrait of the God-fearing person is virtually a mirror image of that of the scoundrel in Prov 6:12-15 who is wicked in essence, demeanor, inner life, effect upon society, and destiny. One type is *given* life in abundance, whereas the other's strenuous attempts to achieve it end only in disaster.

To what genre of poem does Ps 112 belong? Despite its wisdom concepts and vocabulary, Ps 112 is essentially a hymn, for it praises a wondrous work of God: a human being who fears the Lord. Even God praises such a person, as when the Lord boasts to the angelic adversary about the righteous Job: "Have you considered my servant Job? There is no one like him on the earth, a blameless and upright man who fears God and turns away from evil" (Job 1:8). A truly righteous person is a showcase for the blessings God wishes to bestow on human beings, just as Israel is a showcase for the blessings God wishes to bestow on the whole human race. Blessings are for human beings to use and enjoy. Such blessings invite praise of the God who is their source.

Though dependent on the alphabet for their structure, acrostic poems often have their own logical movement. Such is the case with Ps 112. Verse 1 is a declaration of beatitude and verses 2-10 describe its aspects: prosperous descendants (v. 2), wealth that endures (v. 3), generosity toward one's family and friends (vv. 4-5), security, renown, and ease (vv. 6-9b), honor versus shame for their enemies (vv. 9c-10).

Exegetical Analysis

"Praise Yah(weh)" (NRSV: "Praise the LORD!" v. 1*a*) is an invitation verse, inviting others to praise a divine wonder: a virtuous person blessed by God. The source of the "happiness" is "fear [of] the LORD" (v. 1). Fear of the Lord is the traditional though unsatisfactory translation of a term widely attested in the ancient Near East. It is more accurately rendered, "revering Yahweh," that is, singling out for honor a *particular* deity by observing that deity's rituals and commands. The background of the term is polytheism; one had to choose a single deity (out of many possible ones) as one's patron and resolve to be a loyal and obedient client. Such a client "greatly delights in his commandments" (v. 1*c*). The first blessing that is granted to a loyal follower is vigorous descendants. Contrary to NRSV, verse 2*b* should be rendered "a blessed generation of upright people." Descendants are the preeminent blessing, for individuals conceived their life as so embedded in the family that their identity was preserved by the next generation. Birth of children was a kind of "resurrection" from death, for the patrilineal family system, with its subordination of individual goals to those of the group, ensured the continuity and survival of the family.

In verse 3 the blessing is wealth that endures and can be passed on to one's children. The Hebrew term that the NRSV translates as "righteousness" (v. 3*b*) draws its meaning from its parallel "wealth and riches" in verse 3*a*. Here it means something like "prosperity" (NAB) or "beneficence" (NJPS). The psalm emphasizes the permanence of the blessings, as can be seen from the occurrence of "forever" or the like in verses 3*b*, 6 (twice), 8*b*, 9*b*.

From a purely syntactic viewpoint, the subject of the verb "rise" in verse 4*a* can be "the light" (e.g., NJPS: "a light shines for the upright in the darkness"), but most translators (including NRSV) rightly take the blessed individual as the subject. Isaiah 58:10 also asserts that giving to the needy makes one shine in the darkness like a light (similar words are in italics): "If you offer your food to the hungry / and satisfy the needs of the afflicted, / then your *light* *shall rise in the darkness."* Moved with compassion (v. 4*b*), an individual can benefit others, including generations yet to come, for "upright" refers to future generations in verse 2*b*. Adjectives describing the righteous person in verse 4*b* ("gracious, merciful") also describe the Lord in Ps 111:4*b*. Having more than enough, the "happy" individual can lend to others (v. 5*a*) and need never resort to sharp business practices (v. 5*b*, "conduct their affairs with justice"). Blessed even to the day of death (v. 6*a*), the person will always be remembered as a friend of God (v. 6*b*). Even a bad turn of events ("evil tidings") will not ultimately affect the blessings granted, for it cannot remove one from God's care. Verses 7-8 reflect such a hope.

Verse 9 begins the conclusion, for it refers back to verse 4 by its topic of generous giving and quotes verse 3*b*. Up to this point, there has been no mention of the wicked. Verse 9*c* now introduces them by mentioning the individual's "horn" (symbol of life and potency) that is exalted, that is, publicly recognized. Such public recognition of the individual causes shame in the wicked, for they see their own hopes exposed as false and those of their enemy established. At the beginning of the psalm, the singer declared the individual "happy." At the end, the wicked are forced to make the same declaration, albeit in a negative way.

Theological and Ethical Analysis

The second-century church father Irenaeus described human beings transformed by divine grace in a famous Latin phrase: *gloria Dei vivens homo* ("God is given glory by a human being fully alive," *Haer.* IV.20.7). God's wish is to bless humankind with gifts. Recipients of divine bounty may be a people, as in the previous psalm, or an individual, as in this one. One should not, however, imagine that such blessings are given in exchange for virtuous behavior in a quid pro quo arrangement. Though there is a transaction between God and human beings, the inequality of the persons in the relationship creates in the human partner a profound feeling of dependency and gratitude. God and the human being are not business partners. Rather, the human being is a showcase for God's goodness and generosity, delighting in being gifted by One so good.

How different are the gifts in this psalm from those people customarily prize! The first gift is "eternal life" in accord with the expectations of the time, that is, one's identity continues by being imbedded in the family that endures. The second gift is wealth that accrues to one's family as well and enables one to assist others. The permanence that this psalm celebrates is not rooted in the hope that God will never allow anything bad to happen but rather that God will never let anything sever the relationship. The individual who accepts the blessings throws up no block to God's blessing. Touched by God, the person is declared happy, an example to all of God's love and generosity.

PSALM 113

Psalm 113 concludes the trio of Hallelujah Psalms. It begins the "Egyptian Hallel" ("praise") Psalms (Pss 113–18), which were sung at major Jewish feasts. Psalms 113–14 were sung before the Passover meal and Pss 115–18 were sung after it (cf. Matt 26:30; Mark 14:26).

Literary Analysis

In genre, the poem is a hymn. Verses 1-3 invite "servants of the LORD" to praise the name of the Lord in every age ("from this time on and forevermore") and every place ("from the rising of the sun to its setting"). Hailed in heaven as incomparable, exalted, and all seeing (vv. 4-6), the Lord works justice on earth by helping the needy and giving children to the barren woman (vv. 7-9). The poem begins and ends with the call "Praise the LORD!" There are nine mentions of the divine name (eight of "the LORD" and one of "God"), which underline the central position of God in the poem.

Exegetical Analysis

Praise the name of the Lord! (vv. 1-3)

The first section is marked by repetitions of "the name of the LORD" (three times) and "praise" (three times), and by its focus on the chronological (v. 2*a*) and spatial (v. 3*a*) reach of the divine name. "Praise the LORD!" in the final verse repeats the first verse and concludes the whole. Those invited to give praise are "servants of the LORD." "Servant" could be applied to a wide variety of people, from slaves to high government officials. Some ancient seals refer to high officials as "servant of the king." The social context of the lord must be known in order to understand the meaning of servant. "Servants of the LORD" in Ps 113 is an extremely honorable title, meaning those privileged to be friends and servants of the supreme deity in the whole world. Their task is to acknowledge the powerful presence of the Lord in all times and places. A name represents the one named to others. The first part of the psalm is concerned with name recognition, that is, that the Lord be recognized as supreme in all places and at all times.

The Lord reigns in heaven (vv. 4-6)

In contrast to the final section (vv. 7-9), which is concerned with God's presence on earth, verses 4-6 are about God's presence in heaven. The acclamation of incomparability, "Who is like the LORD our God" (v. 5*a*) is elsewhere associated with *doing* an act no other god can do (e.g., Exod 15:11; Ps 89:6-8). Having demonstrated absolute supremacy, the Lord rules over all without hindrance. "Looks far down" (v. 6*a*) is a gesture of dominance; the Lord has authority over heaven and earth.

The Lord reigns on earth (vv. 7-9)

In contrast to God's effortless and universally acknowledged rule over heaven (vv. 4-6) is God's effortful and sporadically recognized rule over earth. The Lord must act to counter those forces that make people poor (vv. 7-8) and cause barrenness that ends family lines (v. 9). The poem uses the metaphor system of up and down. "Up" is God, heaven, and exaltation. "Down" is human beings, earth, and deprivation. In people's movement from down to up, from deprivation to satiety, God is shown to be supreme. The Lord's exalted position makes it easier, not harder, to be with the lowly.

Verses 7-9 succinctly expresses the tradition of God lifting up the poor and making the barren fruitful. One thinks of biblical examples of poor people being raised up: Sarah, Rebekah, and especially Hannah whose song is preserved in 1 Sam 2:1-10. Mary's response to becoming a mother, modeled on Hannah's, is in Luke 1:46-55. Psalm 113:7 echoes Hannah's song in 1 Sam 2:8,

> "He raises up the poor from the dust;
>   he lifts the needy from the ash heap,
> to make them sit with princes
>   and inherit a seat of honor."

Psalm 113:9 echoes 1 Sam 2:5cd: "The barren has borne seven, but she who has many children is forlorn."

Theological and Ethical Analysis

The servants of the Lord who are called to sing this song are enthusiastic about their friendship with the Lord and eager to offer the worship and obedience that befits such a title. This psalm gives such servants a text to express the Lord's universal dominion, supremacy in heaven, and compassionate and just rule on earth.

In reflecting on the deity, one is often torn between affirming a transcendence that removes God from the world and an immanence that reduces God to the world. This psalm manages to affirm God's transcendence and presence (the name) in the world especially in the poor. Though majestically enthroned in heaven, God looks kindly upon the least person on earth, eager to come down and bestow abundance and fertility.

PSALM 114

Literary Analysis

The second of the Hallel hymns (Pss 113–18) treats the exodus explicitly as befits a psalm recited at principal Jewish festivals and especially at the Passover meal (cf. Matt 26:30). In genre, Ps 114 is nearest to a hymn in that it celebrates a divine act (the exodus), though it lacks the usual verse of invitation. The context, perhaps a liturgical performance, is unknown to us. One indication of the missing context is that there is no proper antecedent of the third-person singular pronoun in verse 2.

Verses 1-2 set the scene as the exodus of Israel from Egypt to Canaan. In the perspective of this psalm, Israel seems to have passed directly from Egypt to Canaan when it traversed the sea. At least the psalm shows no interest in the wilderness traditions that occupy so large a part of the Pentateuch and of psalms such as Pss 78, 105, and 107. In verse 3, the poet makes "the sea" (that is, the Red or Reed Sea) parallel to the river Jordan. The parallel of "sea" and "river" is an easy one to make because "sea" and "river" is a common word pair in the Canaanite and Israelite poetic traditions, for example, Pss 24:2; 66:6; 72:8; and 89:25 as well as in Ugaritic texts.

As the people march through the sea to the other side, the speaker taunts the sea and the mountains in the manner of a warrior taunting fallen enemies (vv. 3-6). Next, the speaker warns the earth to tremble before the Lord who has the power to turn solid ground into water. Israelite poets employed both "historic" and "mythological" language to describe the exodus, frequently blending the two perspectives. An example of the historic perspective is Exod 14; an example of the mythic perspective is Exod 15.

Structurally, there are two almost equal parts, the description of the crossing and the behavior of the elements (vv. 1-4) and the speakers's taunt and warning (vv. 5-8).

Exegetical Analysis

The crossing of the sea and its effects upon sea and mountains (vv. 1-4)

"The house of Jacob" is an apt name for Israel in Egypt, for the people at the time were indeed the family of the ancestor Jacob/Israel (Exod 1:1-7). Verse 2 is elliptical; it can mean that Canaan was already sacred to the Lord or that when Judah as a chosen people entered, it became a "sanctuary." The goal of the journey is Yahweh's shrine, as in Exod 15:17:

> "You brought them in and planted them on the mountain of your
>   own possession,
>   the place, O LORD, that you made your abode,
>   the sanctuary, O LORD, that your hands have established."

The Lord took the people from the domain of Pharaoh (Egypt) to bring them into his own domain (Canaan).

Verses 3-4 personify the sea and the mountains as warriors fleeing in panic before Yahweh the warrior. The explicit identification of Yahweh as a warrior, however, is delayed until verse 7 ("tremble . . . at the presence of the LORD") just as the identity of the antecedent of the pronoun "his" in verse 2a is delayed until verse 7. The waters of the Jordan River are personified as soldiers fleeing in panic before superior forces. The picture is like Ps 104:3-4: "Over the mountains the waters stood. At your rebuke they fled, at the sound of your thunder they rushed away. They went up the mountains, they went down the valleys, to the place you founded for them" (my translation). Another example of cosmic waters fleeing in panic is in Ps 77:16. It is quite possible that the verses presuppose a liturgical reenactment of crossing the Jordan such as seems to be described in Josh 3:15-17:

> So when those who bore the ark had come to the Jordan, and the feet of the priests bearing the ark were dipped in the edge of the water, the waters flowing from above stood still, rising up in a single heap far off at Adam, the city that is beside Zarethan, while

those flowing toward the sea of the Arabah, the Dead Sea, were wholly cut off. Then the people crossed over opposite Jericho.

The skipping of the mountains is the result of the Lord thundering in the sky as in Ps 29:5-6:

> The voice of the LORD breaks the cedars;
> the LORD breaks the cedars of Lebanon.
> He makes Lebanon skip like a calf,
> and Sirion like a young wild ox.

Yahweh attacks, and the sea panics; the crashes of thunder cause the mountains to jump. "Tremble" in verse 7 also refers to warriors reeling from the effects of battle. One can tremble before the Lord as in Ps 96:9 and Deut 2:25: "This day I will begin to put the dread and fear of you upon the peoples everywhere under heaven; when they hear report of you, *they will tremble* and be in anguish because of you."

Why do you flee in panic, O Sea, Mountains, and Earth?
(vv. 5-8)

The speaker taunts the sea and mountains for their retreat before a greater force (vv. 5-6). Presupposed, though not made explicit in the text, is the awesome manifestation of Yahweh the warrior leading the people through the sea into Canaan, the sanctuary of Yahweh. The procession is like that in Exod 15:13-18 where panic falls upon all who view the events.

"Tremble, O earth" (v. 7a) is a warning directed, it seems, against the inhabitants living around or in the Holy Land. They must bow before the superiority of the God who enters with his people. The God who created by forcing the cosmic waters into their proper place continues control over the water, presumably making it available to all peoples. The thought is exactly like Ps 104, which begins with God defeating the waters (vv. 5-9) and then making the waters available to the creatures of earth (vv. 14-18, 24-26).

Theological and Ethical Analysis

It would be hard to imagine a more appropriate Hallel Psalm than Ps 114, for it was sung at the important Jewish festivals including Passover. The victory that gave birth to Israel is expressed succinctly and with zest ("Why is it, O sea, that you flee?"). A narrative suitable for Passover is thereby suitable also for Easter. The people are freed from slavery to Pharaoh in Egypt and led to serve the Lord in Canaan. They have been saved by their faithful and powerful God. Christian readers will be especially sensitive to certain symbols: the waters through which one passes to freedom have traditionally been interpreted as the waters of baptism; the waters represent chaos and death; the resurrection of Jesus is victory over the forces of chaos. The psalm is a good choice for a baptismal ceremony. It can also be used for private recitation when one wants to remember before God the great constitutive event from which all else follows.

PSALM 115

Literary Analysis

Psalm 115 does not fit into any of the traditional psalm genres. In content, it is a communal petition for God to act for Israel (vv. 1-2) and expose the folly of those who worship other gods (vv. 3-8). It is also an exhortation to Israel to remain loyal to the Lord in the present crisis (vv. 9-11), ending with a blessing and congregational response (vv. 12-18). The psalm seems to have been sung antiphonally, that is, by two groups (or an individual and a group). This supposition would account for variations in personal pronouns. The Septuagint reckoned Pss 114–15 to be a single poem. Psalm 135:15-18 quotes Ps 115:4-8.

A national crisis seems to be the immediate situation, though the poem gives no information about it. It is possible, however, that the psalm is concerned with a typical situation: Israel's distress causes the nations to scorn God; Israel expresses faith in God and scorn for the nations; Israel experiences blessings to which it responds with gratitude and confidence. Possibly, the psalm may be part of a liturgical ceremony in which the community defined itself over against the nations.

Exegetical Analysis

Show forth your glory to the nations (vv. 1-2)

The literal translation of verse 1 (such as NRSV) is misleading, for the poet uses the Hebrew figure of dialectic negation that exaggerates the negative member to express emphasis. To emphasize "for *your* sake," the poet denies "for *our* sake." The meaning is that the act is much more for your benefit than for ours. Moreover, the usual rendering of verse 1*a* "give glory" is not an accurate rendering of *nātan kābôd*, as is shown by the same phrase in Ezek 39:21: "I will *display my glory* among the nations; and all the nations shall see my judgment that I have executed." One must therefore paraphrase Ps 115:1-2 to convey its sense: "Display your glory to the nations who treat your people with contempt; we ask this out of concern for your name rather than for our welfare." More literally, one can render: "Not for our sake, O Lord, not for our sake, but for the sake of your name display your glory." The complaint in verse 2, "where is their God," implies that the nations have claimed Israel is defenseless because its God is powerless or has abandoned them. Under attack, the people beg God to appear on their side.

Our God in the heavens acts, but their gods on earth do nothing (vv. 3-8)

Two contrasts provide structure to the section: between our God (singular) in heaven and their gods (in the form of images, plural) on earth; between God who acts and gods who cannot. "Our God is in the heavens" is a bold cry in response to the nations' contemptuous "Where is their God?" It is an apt response, for the phrase "in the heavens" implies God is sovereignly free; the phrase is parallel to "he does whatever he pleases." The nations' gods, in the form of images, are regarded with contempt. Contemptuous descriptions of divine images were common from the exile on. Examples are Jer 10:1-16; Isa 40:18-20; 41:6-7; and 44:9-20. In the ancient Near East, the image mediated the presence of the deity; it re-presented the deity to the worshiper. Israelite religion officially forbade images (e.g., Exod 20:4-5; Deut 4:15-18; 5:8-9) and criticized religions that used them. To Israelite thinkers, images represented the gods all too well: as the images are inert and lifeless, so also are the gods they represent. "Trust in" (v. 8b) means to depend on a god for protection and life.

Israel, trust in the Lord (vv. 9-11)

As those who trust in images will be frustrated (v. 8), those who trust in the Lord will experience him as their help and shield (vv. 9-11), that is, as actually protecting them. Divine protection is not automatic; one must be in a relationship with God, in other words, trust in the Lord. The third-person pronoun "their" in verses 9-11 seems odd. One would expect "your" after the verb ("trust in the LORD!") in the imperative mood. The best solution is to suppose that the verb "trust" in verses 9 and 11 was originally in the perfect tense rather than in the imperative mood (Septuagint, NAB, REB): "Israel trusts in the LORD: / he is their help and their shield."

The people are addressed under three titles: "Israel," "House of Aaron," and "You who fear the LORD." The three titles refer to the entire nation under three different aspects; they do not refer to three distinct groups. Though "House of Aaron" refers to priests, Israel as such is a priestly people (e.g., Exod 19:6; Isa 61). Though "you who fear the LORD" is taken by some to refer to proselytes in the postexilic community (1 Kgs 8:41-45; Isa 56:6; Acts 13:16), it refers to Israel as revering Yahweh alone. The latter meaning is supported by the use of the phrase in Ps 115:13.

Blessings and responses (vv. 12-18)

Verses 12-13 announce that God has remembered *us* (NRSV: "has been mindful of us"). God's remembering is similarly crucial in Gen 8:1; 9:15; Exod 2:24; and Ps 74:2. A priestly voice in verses 14-15 announces that God has blessed *you*, echoing the famous priestly blessing in Num 6:22-26. The second blessing in verses 14-15 is another hint that the psalm records an antiphonal liturgy of some kind. The priestly blessing includes more than protection from enemies; it includes increase in population (cf. Deut 1:11; 8:1), which indicates a more general concern than alleviating a particular crisis. It is concerned with Israel's flourishing in the world of nations.

The final statement (vv. 16-18) develops the thought of verse 3-8, where it was said that "Our God is in the heavens" (v. 3) and that the "gods" (represented by their images) are on earth. Verse 16 repeats that the Lord dwells in the heavens. Earth is the domain of human beings, not the domain of the so-called gods, for they are nothings. By divine decree, human beings have earth as their domain. People of the time imagined the universe as having three tiers: heaven, earth, and the underworld. Only in the second tier where human beings lived can someone bless God (v. 18).

Theological and Ethical Analysis

As noted, the psalm may well address a typical situation of Israel rather than be a prayer for an actual crisis. Israel is always the people of God whose weakness and misfortune invite people to accuse their God of neglect or weakness. Israel responds with vigorous trust in their God and scorn toward their neighbors. Their God is not like the divine images of their neighbors. Living in the heavens, their Lord is sovereignly free. Trust in such a God is the only attitude.

Though Robert Browning's famous line, "God's in his heaven— / All's right with the world" (*Pippa Passes*, part 1), is outwardly similar to Ps 115:3 and 16, modern poem and ancient psalm could hardly be more different. In Browning's poem, the phrase denotes an idyllic time of harmony. The psalm, on the other hand, is realistic, being aware that Israel, the Lord's people, is alone in the world of nations. Its singular position can call forth contempt from its neighbors. The psalm records how Israel meets its Lord in public prayer. Even when under attack, they do not lose hope, recognizing God's mysterious ways and desire to bless them. They accept the earth as their sphere in which they have the opportunity to trust in the Lord. The poem enables them to find God and pray always.

PSALM 116

Psalm 116 is the fourth of the six Hallel Psalms sung at important Jewish festivals including Passover. Like several of them, it contains the invitation "praise the LORD!" (v. 19, traditionally Hallelujah). The verse, "I will lift up the cup of salvation and call on the name of the LORD," may account for its choice for the Passover meal. The Septuagint begins a new psalm at verse 10, though no modern translation accepts that division.

Literary Analysis

In genre, the poem is a thanksgiving. Like certain thanksgivings, however (e.g., Pss 16, 34, and 66), the singer seems more intent on expressing gratitude for having found a saving God than for a particular rescue. Much of the poem is concerned with characterizing the deity as attentive (vv. 1-2) and merciful (vv. 5-6) and with expressing the singer's resolve to be a good servant by acts of trust (vv. 7, 9-11) and worship (vv. 12-19). In short, the psalm describes how one person came to fear the Lord. "LORD" occurs fifteen times in the poem, indicating the psalmist's focus on God. People entrusted themselves to a particular deity on the basis of the deity's ability to save them. In this psalm, Yahweh, the Savior of Israel, has proved to be a saving God.

Though the thought of the psalm is relatively clear, commentators differ on its structure. Though there is repetition throughout—a refrain ("call on the name of the LORD," vv. 4, 13, 17), repeated clauses ("in the presence of all his people," vv. 13*b*-14; 17*b*-18), and repeated words ("death" and "sheol," vv. 3, 8, 15; emphatic "I," vv. 10, 11, 16, 16)—the repetition does not seem to have shaped the structure. Dramatic logic suggests four sections: the rescue and the relationship (vv. 1-4); the nature of God revealed by the rescue and the psalmist's response (vv. 5-8); resolve to live as a trusting client of the divine patron (vv. 9-11); resolve to offer appropriate ritual thanks (vv. 12-19).

Exegetical Analysis

The rescue and the relationship (vv. 1-4)

The psalmist celebrates both the rescue from death (vv. 3-4) and the resulting relationship (vv. 1-2). The phrase "I love the LORD" is unique in the Hebrew Bible. "Love" is more than romantic love, for it includes the notion of choice (Prov 12:1; 20:13; Isa 41:8), with overtones of preference and loyalty (Deut 4:37; 10:15). Verses 1-2 describe the relationship of divine patron and loyal client in typical terms: One cries out, and the other hears and helps; one professes long-term loyalty ("I love"; "I call on him as long as I live") and the other "inclines his ear to me." The rescue that initiated or reinforced this bond is told in verses 3-4: struck by a deadly affliction, the psalmist prayed, "Save my life!" and was heard. Such an incident revealed who the Lord is. No wonder the first words of the psalm are "I love the LORD!"

The nature of God revealed by the rescue and the psalmist's response (vv. 5-8)

Faith confessions like that in verses 5-6 are relatively rare in the Bible, which generally prefers to narrate God's acts rather than attributes. The classic biblical confession, and perhaps the source of verses 5-6, is Exod 34:6,

> "The LORD, the LORD,
> a God merciful and gracious,
> slow to anger,
> and abounding in steadfast love and faithfulness."

Psalmic examples include 86:15; 103:8; and 145:8. Such confessions arise from an experience of salvation. In Ps 116, the psalmist, fresh from rescue, expands the traditional confession by elaborating the terms "righteous" and "merciful": They mean that God protects the vulnerable ("the simple," v. 6). Having the Lord on one's side responds to the deepest anxieties of the human heart (v. 7). According to verse 8, the Lord will protect my very self—"my soul," "my eyes," and "my feet."

Resolve to live as a trusting client of the divine patron (vv. 9-11)

To revere Yahweh means carrying out Yahweh's precepts (vv. 9-11) and rituals (vv. 12-19). In this section, the psalmist resolves to "walk before the LORD" (v. 9). The phrase seems to be a shortened form (as in 1 Kgs 8:25) of "to walk before me in faithfulness" (1 Kgs 2:4; cf. Gen 17:1). Though commentators take verses 10-11 in slightly different ways, context makes clear the general sense: The speaker resolves to maintain faith in God even when afflicted and betrayed by others. "I kept my faith" in verse 10 is only one of the psalmist's many strong assertions of love and loyalty: "I love" (v. 1a); "I walk before the LORD" (v. 9); "I am your servant" (v. 16); "I will offer to you a thanksgiving sacrifice" (v. 17a); and "I will pay my vows to the LORD" (v. 18a). In the New Testament, 2 Cor 4:13 interprets verse 10 in a somewhat different way, as faith authorizing one to instruct others: "'I believed, and so I spoke'—we also believe, and so we speak."

Resolve to carry out the appropriate ritual thanks (vv. 12-19)

As verses 9-11 are about obedience, verses 12-19 are about worship. Obedience and worship are the two sides of one coin, revering the deity. The psalmist asks the question, "What shall I return to the LORD / for all his bounty to me?" Though the exchange between God and the psalmist is lively and sincere, it is not based on equality. "What can I give in response for life, salvation, and relationship?" asks the psalmist. God is in need of nothing. I can only give God myself in obedience and worship: "I will lift up the cup of salvation / and call on the name of the LORD" (v. 13). "The cup of salvation" means a drink offering poured out in thanksgiving (e.g., Exod 25:29; Lev 23:37). "Vows" (v. 14) are conditional promises made to God that will be fulfilled if the favor is granted. The cup of salvation and the vows are mentioned as typical rites that the psalmist performs as part of the relationship.

Verse 15, "Precious in the sight of the LORD / is the death of his faithful ones," is puzzling. It cannot mean that God takes pleasure in such deaths, even when freely embraced in martyrdom. The sense must be "*too* precious" or "costly" is their death (as in Ps 72:14). NJPS catches the sense: "grievous in the LORD's sight." In Ps 116 "death" (v. 15) is the third and climactic mention of death; the first is "Sheol" in verse 3 and the second is "death" in verse 8. In each instance, God rescues the client from death. As a client of the Lord of life, the psalmist hopes for protection against death. Verse 16 continues the tone of love and faith, managing in a few words to express loyalty, vulnerability, and gratitude. As in verses 4, 13, and 17, the psalmist calls on the name of the Lord, that is, accepts the Lord as his or her personal God. The phrases "in the presence of all his people" (vv. 14b, 18b), "house of the LORD" (v. 19a), and "Jerusalem" (v. 19b) suggest a liturgical celebration in the Temple. Some suggest that the singer is the king representing Israel. The citation of older psalms and the influence of Aramaic suggests, however, a postexilic date when there would have been no king. It is possible that an officiant sang the song on behalf of the community.

Theological and Ethical Analysis

Prayer can turn into an exchange of favors: You do me a favor, and I offer you a thanksgiving sacrifice. This psalm goes in a different direction, concentrating on the relationship between pray-er and God. Its first words describe the bond between them, "I love the LORD." The act of salvation, though important, is secondary to the abiding rhythm of the Lord's love and the psalmist's response. The response is dictated by the religious forms of the time, "fear of the Lord (revering Yahweh)," which consists of obedience and right worship. Though the dual response may not be in a modern idiom, it is broad enough to include a wide variety of responses to God's action. Modern culture values autonomy as a mark of maturity, so that obedience to another is not an instinctive response. How is obedience to be interpreted? Obedience means wholehearted commitment, listening to the other, and a union of hearts and minds. Though forms of worship have changed as well, it remains true that one is invited to honor the saving God in a bodily and communal way in rites, songs, and communion.

The psalm holds in exquisite balance devotion that is expressed both in the obedience of daily life and the rituals of the sanctuary. A pray-er is defined as one who cries out, and God is defined as the one who hears and saves. Every divine intervention is taken as one more demonstration of the profound relationship between God and a particular community with its members.

PSALM 117

Literary Analysis

These opening and closing words in this shortest of all hymns in the Psalter are *hălĕlû yāh,* "praise!" It is thereby linked to the preceding Hallel hymn, which uses the same verb. This poem's declaration that God's steadfast love endures forever will be developed further by the immediately following poem (Ps 118:1-4). This hymn is a textbook example of the genre: a call to praise (v. 1), the reason for the praise introduced by "for" (v. 2*a*), and a repeat of the invitation verse (v. 2*c*). The reason the nations should give praise is the Lord's steadfast love and faithfulness toward Israel. Israel, the elect people of the Lord, is the showcase for the Lord's generosity and an example of what the Lord wishes for the entire human race. Israel can therefore invite all the nations to look at its prosperity and destiny in order to understand the generous intent of the Most High God.

Exegetical Analysis

Addressing the nations is more characteristic of Isa 40–55 than the psalms. Isaiah 40–55 summons the nations to look at Israel (e.g., Isa 41:1; 43:9; 49:1) and learn from its restoration from exile that its Lord controls the course of world history. According to Isaiah, Yahweh was behind the rise of Cyrus the Persian king who was the instrument for returning Israel from exile (Isa 45:1, 13). So also Ps 117 teaches that the Lord's faithfulness is manifest in the history of the people Israel. Only to look upon them is to see what the love of the Lord can do. "Steadfast love" and "faithfulness" here are not abstract divine attributes; they characterize the Lord's actions done for Israel. In verse 2, "great" and "endures forever" are in parallel. One perhaps could say that the Lord's love and faithfulness are visible ordinarily, but in the case of Israel they are on preeminent and permanent display. The goal is not the exaltation of the people for their own sake, but for the sake of the Lord.

Theological and Ethical Analysis

The claim made by this shortest of all psalms is grand indeed. That a tiny people should be the prized possession of the Lord of the entire universe—the Lord therefore of Babylon and Egypt—might appear arrogant to some modern readers. More than arrogant, even dangerous, for is it not dangerous when one nation claims to be the One God's special people? Yet is it so arrogant and dangerous? The claim is simply that the God who created the entire human race wishes to make an entry into the world of nations and does so through the mediation of one nation. To judge from Israel's own Scriptures, it does not claim to be superior in virtue to others. In fact, its Scriptures indict its leaders and people for their failures to live up to the principles and morality the Lord has given them. Rather, the psalm invites the nations of the world to recognize in one people a pledge of the one Lord's generosity and justice toward all. The little poem is not about imperialism but about God's desires for the human race. Paul quotes verse 1 in Rom 15:11 in support of his conviction that God is calling the Gentiles.

PSALM 118

Psalm 118 is memorably placed between the shortest (117) and longest psalm (119) in the Psalter. It declares "his steadfast love endures forever" (vv. 1-4), as the immediately preceding Ps 117:2b declared "the faithfulness of the LORD endures forever." As the final Hallel Psalm, Ps 118 gathers up important themes of its predecessors: raising up the poor (113), the exodus as manifesting the Lord's rule (114), the threefold invitation to the people named as Israel, house of Aaron, and fearers of the Lord (115), thanksgiving (116), and steadfast love (117).

Literary Analysis

It is generally acknowledged that the psalm is a thanksgiving for victory (vv. 5, 10-18) that was performed in a liturgy involving a procession (vv. 19-20, 26-27). If the psalm was composed in the preexilic period, the "I" who celebrates an actual or ritual victory (vv. 5-21, 28) presumably was the king. If the psalm is postexilic, as many think, then the "I" was a nonroyal leader, perhaps the high priest who seems to have represented the nation to outsiders. The proper name of Israel's God occurs twenty-eight times ("LORD," *YHWH,* 22 times, *Yāh,* 6 times). The number is symbolic, seven (perfection) times four (universality), suggesting that the Lord rules heaven and earth.

The poem itself yields few clues regarding its structure. It may have been composed to accompany a liturgical performance that was well known to its early readers. The main elements of the ceremony can be deduced from the text. Verses 1-4 invite the congregation to praise the Lord's steadfast love. A speaker ("I") narrates how that steadfast love played out in "my" life (vv. 5-18). The narration of rescue is presented twice, each with a different metaphorical system. Such repetition is a kind of large-scale parallelism. According to the first account, the psalmist was led from a tight spot to a broad place, which elicits grateful response (vv. 5-9). According to the second account, the psalmist was rescued from nations surrounding and attacking, which similarly elicits grateful praise (vv. 10-18). The narration was probably sung or spoken in the course of a procession, for verse 19 speaks of the procession arriving at the gate of the Temple. In verse 20, a priestly voice states the qualifications necessary for entering. In verse 21, the individual, now standing within the Temple, repeats the thanksgiving, and in verses 22-27, the congregation adds its own praise. The individual again gives thanks in verse 28, and the poem ends with all giving thanks in a reprise of verse 1 (v. 29). This reconstruction will provide the outline for the exegetical analysis.

Exegetical Analysis

Invitation to the congregation to give praise (vv. 1-4)

The speaker exhorts the people to praise the Lord "for / . . . his steadfast love endures forever." "For" introduces the motive for giving praise, in this case, the Lord's loyalty to the covenant, which will be illustrated in the following recitals of victory. Verses 2-4 characterize Israel in three parallel phrases (as in Ps 115:9-11). Though some suggest each phrase refers to a separate segment of Israel (laity, priests, and proselytes of the postexilic community), it is best to view them as parallel phrases expressing the richness of the people's vocation. The refrain, "his steadfast love endures forever," emphasizes that the Lord is utterly faithful to the covenant promises and able to defeat any enemy interfering with those promises.

The recital of rescue in battle (vv. 5-18)

After inviting the assembly to praise the Lord's steadfast love (vv. 1-4), the speaker narrates how that love showed itself in a particular battle. The distress and the rescue are told twice, verses 5-9 and 10-18, and each story is followed by exultant reflections. Each contains a similar statement: "The LORD answered me" (v. 5b) and "the LORD helped me" (v. 13b). The first experience (vv. 5-9) is described with the metaphor system of constraint and spaciousness. God moves the psalmist from a tight place ("my distress," v. 5a) to a broad place. The salvation itself turns into an act of worship, for it elicited from the rescued person a confession of the Lord as savior (vv. 6-7) and rejection of other sources of salvation (vv. 8-9).

Verses 10-18, the second version of the saving act, employs the metaphor of battle: The singer tells how all the nations surrounded and attacked. With the Lord's help, the singer was able to cut them off (vv. 10-12) and to stand up after being knocked down (v. 13). As in the first report, this one turns into triumphant shouts appropriate for a liturgical ceremony (vv. 14-18).

Word choice and allusions heighten the drama. In verses 10-12, the four-times repeated verb "to surround" and the thrice-repeated verb "I cut them off" effectively convey the back-and-forth motion of battle. Verses 15b-16 constitute a memorable praise of the right hand of the Lord that gained the victory. "Bees" are a metaphor for pursuing enemies also in Deut 1:44: "The Amorites who lived in that hill country then came out against you and chased you as bees do." The victory song in verses 14-18 is based on the song of Moses in Exod 15:1-18, even quoting Exod 15:2 ("The LORD is my strength and my might, / and he has become my salvation"). The paean to the Lord's right hand comes from Exod 15:6, 12. The saving deed in the psalm seems to be the exodus itself or an act modeled on it. In Ps 118:18, "punished" is better rendered "chastened," for God rather allowed the leader to experience sufferings. It is possible that the narratives of suffering and rescue were reenacted in liturgical movement. One can imagine a singer hemmed in by dancers and then led into a secure open space.

Arrival at the gate, announcement of demands, and a new thanksgiving (vv. 19-21)

Arriving at the gate of the Temple, the singer asks to be admitted in order to give thanks in the Lord's own house (v. 19). One has to be granted admittance to such a sacred place. In verse 20, the priest lays down the condition for entrance: One must be righteous, that is, have a record of obeying the commands of the Lord. Evidently admitted into the Temple, the singer proclaims there the praise (repeating v. 14b) uttered in the court before all the people.

The congregation adds its own voices in thanksgiving (vv. 22-27)

The congregation, or a chorus representing it, responds to the singer's story of humiliation-exaltation in a memorable image: A stone rejected by builders as unsuitable turns out to be the very cornerstone toward which all the building blocks are oriented. A cornerstone presumes a large building, perhaps the Temple that symbolized the Lord's choice of Israel and the king. Such a stunning transformation from low to high can only have been done by the Lord. Radical reversal is a sign of divine origin (v. 23). The verse is quoted in Matt 21:42; Mark 12:10; Luke 20:17; and Acts 4:11 to show that the Jewish rejection of Jesus and the church's acceptance of him were in the Scriptures and thus part of God's plan. In Ps 118:23, the people acknowledge once more the divine hand in the rescue (v. 24), respond with joyous sound (v. 24), pray for continued protection (v. 25), and affirm that the singer is blessed (v. 26). Liturgical gestures conclude the chorus's song (v. 27): shining a light and binding branches upon the four corners ("horns") of the altar (v. 27). According to the Mishnah, the procession around the altar on the feast of Tabernacles was accompanied by the recitation of Ps 118:27 on all seven days (*m. Sukkah* 4:5).

One last time the singer gives thanks for the exaltation and exclaims "You are my God" (v. 28). Rescue is a sign of acceptance; there is now a strong bond between the singer and God. Chorus and singer join their voices in repeating the opening verse, a sure sign that the ceremonial song has come to its end.

Theological and Ethical Analysis

Though one must rely somewhat on an imaginative reconstruction of a ceremony to grasp the unity of the psalm, the movement of the poem is clear. All Israel (or its representatives) gathers in the sanctuary to praise the steadfast love of the Lord, moving in a solemn procession as a singer narrates the Lord's grand rescue, evidently the exodus, which is the core event of Israel. The procession evokes the march of Israel from Egypt to Canaan. Exulting in their salvation, procession and singer pause at the gates of the Temple, and the singer repeats the praise in the Lord's own house.

The psalm recognizes that Israel owes its existence to the Lord's initiative and celebrates that steadfast love. Steadfast love becomes actual when enemies are repulsed and Israel is saved. Israel's foundational event—the exodus and conquest—is an act of salvation inviting thanks and praise. The psalm gives thanks in several interplays, between the people and the individual singer and between the Lord and the singer. The people accompany the individual in a procession, realizing that the act the singer commemorates is theirs too. The voices of both alternate in giving praise. The individual is aware that the rescue is not an isolated event but an instance and sign of a steadfast love that endures forever.

Christians will see in the movement from humiliation to exaltation a foreshadowing of Jesus who suffered, died, and was raised from the dead. His rescue from death is a new exodus and a fresh sign that God's steadfast love endures forever. The

Christian community that celebrates the deed is itself intimately connected to Jesus' movement from death to life, for "He is the head of the body, the church; he is the beginning, the firstborn from the dead" (Col 1:18). His exaltation means their own. The psalm is therefore a wonderful song for the Easter season.

PSALM 119

Literary Analysis

Psalm 119 stands by itself, a massive poem between the Hallel Psalms (113–18) and the Songs of Ascents (Pss 120–34). Its one hundred seventy-six verses make it far and away the longest poem in the Psalter, almost two and a half times the length of its nearest competitor, Ps 78 (72 verses). Each stanza of this acrostic poem has eight verses and (normally) eight synonyms of "law," more accurately "authoritative teaching." Such teaching is the theme throughout. In their normal NRSV rendering, the words are: "law" *(tôrāh)*; "word" *(dābār)*, "promise(s)" *('imrāh)*, "ordinances" *(mišpāṭîm)*, "statutes" *(ḥuqqîm)*, "commandments" *(miṣwôt)*, "decrees" *(ēdôt)*, and "precepts" *(piqqûdîm)*. Though a few scholars include "way" *(derek, 'ōraḥ)* or "faithfulness" *('ĕmûnāh)* to bring the total synonyms to ten, the last-named terms do not have the same meaning or frequency as the others. The eight terms are largely synonymous in this psalm, though each contributes its own nuance—illumination ("law," "word"), moral demand ("ordinances," "statutes," "commandments"), guidance ("decrees," "precepts"), and promise ("promise").

The genre of Ps 119 has been the subject of much discussion. Traditionally, the poem has been regarded as a didactic piece, teaching reverence for the law in the Second Temple period, when law was becoming a central religious concept in Judaism. At the beginning of the last century, the great form critic Hermann Gunkel classed it as a "mixed genre" that borrowed freely from other genres. Unfortunately, "mixed genre" implies formalism and decline, and the term reinforced the low opinion of the psalm that many Christian scholars already had because of its supposed legalism. Gunkel did, however, correctly identify the genre as mainly individual petition, and his judgment has stood the test of time. It is crucial for interpreting the poem. Ninety verses (more than half the psalm) contain either a petition or a lament or both, approximately the same ratio found in such laments as Pss 3 and 5. A lament is fundamentally a petition; lament is only one part of it. What sets apart Ps 119 as a prayer is that its desire for life, vindication, and deliverance all involve the word of God. One can only obtain blessings through God's word, and apart from that word nothing is given.

Stylistic features such as acrostic form, repetition of words for torah, and enormous length combine to produce the poem's effect. Literary art has taken a genre born of a specific situation and transformed it into a prayer for the whole of life. The psalm portrays an individual, an "I," struggling to live in accord with God's word. Thanks to the psalm, anyone can be helped to encounter the communicating word in daily life. That word educates, reproves, demands, and promises. Though at times overwhelmed, hopeful, frightened, exultant, the pray-er is intent on listening to the word in the world. Literary art creates a text for lifelong prayer.

What does torah mean in the poem? Since the psalm does not define the term, scholarly answers have been many. For some, torah is the Pentateuch as it had come to be understood in early Judaism; for others, it is torah as used in Deuteronomy and the Deuteronomistic History, that is, authoritative teaching. Others believe, with more reason, that torah in Ps 119 is more general, meaning "divine teaching," a sense that is similar to the meaning of torah in the Wisdom literature. At the time of the psalm's composition, torah had not yet become a term for the Pentateuch. Torah in the psalm is the divine word in its related aspects of teaching, command, and promise. It also designates the dynamic and transformative word through which God carries out his will. These considerations suggest a date of composition in the early postexilic period, the sixth to the fourth centuries BCE, before torah came to be identified with the Pentateuch. Exilic destruction and God's apparent silence have not discouraged the psalmist, who still believes in a revealing and self-communicating God. Borrowing the style and tone of the lament genre, the psalmist crafted something new: a prayer to live by the word of God at all moments of life.

Two factors make a special contribution to the structure. One is the acrostic style (twenty-two eight-verse stanzas, each beginning with a successive letter of the alphabet). The other is the set of words for torah or word of God. The art conveys a sense of totality and completeness, "from A to Z." Within this structure, dramatic movement is discernible. The poem has a clear beginning, the *aleph* (A) and *beth* (B) stanzas (vv. 1-8, 9-16) functioning as a prologue. Complaints and more general petitions begin to appear in the *gimel* (G) stanza in verses 17-24 and are further developed thereafter. Appropriately, the *lamed* (L) stanza in verses 89-96 is the turning point (*lamed* begins the second half of the Hebrew alphabet), moving from the deeply anguished *kaph* (K) stanza in verses 81-88 to more positive views. The final stanza (*taw* [T], vv. 169-76) promises praise and gives assurances that befit a conclusion. Such is the complex process that the psalmist goes through, complaining of peril, rejoicing in hope, begging for enlightenment and fidelity to the commandments. There is no single linear movement. Reality is not like that. The psalmist struggles again and again with the word of God. Space considerations prohibit a stanza-by-stanza exegetical analysis. The following analysis owes much to Will Soll (1991) and D. N. Freedman (1999). After the two prologue stanzas (vv. 1-16), the remaining twenty stanzas are divided into five groups of four stanzas.

Exegetical Analysis

The Prologue (vv. 1-16)

The first two stanzas (*aleph* and *beth*) function as a prologue, stating the goals of the psalmist and sounding the themes of the poem. They also alert readers to the expository method in which a synonym of torah occurs in virtually every verse. The double beatitudes in verses 1 and 2 state the goal in memorable fashion, that pray-ers "walk in the law of the Lord," that is, they live their lives entirely in accord with God's word. Aspects of torah appear in the same stanza: It is the source of good fortune (vv. 1-2), makes ethical demands (vv. 4-6), leads to praise (v. 7), and grounds one's relationship with God (v. 8). Seven synonyms of torah appear in the first stanza. The phrase "his ways" *(derek)* in verse 3 functions as a synonym of torah here and in a few other verses (e.g., v. 37); it ordinarily appears with one of the regular synonyms as in "the way of your decrees" (v. 14; cf. vv. 27, 30, 32, 33). Modern ideas of consistency and symmetry cannot be expected in ancient poems.

The *beth* stanza (vv. 9-16) continues the introduction. An idealistic seeker seeks the word of God that brings happiness and prosperity. Verse 9 expresses the resolve in a grand question typical of youth: "How can a young person keep his way pure, / guarding it according to your word?" (my translation). The answer is through desire and resolve, which are expressed in the following verses. The psalmist is acutely conscious that obedience to the word is entirely a gift of God, as indicated by the phrase "teach me your statutes" (v. 12*b*). The phrase, "blessed are you, O Lord" (v. 12*a*) is at the exact center of the stanza. At this stage, the psalmist chiefly expresses goals and hopes. The anguish and temptation that test youthful ideals and resolve have not yet appeared. They are not far away, however, and will come in the very next stanza (vv. 17-24).

Movement: complaint to petitions to promises of piety (vv. 17-48, gimel to waw [W])

The complaints that begin in vv. 17-24 will grow more pressing in subsequent stanzas: "I live as an alien in the land" (v. 19*a*), "my soul is consumed with longing" (v. 20*a*), and "princes sit plotting against me" (v. 23*a*). Danger and pain have entered the psalmist's life precisely because of loyalty to God's law. Even in the pain, however, it is possible to say, "your decrees are my delight" (v. 24*a*). In the next stanza, verses 25-32, the psalmist becomes even more distressed and confused, provoking further anxiety about whether it is possible to adhere to God's ways (vv. 25, 28, 29, 31). Not all the pleas are uttered in distress, however, nor do all the petitions ask to be saved from a particular danger. The psalmist never loses sight of the goal of being in relationship to the Lord through the word as instruction and promise (vv. 26, 27, 32).

In verses 33-40, verbs in the imperative mood open each line except the last, underlining both the desperation and the longing of the speaker. Verses 33 and 35 employ the metaphor of path for the moral life. In the highly dramatic viewpoint of the psalmist, there are ultimately only two paths: the way of the wicked and the way of the righteous. One way, protected by God, leads to life; the other way is destined to end in death. In a surprising shift of tone, verses 41-48 are without anguish, telling a coherent narrative of how the torah makes one courageous and bold (torah words are italicized in the summary below): May the Lord's steadfast love come to me according to your *promise* (v. 41) that I may answer scoffers as one trusting your *word* (v. 42); do not remove that *word* from my mouth, for I hope in your *ordinances* (v. 43). Subsequent verses describe the effect of keeping the *law* (v. 44), seeking the *precepts* (v. 45); such fidelity toward the torah enables the psalmist to speak the *decrees* before kings (v. 46), delighting in the *commandments* and meditating on the *statutes*. The sudden shift from the mood of the previous stanza is a reminder that Ps 119 does not tell a single story. Life consists of sudden changes and doubling back.

Movement: reflection on the past, admission of guilt in the present, and plea for future help (vv. 49-80)

In verses 49-56, the verb "to remember" *(zākar)* occurs three times (vv. 49, 52 ["think"], and 55) though it appears nowhere else in the poem. Verse 49 asks that the Lord remember the psalmist as the psalmist has remembered the Lord. Though the psalmist chiefly remembers suffering (vv. 51, 53), consolation is not absent (vv. 50, 52, 54). Suffering has resulted from remaining faithful to the Lord (vv. 51, 53). Verses 57-64, the next stanza, contain protestations of loyalty with pleas for help in observing the law. The letter *ṭēt* that heads verses 65-72 is also the first letter of *ṭôb*, "good," which occurs as the first word of verses 65, 68, 71, and 72. The stanza recounts how good and patient God has been toward the psalmist who went astray (v. 67*a*) and was "humbled" (vv. 67, 71) by means of God's statutes. "Humility" in the traditional Christian sense is not a virtue in the Hebrew Bible. Though verses 67 and 71 and Prov 15:33; 18:12; and 22:4 seem to praise "humility," they actually say that humiliation is not inevitably bad, for humiliation can teach one to know one's place in the Lord's world, that is, to revere the Lord and thus attain blessings. In Ps 119, humiliation had a good effect because it taught the psalmist dependence upon the word of God. One may remain arrogant if not taught by torah (vv. 69-70). The divine word is educative. As in the previous sections, the psalmist refers to the past, indeed to the time of God's creative word in the womb (v. 73). Now, says the psalmist, let me be an example of your law to others (v. 79).

Movement: complaint to consolation to reencountering danger with renewed confidence (vv. 81-112)

Verses 81-88 sketch the low point of the psalmist's life. Physically and psychically spent, the psalmist hopes only to be nourished by God's precepts that have always brought life. The prayer is basic, asking only to survive the present crisis ("spare my life," v. 88*a*). The next stanza is another of the psalm's dramatic shifts. As verses 81-88 were the low point, so verses 89-96 are the high point, lifting one's perspective from earth to heaven, from misery to delight. The psalmist had asked in deep skepticism, "how long must your servant endure?" (v. 84*a*) and now is able to declare that "the LORD exists forever" (v. 89*a*) and "your faithfulness endures to all generations" (v. 90*a*). Verses 97-104 continue the mood of exultation in the word of the eternal God.

The psalmist loves the law (v. 97), drawing on its wisdom and delighting in its sweetness. With verses 105-12, the psalmist reenters the world, where the word becomes (in a memorable image) "a lamp to my feet / and a light to my path" (v. 105). Though severely beset by others ("I hold my life in my hand continually," v. 109*a*), the psalmist remains faithful (vv. 109*b*-12).

Movement: assertions of loyalty, from complaint to affirmation of the Lord's righteousness (vv. 113-44)

Assertions of loyalty, longing for personal integrity, and awareness of the Lord as judge characterize verses 113-20. The following stanza (vv. 121-28) develops the complaint from the previous section: Though innocent of wrongdoing (vv. 121, 125*a*, 127-28), I suffer from the attacks of your enemies (vv. 121, 122), and I long to know your precepts. Verses 129-36 vividly express both desire to keep God's law and awareness of the need of God's grace. In verses 137-43, the five-times repeated words for righteousness (*şĕdāqāh, şedeq, şaddîq*) serve to underline the righteousness of the Lord in which the psalmist takes refuge. Though troubled, the psalmist is able to find comfort in God's law (v. 143).

Conclusion: movement from address to petition to protestations of loyalty to petitions and promise of praise (vv. 145-76)

The concluding section is concerned with deriving strength from the divine word and with giving praise. In verses 145-46, the psalmist calls upon the Lord ("I cry," vv. 145-46). The Lord is the first thought on waking from sleep (vv. 147-48) and the one who is near when enemies approach (vv. 150-51*a*). In the next stanza (vv. 153-60), the verb "to see, to look" (vv. 153, 158, 159) gives a dominant tone of petition. The phrases "*look* on my misery" (v. 153) and "*look* [NRSV: "consider"] how I love your precepts" (v. 159) are designed to move God to act kindly toward the psalmist. Increasing resolution is expressed in verses 161-68. Though enemies attack (v. 161), the psalmist is not discouraged, resolving instead to give praise (v. 164) and fulfill the commandments (v. 166). The final stanza (vv. 169-76), though framed by humble petition (vv. 169-70, 176), is marked by a firm resolve to give praise and live according to God's promise. As in most of the other stanzas, praise and petition alternate.

Theological and Ethical Analysis

As already noted, individual petition is a more accurate designation for the genre than the traditional "individual lament." Lament is only one component in a prayer designed to win God's blessings. Though individual petitions usually arise from specific crises, Ps 119 is not situation-specific. Removed from a particular situation by the poet's art—acrostic form, interplay of synonyms for torah, and great length—the psalm is one long petition to live one's entire life in accord with God's word. Though the psalm exalts the word of God, it does not remove it from a human context. The word is celebrated as relational, as communication between God and human beings. Thus the psalmist, who represents everyone struggling to obey God's word in the particulars of life, is portrayed as longing for God's word, wearied from not having it, stirred by the prospect of the life it contains. To be in relation with the divine word is to live with the self-communicating God.

In contrast to certain tendencies in modern spirituality, Ps 119 unfailingly locates authority in God's word and command. Obedience to that word is transformative. The psalm presents divine commands as doable (contrary to pessimistic strains in Christian history) because repentance is always a possibility. Life now, however, is warfare with the evil principle; definitive victory lies only in the future. The major weapon in the battle is the divine word, for its observance trains the passions, gives strength in temptation, and elevates the mind to God.

SONGS OF ASCENTS

Psalm 120 begins a long subsection within the Psalter, Pss 120–34, each of which is prefaced by the superscription "A Song of Ascents." Three superscriptions bear the addition "of David" (122, 124, 131) and one has "of Solomon" (127). The meaning of "Songs of Ascents" is disputed. Some, relying on the meaning of "ascent" (NRSV: "journey up") in Ezra 7:9, propose that it means "pilgrim song," sung as pilgrims approached Jerusalem for the three annual pilgrimage feasts. Support for this interpretation is not strong. Though two Songs of Ascents presume pilgrimages or processions (122 and 132) and others mention Zion (125, 126, 128, 129, 133, 134), "ascent" means "approach" only in Ezra 7:9. Others suggest the Songs of Ascents derive their name from the "ascents" or steplike parallelism common in the psalms, for example, in Ps 127, "unless the LORD builds the house, / . . . unless the LORD guards the city" and "in vain / . . . in vain / . . . in vain." Step parallelism, however, is found throughout the Psalter (e.g., Ps 29), not just in these poems, though it is certainly more frequent here. The most likely explanation of "ascents" is that it derives from the steps or stairs in a temple or large building, which is how the Septuagint, Vulgate, and Mishnah took it. According to the Mishnah, "fifteen steps led up within [the Court of the Women] to the Court of the Israelites, corresponding to the fifteen songs of the steps in the Psalms, and upon them the Levites used to sing" (*m. Mid.* 2:5; cf. *m. Sukkah* 5:4). As early as the second century BCE (the date of Septuagint psalms), then, Pss 120–34 were recited in a ceremony on the steps of the Temple or a related structure. (There is a curious parallel in the gradual [Lat. *gradus*, "step"] psalms in the Latin church that were sung on the altar steps in response to the first scriptural reading.) Certainty is impossible on the matter. The most one can say is that the poems existed in a collection used for ceremonies on a step, an ancient instance of "gradual prayers." The important point is that these psalms are among the most memorable in the Psalter.

PSALM 120

Literary Analysis

In genre, Ps 120 is an individual lament, for it contains complaints (vv. 2-3, 5-7) and petitions for the punishment of enemies (vv. 3-4). There is no statement of hope, however, unless hope is implied in the opening line. Most translators (including NRSV) take verse 1 as a cry uttered in a specific danger, for it puts verse 2 in quotation marks as the prayer that the psalmist uttered in that danger. The poem is structured by two parallel complaints: slanderous attacks (vv. 2-4) and unwilling exile in a hostile country far from Jerusalem (vv. 5-7). The complaints, approximately the same length (respectively, 21 and 22 Hebrew words), tell the same story in different versions. Verses 2-4 tell of a verbal assault that destroyed the psalmist's reputation, and verses 5-7 tell of the effects of that loss of reputation—living as an alien in the community. The places named in verse 5, "Meshech" in the remote north and "Kedar" in the remote south, are far from Jerusalem and symbolize estrangement. Reputation, a community, and a home—all these have been taken from the psalmist. Others' words have become weapons (vv. 2-3, 7) and the only rescue the psalmist can imagine is retaliation in military terms (vv. 3-4).

Exegetical Analysis

My God, save me from lying tongues (vv. 1-4)

Human beings call out, and God answers. Though the verbs "call" and "answer" depict actions, they implicitly portray a relationship that is marked by need and trust on the one hand and mercy and power on the other. The word pair "call // answer" occurs sixteen times in the Psalter (e.g., Pss 3:4; 4:1; 17:6; 27:7). It is possible to interpret verse 1 as primarily descriptive of the psalmist's relationship with God even before the present crisis, though most translators (including NRSV) regard "I cry" as uttered for a particular crisis. The matter cannot be decided on purely syntactic grounds. In any case, the beleaguered psalmist instinctively reaches out to the Lord, equivalently asking "Act as my God in this crisis!"

Songs of Ascents make frequent use of step parallelism. The first step is "the LORD" in verse 1a, which is repeated in verse 2a. The next step is "deceitful tongue" in v. 2c and v. 3c. Though "deceitful tongue" may refer to a specific calumny, it may also refer more generally to a society where mutual respect and truthfulness have disappeared (as in Pss 10:7; 12:1-4; 31:18). The poet personifies the "deceitful tongue" in verse 3. Verse 3 is syntactically unusual, literally, "What will he give you, and what will he add to you, O deceitful tongue?" The second verb (lit. "to give in addition") qualifies the first verb, as in 2 Sam 12:8 and 1 Sam 3:17, "may God do so to you and more also, if you hide anything from me of all that he told you" (cf. 1 Sam 14:44; 20:13). Though not named out of reverence, God is the subject of the verbs. As punishment, the psalmist asks God to fire arrows and hurl firebrands. Malicious words are weapons (Ps 64:3; Prov 12:8), and it is only right that those who utter such words be punished by weapons. The "broom tree" (v. 4b) grows four to twelve feet high with deep roots suited to its desert terrain. Its leaves give shade (1 Kgs 19:4-5) and its roots provide fuel (Job 30:4). Psalm 120:4 suggests its roots were made into charcoal.

A stranger in a strange land (vv. 5-7)

In the second complaint, the psalmist is depicted as an alien in Meshech and Kedar. According to Gen 10:2, Meshech is a descendant of Japheth, father of the peoples of Greece and Asia Minor (present-day Turkey). In Ezek 32:26; 38:2, 3, Meshech is a place in Asia Minor, exact location uncertain. Kedar is a designation for a descendant of Abraham (Gen 25:13) and for certain Arab tribes in the northern part of the Arabian peninsula (cf. Jer 49:28). Far from Palestine, the place names symbolize distance from the Lord and the people of Israel. The third step parallel of the poem is "live/dwelling" (from the verb šākan, "to dwell") in verses 5b and 6a. "Woe is me," says the psalmist living far from family and God.

Distance is not the only problem, for the people of the alien land are hostile. They hate peace *(šālôm)*, which is the last step parallel (vv. 6*b* and 7*a*). Moreover, *šālôm* may be a wordplay on Jerusalem *(Yĕrûšālēm)*, which would imply that those who hate peace hate Jerusalem. The psalmist is indeed in a dangerous situation, attacked by others (vv. 2-4) and forced to live in a hostile environment.

Theological and Ethical Analysis

Though rooted in the Lord, the pray-er suffers much. Indeed, the relationship may even increase the pain. Gone is reputation, and gone, too, is the comfort of being at home and sharing common ground with others. The psalmist is alone, vulnerable, and has no one with whom to share ideals and noble goals. Others want war, not friendship. Though the pain expressed in the complaints is highly personal, it has a communal dimension as well. The psalmist is suffering from a dysfunctional community that attacks and ostracizes rather than welcomes and listens. Tongues turn into weapons and destroy reputations. Society embraces violent solutions. Those who speak peace find themselves at the margin. The suffering depicted here is so intense that it must be told twice with different (though related) metaphor systems (tongues as weapons and being in a distant, hostile land). What sustains the sufferer? Two things: friendship with the Lord who hears cries such as these (v. 1) and hope that the Lord is able to defeat the chorus of malicious tongues (vv. 3-4). The distress depicted in this psalm can be devastating. One's beliefs are scorned and left all alone. With no one to share hopes and dreams, one can turn to one's divine friend and patron who is faithful and just.

PSALM 121

Literary Analysis

This Song of Ascent contains step parallelism that is characteristic of the series: "my help" (vv. 1-2), "not slumber" (vv. 3-4), "who keeps/keeper" (vv. 4-5), and "the LORD will keep" (vv. 7-8). It also treats a theme often found in the Songs—Zion, the holy city. An anxious question begins the psalm: "From where will my help come?" Who is the speaker in verses 2-8? There are two possibilities: (1) An officiant responds with an assurance and a blessing; (2) the psalmist answers and the remaining verses are an inner dialogue like that in Pss 42–43. The first interpretation is to be preferred for several reasons: In the inner dialogue of Pss 42–43, "you" refers to God, whereas in Ps 121 "you" refers to the psalmist; the serene assurance sounds more like a blessing rather than an inner dialogue, and the step parallelism conveys a formality that seems out of place in an inner dialogue. One may conclude that the setting was probably a ceremony in which an officiant blessed an anxious traveler setting out on a difficult and perhaps dangerous journey. The psalm makes it possible for prayers to express their anxiety about making a journey and receive an assurance the Lord is with them.

Though some translations divide the poem into four sections (vv. 1-2, 3-4, 5-6, 7-8, NRSV, NIV), others (REB and NJPS) print it without stanza divisions. The step parallelism provides structure: "my help" links verses 1 and 2; "not slumber" links verses 3-4; "who keeps" links verses 4 and 5; "the LORD will keep" links verses 7-8. Structure is also provided by the opening question, which invites the blessing in verses 2-8. "Coming" in the final verse forms an inclusio with "come" in verse 1, bringing the poem to its conclusion.

Exegetical Analysis

My help comes from the Lord (vv. 1-2)

Verse 1 can have different meanings. "The hills" could refer to a mountain sanctuary, presumably Mount Zion, which would mean that the psalmist looks at the hills of Zion and wonders aloud whether the God dwelling there will truly be a saving God. Verses 3-8 are a positive response. Another possibility, less likely, is that the mountains are a hideout for criminals who attack travelers. Looking at them raises fear in a traveler setting out. "To lift up one's eyes" can imply seeing something at a great distance (Isa 40:26; 49:18; Jer 13:20). Seeing the mountainous land from afar, the psalmist is full of ardent longing yet fearful of the dangerous journey. An anxious question arises: From where will protection come? The psalmist's hope, stated in verse 2 ("*my* help"), has the firmest of all bases—the Lord is creator of the universe. There is no place in the world that does not belong to the Lord.

The watcher over Israel will watch over you (vv. 3-8)

The solemn rhythmic tone of verses 3-8 marks the words as different from verse 2. Different, too, is the controlling metaphor of protecting someone on a journey. The promised protection is practical and down-to-earth. The divine guardian will not let the traveler's foot slip (v. 3a, NRSV: "be moved"); a tired traveler could easily sprain an ankle and not be able to walk farther, forcing companions to stop and find makeshift lodging. A long journey would be made lengthier. Stopping for the night was perilous: uncertain lodging, no street lighting, danger of brigands. To have faith in a God who never slumbered (v. 3b) was a challenge. Two pairs of step words occur in verses 3-4, "keep" and "slumber," linking them tightly together. Verse 4 inculcates trust in a memorable way: literally, "look, he does not slumber, he does not sleep—the guardian of Israel!" "Guardian of Israel" is the center of the poem. "Shade" (from the blazing sun) is a metaphor for protection; the Lord personally *is* protection. The practical tone continues as the speaker promises that the Lord will protect against the burning rays of the sun and the light of the moon. Moonlight was apparently regarded as harmful (cf. "moonstruck"). Night and day is a merism, a poetic device that expresses totality by naming opposites. Thus the phrase "night and day" means "at all times." Verse 7 broadens the horizon—may God offer protection from all evil and guard "your life" *(nepeš)*. The latter word is concretely the throat area where the signs of life (breathing, moisture) are most vivid; by metonymy it symbolizes life itself. Wisdom literature speaks of the necessity of guarding one's soul *(nepeš)*. Here God does the guarding. In the final verse, God guards one's comings and goings (one's movements) and does so forever. Thus God's protection is offered at all times, in every place, and in every movement one can make.

Theological and Ethical Analysis

Like other psalms of longing for God, this one imagines that the Lord of the whole universe has a specific place of dwelling and disclosure. In such psalms, pray-ers long to go there and worship and rejoice with their fellows. The longing in this psalm is the same. Ardent longing for God is a form of worship. What makes this poem distinctive is the mix of longing with anxiety about protection on the journey. The pray-er expresses the anxiety in the form of a question—"from where will my help come?"—and hears a promise that God will accompany the journey in its every twist and turn.

The promised blessings upon the traveler might seem simply optimistic, the kind of easy assurance one sometimes gives to anxious children. One should not, however, view the blessing as a guarantee that nothing bad will happen on the journey. It is a blessing, that is, a wish uttered in the hope that the Lord will go with the traveler. God remains sovereignly free. The traveler accepts the assurance as a prayer and an expression of trust. To understand this prayer, one might keep in mind a helpful distinction between true and false religion. False religion prays for protection against evil in the conviction that if one prays with sufficient fervor, no evil will come upon one. True religion prays with the same fervor, but allows for the possibility, even the probability, that evil may well befall one. Its faith is that when trouble comes, God will be there to help one through the pain. This psalm is certain of one thing: God will accompany the journey to its end.

PSALM 122

The third Song of Ascents adds to the superscription the phrase "of David," like Pss 124, 131, and 133 (where the phrase is not printed in NRSV). It has the step words: "Jerusalem," "tribes," "thrones," "peace," and "for the sake of." Immediately following Ps 121, which blesses a dangerous journey, Ps 122 speaks of the goal of the journey, Zion.

Literary Analysis

Like Pss 46, 48, 76, 84, and 87, Ps 122 is a Song of Zion. It celebrates the sacred city as an architectural wonder (v. 3) where the tribes praise the name of Yahweh (v. 4), the king makes decisions (v. 5), and prayers are offered for the peace of the city (vv. 6-9). In contrast to Pss 46, 48, and 76, which view Zion in larger-than-life terms as the site of victory and a towering mountain, Ps 122 sees the city as the goal of pilgrimage and place of prayer.

Psalm 122 appears to reflect a liturgical ceremony, though it is impossible to reconstruct the ceremony in any detail. Psalms were intended to enable people to participate in the worship carried on in the Temple complex. This commentary, following Franz Delitzsch and others, assumes that the origin of the prayer was the return home of someone who had kept one of the pilgrimage feasts in Jerusalem. This supposition best respects the syntax of verse 2, which should be translated, "our feet *were* standing within your gates." It also explains the wish for the peace of the city (vv. 6-7) and the promise to pray for the good of Jerusalem.

Exegetical Analysis

The joy of celebrating in Jerusalem (vv. 1-5)

How wonderful it was to hear the words of family and friends embarking on the pilgrimage, "Let us go to the house of the LORD!" (v. 1b). Any of the three annual pilgrimage feasts—

Passover, Pentecost, or Tabernacles—could have been the occasion of such a wish. As noted, verse 2 syntactically is most naturally interpreted as retrospective, uttered upon leaving, "our feet *were* standing" (cf. the similar Hebrew syntax in Gen 39:22; Deut 9:22, 24; Job 1:14). The phrase in verse 3*a*, "Jerusalem—built as a city," seems to refer to the impressive buildings and mountain site of Jerusalem. The Lord's people "go up" (v. 4*a*) to Jerusalem and give praise in accord with the ancient law ("as was decreed for Israel"; cf. Exod 23:17; 34:23; Deut 16:16).

Jerusalem is a place not only of praise but also of authoritative guidance, for it contains "thrones for judgment," that is, seats on which judges sit (v. 5). Deuteronomy 17:8-13 mentions an "appellate court" in Jerusalem to which difficult cases were brought. If this is the reference here, the psalm views the legal process as carried out under the supervision of the Davidic king exercising his God-given authority. "Judgment" (v. 5) can refer to ordinary governance as well as the giving of legal decisions. The plural noun "thrones" might be like plural nouns for housing in biblical Hebrew and Ugaritic texts ("tents," "tabernacles") that describe a grand dwelling. If so, "thrones" would mean a grand throne such as a king might have. At any rate, Jerusalem is a place of authority as well as worship.

Pray for the peace of Jerusalem (vv. 6-9)

Jerusalem is personified and addressed in the grammatical second person throughout the section. As suggested, the original setting for the command to pray for Jerusalem seems to have been the moment of leaving the city and returning home. Having seen for themselves the joyous worship, their fellow Israelites, and the majesty of the king, people would naturally pray that the Lord continue to protect the city. If the psalm was written when the memory of ruined Jerusalem was still fresh, such prayers for Jerusalem would be doubly fervent. The prayer in verse 6*a*, "pray for the peace of Jerusalem," is remarkable for its alliteration in Hebrew: *ša'ǎlû šālôm yĕrûšālām*. "Peace" is more than the absence of war. As the parallel colon 6*b* shows, it means the flourishing and prosperity of all those "who love you" (v. 6b). Those who love Jerusalem are those who have chosen to come and show their loyalty to it as the Lord's city. Peace and prosperity will surely be theirs. "Walls" (v. 7a) are the outer defensive walls, suggesting that security is indeed an aspect of peace. The final two verses give the text of the prayers and their purpose. In grammar and in sentiment, the verses are like Isa 62:1:

> For Zion's sake I will not keep silent,
> and for Jerusalem's sake I will not rest,
> until her vindication shines out like the dawn,
> and her salvation like a burning torch.

Theological and Ethical Analysis

In few other psalms is there such joy in fellowship. The joy is generated by others' excited cries, "Let us go to the house of the LORD!" Our feet have stood in the very dwelling place of God. That one's own kindred, the tribes of the Lord, and divine decrees are to be found here (vv. 3-5) delights the singer. All Israelites must pray for this graced but vulnerable city.

Worship in Jerusalem includes more than praise of God. It means that diverse tribes come into one city and join their voices with those of their kindred. Worship also includes an ethical dimension, for the people must respect the judgments handed down from the Davidic throne. In authentic worship, the people speak their praise and thanks to God, and God speaks in return to shape their lives by authoritative words. Joy marks the holy encounter between God and people. The meeting ground of God and Israel is a fragile place, however. One cannot take its security for granted. Israel must pray humbly that God maintain this place of presence and grant the peace and prosperity that comes from communion with God. Through this psalm, people of every age can express their appreciation of the Lord's enlivening presence.

Psalm 123

Literary Analysis

Some Songs of Ascents (apart from Ps 132) were written in the postexilic period, when Israel was no longer an independent nation with its own king or control of its borders. The nation was part of Yehud, a district of the vast Persian Empire. It suffered under Persian bureaucracy and was menaced by neighboring states. The literature of this period complains of the ridicule and taunts of the nations (e.g., Neh 2:19; 4:1, 4). Loss of national sovereignty and dignity is reflected in this little prayer. The individual, the "I" (v. 1), who begins the prayer on behalf of the community, is conscious of being dependent and powerless. Someone else has the power. Even the words seem restricted. A single phrase, "have mercy upon us," is repeated three times. The psalmist's hope is not constricted, however, for the prayer is directed to the divine King enthroned in the heavens (v. 1).

NRSV divides the poem into two stanzas, verses 1-2 and 3-4. "Eyes," repeated four times, binds verses 1-2. "Have mercy upon us," repeated three times, lends a tone of urgency, even desperation, to the poem; the phrase links the first stanza to the second. The repeated words "have more than enough" and "contempt" convey frustration and loss of dignity. Step words that are characteristic of the Songs of Ascents appear: "eyes," "hand," "have mercy upon," "have more than enough of," and "contempt."

Exegetical Analysis

Our eyes are on the Lord (vv. 1-2)

"To lift up one's eyes" seems to be an abbreviation of the biblical idiom, "to lift up one's eyes *and see*" (e.g., Gen 13:10; 18:2; Isa 40:26). Looking toward the heavens symbolizes both the singer's trust in God and inability to find succor on earth. "Enthroned in the heavens" (cf. Ps 2:4) is an exalted title, addressing the Lord under the title of king over heaven and earth.

Kingship is understood concretely, the result of a great victory that established the universe and made the Lord the only powerful deity. See Pss 93, 95–99 for more on divine kingship. Belief in the sovereignty of Yahweh was undoubtedly put to the test whenever Israel fell upon hard times, as was the case in this psalm.

Verse 2 develops the metaphor of looking expectantly to the Lord through two examples, male servants looking at their masters and a female servant looking at her mistress. Contrasts are maximized—male and female, plural and singular—in order to express completeness: *all* look to you. The images are well chosen, concise yet vivid: a great house, perhaps even the palace, servants looking intently at the master or mistress waiting for the slightest motion of a hand. When the hand motions, they spring into action without a word being spoken. A more deft sketch of attentive readiness is hard to imagine. The poet draws the conclusion: so are our eyes upon the Lord until he shows us mercy. Female images of the Lord are relatively rare in the Bible, making the comparison of God to "her mistress" particularly noteworthy.

Have mercy on us as we suffer contempt (vv. 3-4)

The stanza division is admittedly somewhat artificial, for the step parallel "have mercy upon us" spans the stanzas. In the Hebrew of verse 3*a*, the petitions "have mercy upon us" actually surround the divine name, "the LORD." The motive for the Lord to act is that the people suffer contempt and scorn. Why should the people's shame move the Lord to act? To all the world, Israel's hope appears to have been disappointed. Though its God is "enthroned in the heavens," Israel is the lowest of the nations. Their shame is thus a motive for God to show that the ancient promises to the people are true. God's honor is at stake.

Theological and Ethical Analysis

Prayer begins and ends with dependence on God and openness to divine action. This familiar axiom concerning prayer is beauti-

fully illustrated by Ps 123. Instead of busy protestations of innocence and demands that God act now, the psalmist lifts his or her
eyes to heaven (v. 1), symbolically forswearing every other means
of support. Aware of the distance between heaven and earth, the
psalmist embraces the status of servant and waits, eyes fixed on
the hand of the Lord. The psalm sketches a classic picture of
prayer. Biblical prayer is not static, however. It involves communication. The psalmist speaks to God, pointing out the need of the
community: They are despised though the Lord has chosen them
and promised to be faithful to them. Even the prayer displays a
servant's modesty and tact: Look at the disrespect shown to *your*
name! Psalm 123 is a primer on prayer, modeling quiet attention
to God and a true servant's concern for the good name of the
Lord.

PSALM 124

Literary Analysis

There is more step parallelism in Ps 124 than in any other Song
of Ascents: "If it had not been the LORD who was on our side,"
"then," "the flood," "gone over us," "snare," and "escaped."
For step parallelism, see the preface to Ps 120. The parallelism
lends swiftness and drama to the poem. In genre, Ps 124 is a communal thanksgiving. The structure of the poem is simple—an
extended if-then clause (vv. 1-5) and a statement of thanksgiving
and praise (6-8). "The LORD" appears twice in each section.
Thrice-repeated *napšēnû,* literally, "our throat; self, soul" (NRSV:
"us" in vv. 4*b* and 5*a*; "we" in v. 7*a*), links the two sections. The
theme is simple: If the Lord had not come to our aid, they would
have swept us away; so give thanks to the Lord.

The time and circumstances of composition are difficult to
determine, for the psalm describes the enemies simply as "people"
(NRSV: "enemies," v. 2*b*). A clue is provided by the word for
"then" (vv. 3*a,* 4*a*), which is an Aramaism from the colloquial

speech of the postexilic period. That fact suggests the poem was written in the late postexilic or Second Temple period. Though the threat is not described in detail, it loomed over the entire community, for "Israel" (v. 1*b*) is summoned to give thanks. The threat must have been serious, however, for the singer compares it to chaotic flood waters. Writing in his 1929 commentary, Hermann Gunkel even proposed that in the occasion was a pogrom. The poet has skillfully captured the deadly threat and vividly expressed the enormous relief and gratitude of those who escaped.

Exegetical Analysis

Rescue from danger (vv. 1-5)

Step parallelism, characteristic of the Songs of Ascents, has seldom been used with more effect than in verse 1. Repetition of the conditional sentence (vv. 1-2, in Hebrew with emphatic "if") makes one feel as if it was shouted out by people who had just gotten beyond the reach of danger. "Let Israel now say" (v. 1*b*) is directed to the congregation, inviting them to give thanks; the singer gives them words to express their intense relief and gratitude. "Then" (vv. 3*a*, 4*a*, 5*a*) has a logical meaning ("so") rather than a temporal meaning ("at that time"). An English translation is more vivid if "then" is omitted (so NAB). Two metaphors are used for the enemies in verses 3-5—devouring beasts and waters flooding the earth. Probably, the two metaphors are one, for Ugaritic and Mesopotamian literature associate a monster with rampaging cosmic waters. The association of monster and waters is also attested in the Bible. An example is Ps 89:9-10:

> You rule the raging of the sea;
> when its waves rise, you still them.
> You crushed Rahab [a monster] like a carcass;
> you scattered your enemies with your mighty arm.

Such metaphors effectively convey the overwhelming savagery of the enemies.

Give thanks to the Lord for the deliverance (vv. 6-9)

In the Psalter, the phrase "Blessed be the LORD" (v. 6) always begins a verse and occurs either in a doxology (e.g., Pss 41:13; 72:18-19; 89:52) or a thanksgiving followed by the conjunction "for" introducing the motive (Pss 28:6; 31:21). In Ps 124:6 "Blessed be the LORD" gives thanks for a rescue, which is implied in verse 6*bc*, "who has not given us / as prey to their teeth." The phrase refers back to the metaphor of the devouring beast in verse 3. The third metaphor for the enemy—a trap set by a fowler (v. 7)—occurs elsewhere in the psalms (91:3; 140:5). Hunters trapped birds by placing two vanes of netting on either side of a clearing or hole strewn with bait while they hid behind a wall holding an attached cord. When the birds landed, the vanes were quickly pulled toward each other trapping the bird. In this case, however, "the snare is broken" (v. 7*c*). The bird (the Hebrew word means small bird) quickly flies up to freedom in the open air. The image of a little bird flying to freedom is a perfect symbol of miraculous deliverance. The bird had absolutely no resources to overcome the fowler. The broken trap is a pure gift.

Appropriately, the psalm ends with fresh expression of confidence "in the name of the LORD," that is, the Lord's self-presentation on earth. Since the Lord has created heaven and earth, Israel can be sure that no danger, human or superhuman, has ultimate power. The deliverance, so vividly told and freshly experienced, reveals the people's savior in action.

Theological and Ethical Analysis

The first two images—a monster ripping human flesh and a flood sweeping away helpless individuals—effectively convey evil lurking at the edge of life. The third image, the little bird flying up from a trap, though more mundane than the other two images, conveys equally effectively deliverance from danger—sudden, complete, and unexpected. Word repetition and three memorable images create an unforgettable picture.

A perennial problem in appreciating God's benefits is the human propensity to take them for granted. One is grateful for an hour and then returns to regarding the world as repetitive and self-enclosed. This vivid psalm forces people to undergo the drama of good and evil in the world, teaching them how life can hang by a thread and how deliverance can come swiftly and unexpectedly. Liberation, though mundane as a bird escaping a trap, is a glorious thing. Pray-ers are invited to fit their community's deliverance, or their own personal deliverance, into this memorable framework.

PSALM 125

Literary Analysis

This Song of Ascents, like Ps 122, is concerned with Jerusalem. Step parallelism appears as in all the psalms in the series (Pss 120–34): "forever(more)," "surround," "the righteous," and "good." For step parallelism see the preface to Ps 120. Psalm 125 is a Song of Zion with the usual themes of the tradition: the stability of Zion (cf. Ps 46:5) and the inviolability of the city, that is, the nations shall never capture it (cf. Pss 46; 48; 76; Isa 7:8-9). Those who trust in the promises about Zion shall therefore be as firm as the city itself (Ps 125:1). Mountains are symbols of stability because they anchor the earth (Pss 36:6; 65:6; 76:4; 90:2), and Jerusalem is in the very center of these massive pillars (Ps 125:2). According to the Zion tradition, those who hold the scepter must rule justly in the Lord's name (Ps 125:3; cf. Ps 2:6; Isa 7:1-9; 33:17-24).

A less noted feature of the Zion tradition appears in Ps 125: the purification of the city through divine judgment. The Lord attacks the city to remove sinners defiling it and to uphold their victims, the righteous "poor." Examples of such purifying judgments are Isa 1:21-28 and chapter 65. In Isa 1:21-28, the Lord as Warrior attacks the city: "I will turn my hand against you; / I will smelt away your dross" (Isa 1:25*ab*). As a result, the city is purified: "Afterward you shall be called the city of righteousness" (v. 26*c*). In another purification, Isa 65 distinguishes between "my servants" (vv. 8, 9, 13, 14) and another group ("you") who are put to shame when God creates new heavens and a new earth (v. 17). Psalm 125:4-5 prays for a similar judgment that will restore Jerusalem to its original holiness. Peace will at last come upon the city. Though robustly confident in Jerusalem, Ps 125 is far from complacent, for it prays for the holiness of Zion. Like several Ascents psalms (122–24, 126), Ps 125 consists of an opening statement (vv. 1-3) followed by a prayer (vv. 4-5).

Exegetical Analysis

Promises about Mount Zion (vv. 1-3)

Relying on God's promise that Zion will not be shaken though the world totter (Ps 46:5), the singer declares that those who trust in the Lord will similarly be unshaken (Ps 125:1). The assurance is not mindless trust, for such trust is misplaced. Jeremiah writes about excessive trust in the Temple: "Do not trust in these deceptive words: 'This is the temple of the LORD, the temple of the LORD, the temple of the LORD.' For if you truly amend your ways and your doings, . . . then I will dwell with you in this place, in the land that I gave of old to your ancestors forever and ever" (Jer 7:4-7).

The singer views the mountains surrounding the city in non-mythological terms, as symbols of the Lord surrounding the people (v. 2) rather than as pillars of the universe. Furthermore, the city itself must be holy as befits its Lord. Therefore "the scepter of wickedness" (a scepter wielded by an unjust ruler) cannot rest (figuratively) on the land allotted to the righteous lest the unrighteous ruler lead the people to do wrong (v. 3). In the dramatic perspective of the psalm, there are only two paths: wicked and righteous. Only a righteous people will enjoy the security afforded by Zion and prosper in the land. Wickedness has no place in these holy spheres, for it endangers peace and prosperity. The psalmist's statements in verses 1-3 are not ironclad guarantees of divine protection, but invitations to trust in God's promises about Zion the holy city.

Prayer that the Lord exercise judgment (vv. 4-5)

Having declared the community's trust and hope in the Lord's choice of Zion (vv. 1-3), the singer invites people to pray that the wicked be uprooted from the holy city and the righteous be affirmed. Though NRSV and NIV take verse 5 as a statement of what the Lord will do, others (NJPS, REB, NAB) rightly take it as a prayer, "let the LORD make them go the way of evildoers" (NJPS). To the psalmist, people fall into one of two classes by their fundamental choices, either friends of God ("the good," "the upright") or enemies of God ("crooked ways"). The Lord will force the latter to leave the city they have defiled. "Peace" for Israel is the result of God's judgment of the upright and the wicked.

Theological and Ethical Analysis

Biblical faith never ceases to proclaim that the Lord of the universe has a local habitation and a name. Zion is the place where the Lord meets Israel, speaks to them, and receives their worship. The relationship between God and people is expressed in the interchange of gifts and the free response of the people. The people can count on the Lord being in a particular place, Zion, and can rely on the protection there offered. But they cannot presume protection and prosperity will be given automatically, without trust in the Lord and prayer. All is grace.

The psalm prizes the gift of God's presence in a particular place and the safety it offers to the people. Wickedness can drive away the divine presence, however, and so the psalm prays that the Lord act as judge and purify Zion of sinners. Even a sacred gift can be corrupted. Psalm 125 is an appropriate prayer for the church. Though holy and the place of authentic worship and encounter with God, the church is also fragile and can lose its way when people forget the God in its midst. The psalm appreciates the holy place; it also prays that God truly "be there."

PSALM 126

Literary Analysis

This psalm, like several Songs of Ascents (Pss 122, 125, 127, 128, 132), is about Jerusalem or at least mentions the city. It also contains the step parallelism characteristic of the collection: "restore the fortunes," "then," "the LORD has done great things," "shouts of joy," and the verb "bearing/carrying" *(nāśāʾ)*. For step parallelism see the preface to Ps 120. Since Ps 126 does not contain an explicit complaint or lament, it is technically not a community lament. It is rather a community prayer for the return of the exiles and the restoration of Israel, hinting at suffering by its passionate desire for healing in verses 4-6. Like other Songs of Ascents (122–25), it consists of an opening statement (vv. 1-3) that serves as the basis of the prayer that follows (vv. 4-5).

Important for the interpretation of the psalm is its temporal perspective. Does it look forward to a return in the future (so NJPS: "when the LORD *restores* the fortunes of Zion—we see it as in a dream"), or does it regard the return as a past event (NRSV: "when the LORD *restored* the fortunes of Zion")? The majority of interpreters and translators (including NRSV and this commentary) take the second interpretation. Syntactical considerations favor it, though syntax alone cannot decisively rule out the first view. Evidently, the situation was something like the following: seeing some exiles returning, the singer rejoices and prays for the return of all. It is clear from the literature of

Second Temple Judaism that many in Israel did not regard the restoration from exile as finished. For them, exilic dispersion was still a reality; God had not finished gathering in the scattered children of Israel. Historically, Israel did not rule its own land except for a brief period of Hasmonean rule from the mid-second to the mid-first century BCE. The glorious promises had not fully come true. People still waited for the proper fulfillment of such grandiose texts as Isa 60:10, "Foreigners shall build up your walls, / and their kings shall minister to you." Daniel 9:15 presumes that divine wrath is still operative in the mid-second century BCE: "And now, O Lord our God, who brought your people out of the land of Egypt with a mighty hand and made your name renowned even to this day—we have sinned, we have done wickedly." Psalm 126 was a fit expression of the sentiments of many people over centuries. Though originating in the late sixth or early fifth century BCE when the first returnees began to trickle home, it is relevant to the situation of the community rejoicing at the return of exiles and praying that all may come home.

Exegetical Analysis

The community's joy at the return of the exiles (vv. 1-3)

Verse 1 says, literally, "the Lord returned the restoration of Zion." The verse uses the rhetorical figure of abstract for concrete, "restoration" for "returning ones." The effect of the return upon the community is a joy beyond normal experience, a dream (cf. Isa 29:8). In Ps 126, positive dreams are fulfilled: The people wake and find the wonderful dream is a reality. One can well understand their exultant shouts. Exilic destruction was coming to an end. Even more important to the psalmist, it is the Lord who has initiated events. Divine wrath has ended and divine favor has returned. The returnees serve as a kind of pledge that more will come: "the LORD has done great things for us" (v. 3a). Ancient deeds are redone; the exodus is renewed. Even the Gentiles see.

"We rejoiced" (v. 3*b*) echoes the syntax of "we were like those who dream" (v. 1*b*), bringing the section to a close.

Complete the work you have begun (vv. 4-6)

"Restore our fortunes" picks up the opening verse "restored the fortunes," indicating that the prayer is for the completion of what has already begun. "The watercourses in the Negeb" are riverbeds in the dry southern area of Palestine. Bone dry except for rainstorms that create instant torrents carrying away all in their path, the image of a water-filled wadi is bold and unexpected for sudden transformation of infertile land. Such is the power of the Lord who in the blink of an eye transforms arid wastes into fertile land. Divine control of water, whether it be of cosmic floods or roaring wadis, is a sign of divinity, for water is the stuff of life.

Theological and Ethical Analysis

The psalmist has a discerning eye and a responsive heart. Faced with the wreckage of the community, the psalmist senses hints of restoration in the return of a few dispersed members. They are the firstfruits of a larger restoration to come, the psalmist dares to hope, and so prays for the Lord of the harvest to gather everyone in. The poet's eye sees wholeness and continuity where others might see "ordinary" or "natural." A new exodus is taking place and will not be complete as long as there are still scattered and dispersed members of Israel.

One can easily imagine different judgments and responses than those of this poem. Some stragglers return. How far short of the dreams inspired by the grand dreams of the prophets! They count as nothing because we are still under the power of a great empire. They are merely a reminder of the failure of ancient dreams and promises. The psalm, however, sees glimpses of divine power in little things, such as a family returning home, and allows God a timetable that does not match human ones. It discerns God's hand when others refuse to notice, rejoices when others are grim, and prays for completion when others go their own way.

PSALM 127

Literary Analysis

The eighth of the fifteen Songs of Ascents, Ps 127, contains the common thematic and stylistic features of the series. It talks about "the house," which many commentators identify with the house of David, or with the Temple, and it has step parallelism: "unless the LORD," "in vain," and "sons." For step parallelism see the preface to Ps 120. Wordplay—"builds" *(yibneh)*, "those who build" *(bônāyw)*, and "sons" *(bānîm)*—has an effect similar to step parallelism. The reference to "the house" (v. 1), which can be understood as a reference to the Temple, probably led copyists to add "of Solomon" to the superscription.

The psalm does not belong to any of the traditional genres. Many class it as a wisdom instruction; others regard it simply as two juxtaposed proverbs. Still others describe it in purely thematic terms, asserting that it concerns human work and divine blessing like its neighbor, Ps 128. Formally, Ps 127 most resembles Ps 124, which also immediately repeats its opening line. Repudiation of purely human means of salvation (Ps 127:1-2) is found also in Pss 60:11; 108:12; 146:3; and 147:10. More significant, however, is its use of the formula "happy is" (v. *5a, 'ašrê*), which plays a key role in many psalms (e.g., 1:1; 32:1, 2; 41:1; 119:1, 2; 128:1). In Ps 127 it concludes the poem; all else leads up to the declaration that the man with many sons is "happy." All commentators point out that Ps 127 has characteristics of Wisdom literature. It is not therefore surprising to find that Prov 19:14 provides a clue to the meaning and rhetoric of Ps 127: "House and wealth are inherited *[nahālāh]* from parents, / but a prudent wife is from the LORD." Like Ps 127, the proverb contrasts house and wealth with a gift only God can give: a suitable wife. Psalm 127 makes the contrast between human labor and divine gift even sharper by asserting that human toil cannot even build houses and guard cities.

Though some commentators distinguish sharply between verses 1-2 and 3-5, the connection between the verses is, in fact, seamless. According to verses 1-2, builders *(bônāyw)* alone cannot build *(yibneh)* a house. In contrast, verses 3-5 imply that sons *(bānîm,* vv. 3-4) merely by their existence constitute a house. "House" in Hebrew (as in English) means both a building and a family. Verses 1-2 assert that sentries alone cannot guard a city. In contrast, verses 3-5 assert that sons are effective guards. Like arrows in the hand of a warrior, they will protect their father when he faces enemies "in the gate." Courts met "in the gate," which functioned like a modern courthouse. Happy, therefore, is one who is blessed by the Lord with gifts one can never bestow on oneself—sons. The declaration, which is so typical of ancient Near Eastern culture, is transformed by the poem into something more transcultural: Only God can build a worthwhile community and protect it from the inevitable assaults of evil. Family and community are completely gifts of God. God bestows them, and humans receive them.

A good commentary on the logic of the psalm is 2 Sam 7, when the prophet Nathan responds to David who wants to build a temple (house) for the Lord: "Thus says the LORD: Are you the one to build me a house to live in? . . . Moreover the LORD declares to you that the LORD will make you a house. When your days are fulfilled and you lie down with your ancestors, I will raise up your offspring after you, who shall come forth from your body, and I will establish his kingdom" (2 Sam 7:5, 11-12). Psalm 127 affirms that, like David, Israel must learn to allow the Lord to build them a house.

Exegetical Analysis

Only God can build and protect the community (vv. 1-2)

Step parallelism is handled with great skill. Three identical words ("unless the LORD"), identical syntax, and the repeated "in vain" in verse 1 create a solemn and proverbial tone. Building a house and guarding a city are nicely parallel. It is attractive, as commentators have suggested, to assume that the situation is the postexilic rebuilding of the Temple and city. At such times people are tempted to think that human effort is all that is needed. There is an effective play between the thrice-repeated "in vain" (*šāw'*, vv. 1-2) and the single word "sleep" (*šēnā'*, v. 2). Verse 2 is a beautifully constructed tricolon with a hard-hitting and unexpected final colon: In vain do you wake up early, stay up late, eat your hard-earned bread—God provides for his beloved while they sleep (NRSV footnote). So, on the one side we have sleep-deprived workers, and on the other, the Lord's loved ones peacefully sleeping.

Sons are a gift of God and provide protection (vv. 3-5)

Asserting the uselessness of human effort alone, verses 1-2 claim that only the Lord truly can build and protect. Verses 3-5 declare that it is through sons, unquestionably a gift of God, that the Lord builds and protects. The point is made both by statement and wordplay—"build," *bānāh,* and "sons," *bānîm.* "Heritage" in verse 3 means a free gift of God, the land given to the ancestors. Its parallel, "reward," here means a benefit bestowed because of a promise, not because of work done. The singer uses military metaphors, "arrows," "warrior," and "quiver," to emphasize sons' role as protectors. Protection as an issue is raised already in verse 1. Verse 5cd apparently has to do with legal disputes, for "in the gate" can be a place of assembly and legal trial (e.g., Deut 21:19; Isa 29:21; Amos 5:12, 15). Perhaps having many sons present would sway judicial decisions in one's favor, or at least prevent unjust decisions. The phrase "his enemies" suggests perhaps that powerful personages misused the law court for their own gain.

Theological and Ethical Analysis

If, as seems likely, the period of composition is the exilic period when all eyes were focused on rebuilding the house of Israel, the symbolism of this little psalm must have had a special power. That period had a special interest in the traditions about the ancestors in Gen 12–50 as is shown by such texts as Isa 41:8; 51:2; 63:6; and Jer 33:26. These traditions were concerned with sons who became the ancestors of all Israel. Psalm 127 evinces a similar interest in sons and emphasizes their value through negative contrast with purely human attempts at rebuilding. Sons were a symbol of divine fidelity and grace.

Rebuilding has a special kind of excitement. When peace comes, one is able to join with others to build up what has been destroyed and restore hope to a dispirited community. This poem seems written against excessive confidence in human means of rebuilding, no matter how noble the enterprise. It brands such efforts "in vain." Only God can rebuild in a lasting way and afford protection from all enemies. To make the point, the psalm holds up children. No one doubts that a child is the greatest symbol of a gift there is. Parents may try to conceive, but a living child comes only from God. The psalmist builds on this simple experience in order to show people how to receive the divine gift of a restored house of Israel.

PSALM 128

Literary Analysis

Psalms 127 and 128 form a pair. The first ends with "happy is the man/everyone" and the latter begins with it; both are concerned with human labor and offspring and with house and city, and both introduce the second part of the poem with the Hebrew demonstrative particle *hinnēh* (127:3*a*, 128:4*a*, left untranslated by NRSV). Psalm 128 has the step construction characteristic of the Song of Ascents series ("happy," "bless/blessed," and "may you see") though in more muted form than other songs. For step parallelism see the preface to Ps 120. Psalm 128 also resembles Ps 1, which likewise declares "happy" an individual who obeys the Lord. Both Ps 1 and Ps 128 employ the metaphor of "the way" and both express "happiness" in terms of fruitfulness. Though Ps 128 has similarities to Wisdom literature, especially Proverbs—fear of the Lord, the metaphor of walking in the way, the pronouncement "happy is/are," happiness as family flourishing—it is not an instruction. Rather, like Ps 1, Ps 128 is a declaration that everyone who obeys and worships Yahweh alone ("fears the LORD," v. 1) will flourish in their family, national, and religious life. The three spheres were closely related since the king functioned as paterfamilias of the (tribal) state, the father functioned as paterfamilias of "the house of the father," and Yahweh was the supreme patrimonial lord to whom Israel was bound through covenant as kindred or kindred-in-law. The blessings in the psalm span family (fruitful wife, many children), nation (prosperity of Jerusalem, seat of the dynasty), and God (font of blessings).

Like most of the Songs of Ascents so far considered, the poem has two parts: a statement of faith and a prayer that builds on the statement. Verses 1-4 are the statement and verses 5-6 are the prayer. "Fear of the LORD" in v. 1a forms an inclusio with verse 4a.

Exegetical Analysis

Happy the one who reveres the Lord (vv. 1-4)

"Happy is/are" (v. 1a) is a declaration of beatitude (sometimes called a macarism). A beatitude declares someone fortunate because of a quality possessed or a choice made, in this case, revering Yahweh alone through obedience and worship ("fears the LORD"). Happiness is expressed in agricultural terms ("you shall eat the fruit of labor of your hands," v. 2a) and family terms (fruitful wife and many children). As mentioned, family was a far broader symbol in the culture than today, so the blessing pervades all aspects of society. As is evident from the structure of verse 3, "your wife" and "your children" are in parallel. The pairing of wife and children is reminiscent of Proverbs, where a man's greatest joys and greatest sufferings derive from the compatibility of his wife and the wisdom of his children. Revering Yahweh thus brings the greatest blessings that anyone can desire—a fulfilled and fruitful family community.

May you see the prosperity of Jerusalem (vv. 5-6)

Family life spills over into national life. Zion was the dwelling place of the Lord and the residence of the Davidic king. The blessing that comes upon the family of a person revering the Lord comes from Zion, where the Lord dwells (v. 5*a*). Blessing is a gift and must be sought and prayed for, thus the final wish expressed in parallel phrases, "may you see." The two blessings sought are to experience the prosperity of Jerusalem and of one's family (symbolized in children). To see Jerusalem prospering is to experience the nation at peace, and to see one's grandchildren is to know that one's identity lives on.

Theological and Ethical Analysis

Both Pss 127 and 128, probably by the same author, confidently express faith in a generous and faithful God who delights in bestowing life in a happy family and secure nation (symbolized by its capital city). Though framed in idyllic terms, the psalm is far from utopian. To fear the Lord is difficult; it means being loyal to one Lord to the exclusion of others. Exclusive choice, foreign to prevailing ancient Near Eastern religions, was not easily done. Other religions permitted one to deal with several gods in order to find blessing. This psalm forbids such deals, demanding instead a loyal and ethical response to the one Lord. Only then can the blessings of the Lord operate. And they come as gifts, not as the result of deals.

Psalm 129

Literary Analysis

Psalm 129 features the theme of many Songs of Ascents, Zion, as well as step parallelism, "often have they attacked me from my youth" (vv. 1-2) and "blessing/bless" (v. 8). For step parallelism see the preface to Ps 120. It is a communal lament, though it does not conform perfectly to the model. It tells of past sufferings (vv. 1-3), divine rescue (v. 4), and asks for punishment on "all who hate Zion" (vv. 5-8). Like other Songs of Ascents, the structure is simple: first a statement (vv. 1-4) and then a prayer based on the statement (vv. 5-8). "All who hate Zion" is evidently a new expression for those who oppose Judaism. "Let Israel now say" (v. 1) is either an invitatory verse, which would suggest that a congregation sings the poem, or a command that the poem be subsequently recited as a sacred song.

Differences from other communal laments should be noted: in Ps 129 the people do not complain of a specific suffering but of sufferings endured since their youth. "From my youth" evidently looks back to Egyptian bondage, which was the time of the nation's youth according to Hos 2:15*cd* ("There [Israel] shall respond as in the days of her youth, / as at the time when she came out of the land of Egypt"); 11:1; Jer 2:2; and Ezek 23:3. The imagery of verse 3 echoes that of Isa 51:23, which quotes Israel's tormentors in the exile as saying,

> "Bow down, that we may walk on you";
> and you have made your back like the ground
> and like the street for them to walk on.

Psalm 129 therefore complains about the sufferings connected with being the Lord's people in the world; it selects two typical instances of suffering, one from the exodus (v. 2*a*) and the other from the sixth-century BCE exile (v. 3). They stand for all that the nation has had to endure as the Lord's people. Despite the sufferings, the people have experienced the Lord as righteous (v. 4), that is, upholding them as the aggrieved innocent party and putting down their wicked oppressors. In a nutshell, the poem sketches the relationship of the Lord and the people. On the one hand is their suffering, and on the other, their righteous God. Relying on that righteousness, the singer makes a plea that "all who hate Zion" (v. 5a) be uprooted, nevermore to put their hate into practice.

Exegetical Analysis

Israel's sufferings and the Lord's protection (vv. 1-4)

The repetition of the phrase "often have they attacked me from my youth" conveys weariness from being attacked because they are the Lord's people. The people survive, however, and their enemies do not prevail. Verses 1-2 establish a pattern—suffering-yet-prevailing—that verses 3-4 develop in a memorable image—plowing a person's back. Plowing at the time was done by oxen turning over a single strip of land at the end of which the oxen stopped to rest while the plowman cleaned the plow; they then reversed direction and came back. Because the oxen were relatively small and had to rest frequently, it was in the farmer's interest to make the rows short so that the oxen could rest at each turn. The reference in v. 3b to long furrows shows that Israel's enemies went out of their way to inflict serious injury. As verses 1-2 ended on a note of defiance ("they have not prevailed against me"), so also do verses 3-4, though the latter passage goes beyond defiance to triumph ("the LORD is righteous"). Cutting the cords of the wicked (v. 4b) may refer to cutting away the oppressive plow.

Prayer that those who hate Zion will be uprooted (vv. 5-8)

Hating Zion (v. 5a) refers to action and not simply attitude; such haters attack the residence of the Lord. The psalmist's prayer is not primarily for national triumph but for the defeat of those who attack the Lord. Being shamed and turned back means that their malicious plans are frustrated so that all can see. Grass on the housetops is an image found also in Isa 37:27.

> "they have become like plants of the field
>   and like tender grass,
> like grass on the housetops,
>   blighted before it is grown."

Without deep roots, such grass withers quickly and does not reseed itself. Reapers cannot fill their cupped hands with it, nor can anyone bind sheaves with it. Greetings ("the blessing of the LORD be upon you!") that passersby and harvesters exchange in the joyous days of harvest will never take place. Ruth 2:4 is an instance of such harvesttime greetings: "[Boaz] said to the reapers, 'The LORD be with you.' They answered, 'The LORD bless you.'" Psalm 129:6-7 prays that the enemies be annihilated and that their family line be ended. The psalm regards the enemies of Israel as enemies of the Lord.

Theological and Ethical Analysis

This prayer is for people who accept the difficult and painful vocation of being the Lord's people in the world. For reasons that are not explained in the psalm, that vocation involves suffering and attacks. While describing the sufferings, the psalmist declares that the enemies have not prevailed. The reason is that the Lord is righteous, that is, upholds the aggrieved innocent and punishes the wicked oppressors. The Lord is faithful to the covenant made long ago with the ancestors. This part of the poem evokes a New Testament text, 2 Cor 4:7-12: "But we have this treasure in clay jars, so that it may be made clear that this extraordinary power belongs to God and does not come from us. We are afflicted in every way, but not crushed; perplexed, but not driven to despair" (vv. 7-8).

Prayers for the eradication of the Lord's enemies make modern readers uncomfortable. Though one may concede that the psalmist technically makes a distinction between the people's enemies and God's enemies, in practice the enemies are the same population. Should not one pray rather for the illumination of the Lord's enemies that they too might offer worship? Why should one pray for the annihilation not only of the attackers but also of their children and future descendants? Responsible pray-ers must make distinctions the psalmist did not bother to make. One should pray verse 5 as meaning that attackers of the Lord (not just of the holy community) be defeated and revealed as foolish. Regarding their descendants, one may pray (leaving the timetable and means in God's hands) that the violent find no followers to continue their work.

PSALM 130

Literary Analysis

Though Ps 130 is not concerned with Zion (unlike most Songs of Ascents), it has the step parallelism characteristic of the series: "I wait for the Lord, my soul waits"; "I hope // O Israel hope in the LORD"; "those who watch for the morning"; and "redeem." For step parallelism, see the preface to Ps 120. It is one of the seven penitential psalms of the church (6, 32, 38, 51, 102, 130, 143), which had a special role in the lenten liturgy of the medieval church. Though having components of an individual lament, Ps 130 takes a unique direction. The crisis provoking the prayer, for example, is not described, being evoked by a single metaphor, "the depths," which implies drowning in a watery mass, as in Pss 32:6; 42:7; 69:2, 14; 88:7, 17; and 124:4-5. Rather than seeking rescue from the physical danger symbolized by the waters, the psalmist asks to be heard by God and forgiven of iniquities. The statement of trust, normally found in laments, consists of resolutions to hope in the Lord (vv. 5-6). A feature characteristic of thanksgivings, teaching others to revere the Lord (cf. Pss 32:8-9; 34:11-14) appears in Ps 130:7-8. It appears that the traditional genre has been reworked to describe the relationship of a repentant individual to a God who seems silent and far off. God is named often: Yahweh ("LORD") appears four times, Yah once (v. 3*a*, NRSV), and the Lord *('adōnāy)* three times. One suspects the poem was written in a difficult time for the nation as well as for the singer.

Translations vary in their paragraph divisions. NRSV has four stanzas; NJPS, three; and NAB, two. Though diverse divisions can be justified, this commentary presumes two stanzas, the first dominated by the psalmist's desire to be heard and forgiven (vv. 1-4), and the second dominated by the psalmist's and Israel's waiting for the redeeming Lord (vv. 5-8).

Exegetical Analysis

Hear me, O Lord, and forgive (vv. 1-4)

The title commonly given to the psalm, *de profundis,* is the Latin Vulgate rendering of its first two words. Though the anguished cries arise from a dangerous situation, the psalmist asks for only one thing: that the Lord hear and be attentive. Why the stress on being heard rather than being rescued from "the depths"? The reason is that the pray-er is keenly aware of having sinned, and God cannot tolerate sin. How can Holiness have anything to do with sinful people. The first task, therefore, is to overcome the distance between the sinner and God. Only God can bridge the chasm. For this reason, the psalmist begs, "hear my voice!" and immediately adds "if you, O LORD, should mark iniquities, / Lord, who could stand?" (v. 3). NJPS "keep account of sins" is a more expressive rendering. In the context, "hear" and "forgive" are virtually synonyms. For God to hear the plea is to turn an eye from the list of sins and receive the sinner. Verses 3-4 provides the motives to hear the plea: If the Lord does not forgive, no human being can stand, that is, be established (cf. Pss 33:11; 102:28; Isa 66:22); God's nature is to forgive ("there is forgiveness with you"); forgiveness makes worshipers ("so that you may be revered"). The appeal is unashamedly to the divine mercy. The personal "iniquities" (v. 3a) that the psalmist seeks to have forgiven are related to the national iniquities (v. 8) Israel seeks to have forgiven.

Wait for the Lord (vv. 5-8)

The statement of trust takes the shape of a resolution to wait for the Lord. Waiting is a form of trust. Determination is conveyed by the repetition of "wait" (v. 5) and "hope" (vv. 5, 7). Repetition of the latter verb is deferred until verse 7 at which time it is applied to the nation rather than an individual. Night symbolizes divine absence; one waits for darkness to disappear at the appearance of dawn. Sentinels (NRSV "those who watch for," v. 6) are either officers on regular evening patrol in the city (Song 3:3; 5:7) or soldiers on guard duty in a time of war (Isa 62:6; Jer 51:12). In either case, anxious cares end with the dawn and return of light.

The poem moves from hoping on a personal scale to hoping on a national scale. A similar movement from individual to nation is found elsewhere in the Psalter. Just as forgiveness (affecting the individual) is "*with* you" in verse 4a, so steadfast love and great power to redeem (affecting the nation) is "*with* the LORD" in verse 7. Verse 8 opens with the independent pronoun "he," implying there is no other source of redemption. In both instances, personal and national iniquities, only the Lord can redeem. "Redeem" (repeated for emphasis) is a term of family law; a relative redeems by avenging harm done to family members, assists poor members (Lev 25:25), and can even take the responsibility of fathering a child with his brother's widow (Deut 25:5-10). Though "redeem" might seem more applicable to an individual's need, it applies equally to national needs, for Yahweh was linked to the people through (adoptive) kinship and was father or kinsman to the *house* of Israel. The psalmist's appeal to the nation to wait for the Lord has a firm basis in the tradition.

Theological and Ethical Analysis

Penitential psalms can give the impression of being negative and obsessed with sin. This one, for example, is uttered "out of the depths." Psalm 130 is not guilt-ridden in a modern sense, however. It is rather concerned with restoring a relationship with God that had been ruptured by sin. The break means no more conversation, no more speaking and listening, no more being welcomed. Iniquities have forced God to withdraw. In this psalm, the distance between God and the psalmist is symbolized by silence. To be silent and to keep track of sins is the same thing. The prayer wants to end the silence and be heard, wants God no longer to keep track of sin.

No assurance is given that God is willing to reenter the conversation, to "hear" once again. The psalmist has to wait expectantly. If one cannot yet speak in the certainty of being heard (vv. 1-2), one can always look, as sentinels look, for the dawn (vv. 5-6)—not only the individual but the nation as well.

Many people pour out words to God but have profound doubts that anyone is listening. What should one do in such a situation? Cease praying, be crushed by the silence, retreat into private concerns? Psalm 130 gives such doubters the words to express hope and wait hopefully.

PSALM 131

There is only one instance of the step parallelism of the Songs of Ascents in Ps 131, "like a weaned child." For step parallelism see the preface to Ps 120. The poem picks up phrases from earlier Songs in the series: "of David" in the superscription from 122, 124, and 133 (not in NRSV), perhaps inspired in Ps 131 by David's self-humiliation in 2 Sam 6:21-22; "O, Israel hope in the Lord" from 130:7; and "from this time on and forevermore" from 121:8 and 125:2. Psalm 131 has a special similarity to Ps 130 because both invite Israel to imitate the psalmist's hard-won attitude of trustful hope.

Literary Analysis

In genre, the poem is a song of trust. Its central metaphor is striking: a weaned child between two and three years old. The poem is framed by its opening and closing occurrences of "the LORD" (vv. 1 and 3) and by its opening and closing sentiments, the first put negatively ("my heart is *not* lifted up") and the second put positively ("I have calmed and quieted my soul"). The opening confession is made through a threefold denial: my heart is not lifted up, my eyes are not lifted up, and I have not occupied myself with matters too high for me. The same confession is made in verse 2 though a double affirmation ("calmed and quieted") expanded by the doubled image of the weaned child. Finally, all Israel is invited to imitate the singer's calm and trust (v. 3). NRSV and several other versions make separate stanzas of the expression of personal trust (vv. 1-2) and invitation to Israel (v. 3).

Exegetical Analysis

I have calmed my soul (vv. 1-2)

"Not," repeated three times, shows how vehemently the singer rejects all self-reliance. Repeated denials indicate strong feelings. The image of the peaceful child in verse *2bc* can be misleading. Peace and calm have come only through bitter struggle. The heart is the organ where impressions from the senses are stored, decisions are made, and actions initiated (to be carried out by tongue, hands, and feet). "Heart" and "eyes" express the inner and the outer person. A heart "lifted up" normally has a negative connotation, meaning haughty and proud, neglecting God's rule (e.g., 2 Chron 26:16; Prov 18:12; Ezek 28:2). Raising one's eyes is a sign of pride also (e.g., Prov 6:17; 30:13); one surveys the world as if one owned it. Occupying oneself with things beyond one's capacities is an act of arrogance, going beyond what humans should do. Verse 1 is therefore not a surrender of all dreams and plans, but of sinful and arrogant behavior. As noted, the singer's rejection of such behavior has not been easy. It has been learned through bitter experience. A process (did it include disappointment and suffering?) has taught and seasoned the singer. As one learns from the singer's summons to all Israel, the process has not dulled his or her magnanimity and vision. It has rather taught where true and lasting help is to be found.

It is puzzling that a *weaned* child (no longer drinking its mother's milk) should be held up as a model of calm and quiet. Children were weaned around the age of three years, and the occasion was significant enough to be celebrated with a feast (Gen 21:8). Since the poem mentions the mother as well as the child, the reason may be because a three-year-old would be old enough to appreciate its mother's love and constancy. The child, like the singer, had gone through a process of being nurtured daily and would not doubt the mother's further nurture and care. The image of God as female is the second in the Songs of Ascents, the first being Ps 123:2:

> as the eyes of a maid
>   to the hand of her mistress,
> so our eyes look to the LORD our God,
>   until he has mercy upon us.

O Israel, hope in the Lord (v. 3)

Sometimes in thanksgivings the singer, with the experience of the rescue still fresh, teaches others how kind and reliable the Lord is (e.g., Ps 32:8-9; 34:11-12; 40:9-10). Psalm 131 does the same on the basis of the powerful process (vv. 1-2) that taught the psalmist to give up self-reliance and rely on the Lord alone. As often in the Psalter, there is a parallel between personal and national history. The people, like the singer, must no longer proudly raise their hearts and eyes as if they alone controlled the outcome of events. Like the singer (and the child that inspired the singer), they must allow the Lord to care for them.

Theological and Ethical Analysis

Psalm 131 is a surprisingly modern poem. It describes a universal process in which one surrenders to a higher power and then urges others to do the same. As one discovers a limited self and a caring God, the result is, surprisingly, not disappointment but peace. Though the psalm gives no details of the process leading up to the passionate cry, "my heart is not lifted up, / my eyes are not raised," one surmises it involved a powerful experience accompanied by honest reflection.

The peaceful child as a model for the (adult) psalmist is a striking paradox. One must become weak in order to become strong. Moses' inability to speak as an adult (Exod 4:10), Jeremiah's youth (Jer 1:6), Paul's embrace of weakness (2 Cor 12:10) can become occasions of surrender to God. Experiencing failure and suffering, Paul received the word: "My grace is sufficient for you, for power is made perfect in weakness" (2 Cor 12:9). The child as model will figure in the Gospels, for instance, "[Jesus] called a child, whom he put among them, and said, 'Truly I tell you, unless you change and become like children, you will never enter the kingdom of heaven. Whoever becomes humble like this child is the greatest in the kingdom of heaven'" (Matt 18:2-4). The psalm focuses on one point—the child knows that its mother will take care of it—and makes it a metaphor for the life of faith. A simple truth, a challenging reality.

PSALM 132

Literary Analysis

Psalm 132, like most Songs of Ascents (120, 122, 125, 126, 128, 129, 133), mentions Zion and the Davidic king. Typical of the series, it places whole phrases in parallelism: "the Mighty One of Jacob" (vv. 2 and 5), "priests . . . clothed with righteousness . . . faithful shout for joy" (vv. 9 and 16), and "he has/I have desired it" (vv. 13 and 14). Individual words are also repeated: ten words occur twice (e.g., "sit/reside," "throne," "priests," "[the] faithful," "son"), two words occur three times ("clothe" and "shout for joy"), and one word ("David") occurs four times. Repetition is thus an important rhetorical feature.

Psalm 132 belongs to the genre of royal psalm with elements of Zion songs. The linking of David and Zion is not at all surprising, since Zion was the site of the king's palace as well as the Temple. The poem tells of the transfer of the ark from its temporary location at Kiriath-jearim ("the fields of Jaar") to its permanent location in Jerusalem. Second Samuel 6–7 narrates the same events, though with significant differences from Ps 132. According to 2 Sam 6, after David's first attempt to bring the ark from Baale-judah (i.e., Kiriath-jearim) to Jerusalem was foiled by an outbreak of divine wrath, he brought it from its temporary resting place at Obed-edom's house to Jerusalem and placed it inside the tent he pitched for it. In the version in 2 Sam 7, David's offer to build a house (temple) for the Lord was not accepted, but the Lord promised to build him a house (dynasty).

Psalm 132 tells it differently: David vows to bring the ark and tabernacle *(miškān)* from Kiriath-jearim (Jaar) directly to Jerusalem (vv. 1-5); nothing is said about building a house for the Lord. David's vow and prayer (in which his servants joined) occupy the first half of the poem (vv. 1-10). Will the vow and prayers be heard? Everything hangs on the divine response. If no answer comes from the Lord, David is finished as king of Judah and Israel. The Lord's positive response is given in the second half (vv. 11-18), relieving the tension: Not only will I make Jerusalem my resting place forever, I also choose the dynasty of David. Psalm 132 does not mention several points highlighted in 2 Samuel: the outbreak of wrath at Kiriath-jearim (i.e., Baale-judah), the temporary stay at the house of Obed-edom, David's resolve to build the Lord a house (permanent structure), the dichotomy between a tent and a house of cedar, and Nathan's oracle. And the poem highlights points scarcely mentioned in 2 Samuel: Zion as a sacred city, its link with the choice of David, and the importance of the tent shrine in Jerusalem. The psalmist has selected only those details that dramatize David's vow and heighten the grandeur of God's reply.

Differently from NRSV, this commentary suggests that there are four stanzas of equal length: verses 1-5, 6-10, 11-13, and 14-18. Each stanza has five bicola and each contains the name "David"; the last line of each stanza is linked to the first line of the following stanza by word repetition ("find/found" in vv. 5 and 6; "David" in vv. 10 and 11; "desired" in vv. 13 and 14). The story itself provides the unity: David's oath to provide a dwelling place for the Lord (vv. 1-5); the finding of the ark and the procession to Jerusalem (vv. 6-10); the Lord's oath to give David an eternal dynasty and to affirm the choice of Zion (vv. 11-13); affirmation of the promises to Zion and to David (vv. 14-18).

Exegetical Analysis

David's oath to provide a dwelling place for the Lord (vv. 1-5)

The poem begins with a prayer that God be mindful of David's hardships. "All the hardships" refers to David's labors in fetching the ark. Like a good servant, David puts his Lord's interests above his own. How can David live in a palace in Jerusalem while his Lord lives in a remote village? His Lord shall live in Jerusalem! The prayer that the Lord accept David as servant will be continued in verses 6-10. "Mighty One of Jacob" (vv. 2, 5) is an ancient title for Yahweh, its earliest occurrence being the Testament of Jacob (Gen 49:24; cf. Isa 49:26; 60:16). "Bull of Jacob" is its root meaning; animal names were used for gods and human heroes because they embodied the virtues of the animal. "Bull" symbolized strength and procreative power. Citing the ancient title shows that the ancestral God is taking up residence in David's new capital city. "Mighty One of Jacob" in verse 5b echoes verse 2b, concluding the first section.

What does David vow? To bring the tabernacle (*miškān*, NRSV: "dwelling place") of the Lord into his new city. Politically and religiously, the transfer of the central religious symbol to

Jerusalem was absolutely necessary. David could not command the loyalty of the tribes if they went somewhere other than Jerusalem to worship and deliberate. The ark-throne of Yahweh had to be in Jerusalem. The ceremony reflected in this psalm advertises David's loyalty and the Lord's choice of David's family and city.

The finding of the ark and the procession to Jerusalem (vv. 6-10)

Stanza 2 tells how David and his servants (including some priests) carried out the vow. The verbs in verse 6 ("we heard of it . . . / we found it") suggest they had to look for the shrine, still in the backwater where the Philistines returned it twenty years before. Arriving at the shrine, David and his servants did obeisance, "let us enter his tabernacle" (NRSV: "go to his dwelling place"). Now comes the delicate issue of moving the ark and tabernacle. David's servants utter an earnest prayer that the Lord enthroned on the ark will consent to go. They borrow a venerable prayer that was part of the ark ceremonial (see Num 10:35): "Rise up, O LORD, and go to your resting place" (v. 8a). In verse 14, the Lord will answer the prayer and embrace Jerusalem ("This is my resting place forever"). (The Hebrew of verse 8a may also be translated "go *from* your resting place," which fits the context better.) The people continue the prayer, asking God to bless the priests and the faithful accompanying the procession. Verse 10 asks God not to refuse the request of the loyal servant David, "do not refuse your anointed one" (NRSV: "do not turn away the face of your anointed one," cf. 1 Kgs 2:16, 20).

Where are Ephrathah and Jaar mentioned in verse 6? "The fields of Jaar" is simply a shortened name for Kiriath-jearim, a town that has several names in the Bible (e.g., Baale-judah in 2 Sam 6:2, Baalah in Josh 15:9). "Fields" is a place designation as in Ps 78:12, "the fields of Zoan." Kiriath-jearim was where the ark was kept after the Philistines returned it. "Ephrathah" is a name for Bethlehem, but the ark was never kept there. "Ephrathah" must therefore designate the district of Kiriath-jearim, for it is parallel to Jaar. Genealogies in 1 Chronicles explain its connection to Kiriath-jearim: Caleb had Hur by Ephrath, his second wife (1 Chron 2:19), and Hur had Shobal father of Kiriath-jearim (1 Chron 2:50). According to Ps 132, the ark went directly from Kiriath-jearim to the tabernacle in Jerusalem (cf. 2 Sam 6:17). The psalmist wishes to emphasize that the ark went from its humble location after its capture and return by the Philistines to its glorious place in Jerusalem of David, the conqueror of the Philistines.

The Lord's oath to give David an eternal dynasty and to affirm the choice of Zion (vv. 11-13)

The two requests in verses 6-10 are answered: the pleas concerning David (vv. 1, 10) are answered in verses 11-12, and the plea concerning the shrine (vv. 6-9) is answered in verse 13. The Lord does not refuse and swears to accept David's dynasty and choose David's city "for his habitation." Though some scholars distinguish God's conditional promise to David here (v. 12, "*if* your sons keep my covenant") from unconditional oaths elsewhere (e.g., Ps 89:3-4, 19-27), one must question whether the distinction between conditional and unconditional was significant to ancient writers. Covenants, after all, even those between God and human beings, establish a relationship in which both sides freely assume obligations. It would simply be assumed that both God and David's descendants would be loyal to the relationship. The major point is that the Lord graciously accedes to the request of David and the people and chooses David's family and David's city as his residence.

Affirmation of the promises to Zion and to David (vv. 14-18)

The order of treatment of the themes of the previous section is chiastic, ABBA. Zion ended the previous section and begins this one. The Davidic dynasty is treated last. Verse 8*a* had urged "Rise up, O LORD, and go to your resting place," and verse 14 is the emphatic answer: "This is my resting place forever!" As befits the shrine of the all-powerful and generous patron of the Davidic dynasty, there will be no poor in the city (cf. Deut 15:4). Priests and faithful will reflect the Lord's glory in their splendid garments and joyous singing. "I will cause a horn to sprout" (v. 17a) combines two Hebrew idioms. "Horn," a symbol of strength, can refer to a strong individual (e.g., Deut 33:17; 2 Sam 22:3 = Ps 18:2; Dan 7:7-8). Princes could be called young plants (e.g., Isa 11:1, "A shoot shall come out from the stump of Jesse, / and a branch shall grow out of his roots") so that "sprout up" could be used of a future ruler (e.g., Zech 6:12). In Ps 132:17a, the Lord promises to raise up mighty sons for David and, in the parallel colon, promises to keep the dynasty lit as if it were a lamp (cf. 1 Kgs 11:36). In striking contrast to the bright clothes of the priests and gleaming crown of the king, God's enemies are clothed with shame (v. 18).

Theological and Ethical Analysis

Though the psalm might initially strike one as overly triumphal, it is actually a humble prayer that the Lord look kindly on the Davidic king and ratify his desire to have the Lord with him in his rule (vv. 1, 8-10). Confident of divine protection up to this point, the king wants to make his Lord the center of his life and that of his people as he builds his city and prepares his family to rule. He swears an oath to bring the ark into his city. The divine answer to his oath is out of all proportion to his prayer. The Lord will abundantly give him everything he asked for and more besides—a dynasty and a city, both gifts without limit of time.

For Jews and Christians, this psalm records a wonderful moment in the history of God's dealings with Israel. As kingship is introduced, David incorporates the previous history of the people into the new style of governing. The Lord graciously chooses the Davidic dynasty and the city of Zion. Psalm 132 is a prayer for any servant of the Lord who seeks first and foremost the honor of the Lord. A brave and generous promise is crowned with abundant blessings. Christians will see hints of the relationship between the Son of David and the God who has placed him on the throne.

PSALM 133

Literary Analysis

The fourteenth of the fifteen Songs of Ascents (120–34) is concerned with Zion. It also has step parallelism: "running down upon the beard," "on the beard of Aaron," "running down," "running down [NRSV: "falls on"] the mountains of Zion." For step parallelism, see the preface to Ps 120. Psalm 133 is a song of Zion. Like Ps 122, it celebrates the city as a gathering place for the tribes of Israel when they come on the three annual pilgrimage feasts. The famous first line of Ps 133 in a sense restates Ps 122:4,

> To [Zion] the tribes go up,
>> the tribes of the LORD,
> as was decreed for Israel,
>> to give thanks to the name of the LORD.

Exegetical Analysis

An exclamation of affectionate wonder begins the poem: "How very good and pleasant it is / when kindred live together in unity!" NRSV "kindred" is more accurate than the traditional "brothers," for the Hebrew word refers to men and women in kin relationship with each other; they are descendants of a common ancestor and share the same history. The people themselves are a witness to God's call.

After verse 1, metaphors of oil and dew are introduced, which are difficult to understand. What is the meaning of oil running down the beard of Aaron and the dew of Hermon running down (NRSV: "falls on") the mountains of Zion? One clue is provided by the Song of Songs, which also uses startling metaphors (e.g., Songs 2:1-3, 8-9; 4:1-5; 5:10-16) and shares several words with Ps 133, for example, "behold" (*hinnēh;* Song, nine times; NRSV, left untranslated), "good" (Song 7:10; NRSV: "best"), "pleasant" (Song 1:16; NRSV: "lovely"), "How!" (*māh;* Song, ten times), "dew" (Song 5:2), "precious oil" (Song 1:3; NRSV: "fragrant oils"), "Hermon" (Song 4:8), "mountain" (Song, six times). The similarities suggest the psalmist borrowed from traditional lyric poetry to describe the family of the Lord at the feast in Jerusalem.

Metaphors in Hebrew lyric poetry can be extended by descriptions pertaining primarily to the metaphor, not to the referent. An example is the man's praise of the woman in Song of Sol 4:2:

> Your teeth are like a flock of shorn ewes
> that have come up from the washing,
> all of which bear twins,
> and not one among them is bereaved.

Whiteness is expressed in an image of ewes sheared of their dirty outer wool and given a wash. The poet then concentrates on the image itself, describing the ewes as fertile. Though fertility has nothing to do with the woman's teeth, the word implies she is fertile, and so has a secondary reference to her. Images in this kind of poetry have more "substance" than images in English poetry, being capable of elaboration on their own.

In Ps 133, the primary reference is to the oil on the head of Aaron. The oil running down his beard is an elaboration of the image (like the fertility of the ewes in the example above). Abundance of oil suggests plenitude and generosity. Moses ordained Aaron to the priesthood by anointing his head with oil (Lev 8:12). All priests have the oil of Aaron on their head. Priests presided over the sacrifices and rituals of feast days. The priests' beautiful vestments, the happy people, the colorful ceremonies delighted the senses. The brilliance is perfectly symbolized by the metaphor of oil, glistening and symbolizing legitimate priestly ordination. Oil can have a further meaning: the oil dispensed by generous hosts so their guests can anoint themselves before a meal.

Luke 7:44-46 is a New Testament example: "I entered your house. . . . You did not anoint my head with oil, but she has anointed my feet with ointment." The metaphor refers to both worship and festive meals, which is precisely the theme of the psalm.

"Hermon" is an instance of an exotic locale, as in Song 4:8, where it occurs with several other place names. Mount Hermon was famous for its heavy dew. Though the Mediterranean climate of Palestine had no rainfall from May or June to September, it had dew. Dew was important in the summer and a supplement to rain. Zion was therefore a place of fertility which even in the rainless season has an abundance of dew, like that of mighty Hermon to the north. So plentiful is it that it "runs down [NRSV: "falls on"] the mountains of Zion" (Ps 133:3).

Theological and Ethical Analysis

The community that is gathered in Jerusalem, eager to worship, open to fellow Israelites, is itself a sign of God's favor. People are encouraged as they sense the kindness and generosity of God in members of the community. The psalm states an ideal. In reality, communal life is often difficult. There are difficult people, different opinions on worship and Christian practice, and animosities, some of long duration. It sometimes seems easier to go it alone. This psalm directs attention to a different reality—the people are brothers and sisters, members of the family of the Lord. Seeing the community united, the psalmist draws on the resources of lyric poetry to portray its wonder. How marvelous a gift is their unity, their worship, and their blessings in the holy city.

PSALM 134

Literary Analysis

The fifteenth and final Song of Ascents is a doxology or blessing. A final doxology is not surprising, for each book of the

Psalter ends with a doxology (41:13; 72:18-19; 89:52; 106:48; 150:1-6). Psalm 134 mentions themes common in Songs of Ascents, the house of the Lord and Zion, and it repeats phrases, "bless the LORD" and "may the LORD . . . / bless you from Zion."

Structure is provided by the repetition of the invitation "bless the LORD" in verses 1 and 2 and by the response to the blessing in verse 3. "Bless the LORD" in verse 2b echoes "bless the LORD" in verse 1a, bringing the first part to its conclusion and preparing the way for a blessing in response. Performance of the song was perhaps antiphonal, between two choirs or a choir and a speaker.

Exegetical Analysis

Blessing dominates this poem in which humans bless God, and God is invited to bless humans. How can a human being bless God who lacks nothing, who possesses everything as "maker of heaven and earth" (v. 3a)? The only thing God lacks is the recognition, obedience, and love of beings on earth. When humans bless God they make known God's past and present benefits to the human race, their community, and themselves. "Servants of the LORD" (v. 1a) will never tire of giving such blessing. Though the designation "servants of the LORD" does not usually refer exclusively to priests, it seems to designate them here, for only they "stand by night in the house of the LORD" (v. 1b). Priests are mentioned in Pss 132:9, 16; 133:2; and 135:1-2. The verb "stand" implies they are not visitors but attendants, for the word is used of the service rendered by priests and Levites (e.g., Deut 10:8; 1 Chron 23:30; 2 Chron 29:11). First Chronicles 9:33 speaks of Levites being on duty day *and night,* and rabbinic sources describe priests guarding the Temple at night and preparing for morning sacrifices. Some suggest that the act of blessing took place when those on night duty were relieved by a new group of priests. It is possible, however, that the phrase "by night" is an implied merism (i.e., standing for "day and night") and the phrase means "at all times." To lift up the hands (v. 2a) is to pray (Pss 28:2; 63:4; 141:2).

In verse 3, another voice answers the first summons: May the Lord give a blessing in return. The Lord's blessing differs from that of human beings, however. First, it comes from Zion, where the Lord dwells and meets Israel. Second, those who are blessed have profound needs, for they do not possess all things. Their hold on life is slim; they are subject to illness, poverty, crop failure, collapse of kingship, and invasion by enemies. Moreover, their hearts are wayward and their sinful conduct invites divine retribution. As "maker of heaven and earth," the Lord has an array of gifts and a desire to bestow them. Divine blessing is the most precious thing anyone can receive.

Theological and Ethical Analysis

At first glance, Ps 134 seems conventional. It requires a special effort to hear the summons in verses 1-2 as addressed to oneself. Though the original group addressed were priests, the summons is applicable to all, for the priests represented all Israel before the Lord. Every Jew and Christian can be called a servant of the Lord. The Lord can never be praised enough nor be given sufficient thanks. Gifts of God are freely given and invite a spontaneous and heartfelt response. When one blesses God, one's words do not disappear into infinity never to be answered. The psalm shows God responding. From Zion, a particular place of dwelling and self-disclosure, the Lord grants fresh blessings. Divine generosity initiates an exchange of gifts. The psalm inserts pray-ers into this generous relationship.

PSALM 135

With Ps 134, the Songs of Ascents have come to an end. Psalm 135 forms a new subsection with Ps 136, yet it has several links to the Songs of Ascents: verse 2 appears also in 134:1, and both psalms favor the verb "to bless" (three and five occurrences, respectively). Psalms 135–36 also have affinities with the psalms that immediately precede the Songs of Ascents, the Hallel Psalms 113–18. The phrase "praise the LORD," which opens and closes Ps 135, appears also in Pss 111:1; 112:1; 113:1, 9; 115:18; 116:19; and 117:2. Phrases from Ps 115 appear also in Ps 135 (e.g., 115:3 in 135:6; 115:4-8 in 135:15-18; 115:9-11 in 135:19-20). Editors of the Psalter may have conceived Pss 111–18 and 135–36 as a frame to the Songs of Ascents.

Literary Analysis

Psalm 135 is a hymn praising the Lord for defending Israel against Pharaoh and defeating the nations who held the land intended for Israel. The psalm draws heavily on traditional material, and it is not easy to say if it borrows or simply shares common traditions. To mention only a few of its borrowed or shared traditions: Ps 135:4 and Deut 7:6; Ps 135:7 and Jer 10:13; Ps 135:10 and Deut 4:38; 7:1; 9:1; 11:23; Ps 135:13 and Exod 3:15; Ps 135:14 and Deut 32:36. Such extensive borrowing, especially from Deuteronomy, indicates the psalm was composed in the post-exilic period. Further evidence of a late date is provided by certain linguistic features (l as object marker, $\check{s}e$ as a relative particle) and the polemic against divine images (Ps 135:15-18) that was common in exilic and postexilic writings (Jer 10:1-16; Isa 40:18-20; 41:6-7; 44:9-20). Reuse of older writings is sometimes called the "anthological style" because it gathers (anthologizes) revered writings. Anthologizing suggests that the concept of "scripture" is developing. A library of authoritative *writings* is available that authors can cite and upon which they can build.

Psalm 135 has a concentric structure (Allen 2002, 226). "Praise the Lord" forms the outermost frame (vv. 1*a*, 21*b*). The next layer is verses 1*b*-4 and 19-20, which are summonses to prayer plus motive. Verses 1-4 exhort the servants of the Lord to praise (*hillēl*, three times) the Lord, "for the LORD has chosen Jacob for himself," and verses 19-20 exhort Israel to bless (*bērēk*, five times) the Lord. The next layer in the concentric circle is verses 5-7, affirming the Lord's sovereignty over the gods, and verses 15-18, attacking the images of the gods. At the center is verses 8-14, which tell of the Lord's great acts on behalf of Israel. Within the concentric structure, there are several contrasted relationships: the Lord and the gods, the gods and the nations, the Lord and Israel, and the gods and their images. Yahweh's act of creation, described in an indirect way in verses 6-7 (rule over heaven, earth, and cosmic waters), wins special acclaim: "the LORD is great; / our Lord is above all gods" (v. 5). Since the Lord has displaced the gods, the images that represent the gods to human beings are useless, conferring no benefit upon those who count on them for help (vv. 15-18). As clients of such gods, the nations come under the sovereignty of the Lord. Implied though not explicitly stated is that the Lord has an "image" or representative on earth: Israel. The images of the gods are inert (vv. 15-18), whereas Israel is a living people. Through them, the name of the Lord endures forever (v. 13), "for the LORD will vindicate his people" (v. 14).

Exegetical Analysis

Praise the Lord! (vv. 1-4)

As noted, the opening summons, "praise the LORD!" is repeated at the end. The opening invitation is repeated in verses 19-21. Psalm 135 invites the group also named in Ps 134—servants of the Lord who stand in the house of the Lord. Though normally designating priests and Levites (no one else would have access to the house of the Lord), it here means all Israel, for clergy had a representative function (cf. Exod 28:29-30), and the matching verses 19-20 envision priests and laity worshiping together. The psalmist apparently wants to associate all worship with the sanctuary. "Name," the self-presentation of the deity, is important in the psalm, appearing in verses 1, 3, and 13. Its appearance in verse 3 is parallel to the divine names Yah and Yahweh (both rendered "LORD" by NRSV). Verse 4 gives the motive for praise, "the LORD has chosen Jacob for himself, / Israel as his own possession *[sĕgullāh],*" a term used inside and outside the Bible for something prized by a god or a king. The motive for praise is that the Lord has chosen them as a dear and special people.

The greatness of the Lord in creation (vv. 5-7)

This section opens with a confession of faith similar to Jethro's confession in Exod 18:10-11 (identical words in italics): "Blessed be the LORD, who has delivered you from the Egyptians and from Pharaoh. Now *I know that the* LORD *is greater than all gods,* because he delivered the people from the Egyptians." The deeds on which the psalmist's confession of faith is based are greater than in Exod 18, for they include creation (arrangement of heaven, earth, and seas in vv. 5-7), deliverance from Pharaoh, and conquest of kings (vv. 8-12). Arranging the waters of the cosmos to benefit the world (vv. 6c-7), especially the human race, is part of the creation process (e.g., Pss 74:15; 89:9-12; 104:5-18). Such arrangement stands for the whole act of creation, the part for the whole. Creation demonstrates the total mastery of Yahweh over the world, dethroning other gods and rendering useless their images.

The greatness of the Lord in caring for Israel (vv. 8-14)

The act of God that is particularly decisive for Israel is the exodus. The psalm divides its account of the exodus into two panels, each introduced by the relative pronoun *še* (vv. 8a, 10a, lit. "*who* struck down"). The first panel concerns Egypt (i.e., the exodus) and the other concerns Sihon, Og, and all the kingdoms of Canaan (i.e., the conquest). In the first panel, the author mentions only the last of the ten plagues, the killing of the firstborn (cf. Exod 12:12, 19), which symbolizes the forced obeisance of Egypt to the Lord. The second panel lists the kings who stood in the way of Israel's advance, Sihon and Og, and the kings who stood against Israel in Canaan itself (Num 21:21-35; Deut 2:26–3:7; Josh 12). The kings' lands became the heritage of Israel (v. 12). "Heritage" (v. 12), repeated for emphasis, refers to the land of Canaan under only one aspect, that it was inherited by the tribes of Israel. "The primary productive asset of ancient Israel—namely the land—was not allocated by market forces. Land was inalienable (at least in principle) and was not a commodity but patrimony, subject to the customary rules of inheritance" (King and Stager 2001, 193).

"Your name" (v. 13) is important in the logic of the psalm. When Israel flourishes on the land, the Lord's name endures forever. It seems that Israel dwelling in the land of Canaan is the functional equivalent of an image of the Lord. Verse 14 continues in the same vein: the Lord stands by Israel, rescued from Pharaoh, defended from hostile kings, and now safely living in the land of Canaan.

The images of the gods are without life and power (vv. 15-18)

As noted, contemptuous descriptions of divine images (NRSV: "idols") were common in biblical literature from the exile forward. Though biblical authors portray the nations as worshiping statues, ancient worshipers in reality regarded statues as mediating the presence of the deity. Biblical writers satirized through caricature because their own religion forbade images (e.g., Exod 20:4; Deut 4:15-18; 5:8). To biblical writers, physical images represented the gods all too accurately—inert images representing powerless gods. Verses 15-18 are a corollary of verses 5-7, which describe the victory that made Yahweh supreme and dethroned other gods.

Bless the Lord! (vv. 19-21)

Corresponding to the opening summons to praise the Lord is the final summons to bless the Lord. "Praise" and "give thanks" are here virtual synonyms. As in Pss 115:9-10 and 118:2-3, the parallel phrases, "house of Israel," "house of Aaron," "house of Levi," and "you that fear the LORD" portray the people of Israel in all their fullness (including the priestly role of giving praise).

Theological and Ethical Analysis

The poem is Israel-centered. Its God was demonstrated to be supreme at creation; other "gods" lost their position. Israel was protected against Pharaoh; kings and their peoples were displaced that it might have their land. Not a thought is given to the rights of any nation except the Lord's nation. Many modern believers are understandably uneasy by the privileging of one nation and the dismissal of others. Two points may be made in response. First, worship inevitably *focuses* on one god to the exclusion of others even in polytheistic religions; pray-ers demand the attention of one god among others and use petitions and praise special to that god. Though a biblical hymn may not *recognize* any salvation for noncommunity members, it cannot be taken to mean that no salvation is ever offered. A hymn is not a treatise on the value of other religions and the validity of other gods. Other biblical books do display sympathetic awareness of the nations, for example, Gen 1–11; Isa 40–55; Ruth; Jonah, and Job. Second, modern outlooks are also products of a particular history, with their own limited views of God, the holy community, and the nations. It is important therefore that there be a dialogue between biblical accounts and modern viewpoints.

Having noted differences in ancient and modern perspectives, one can appreciate the achievement of this hymn. Rather than praising God in a general way, it praises one deity who had done specific deeds and who loves a particular people and is committed to their flourishing. The psalm names the God, the deed, and the people, so that the people can respond to divine largess with thanks and praise. Israel believes that they were dear to the Lord from the beginning of time and that the Lord has protected them from oppressors and given them their land on which they live safely and from which they derive their livelihood. Modern pray-ers who believe that sacred history continues into their day can recite Ps 135 with gratitude and confidence.

PSALM 136

Literary Analysis

Psalms 135 and 136 form a pair. Both are hymns, narrating the creation of the world and of Israel with the goal that Israel will give praise for God's wonders. They share vocabulary and the same view of the sacred history. Psalm 136 is unique in preserving the antiphonal reply "for his steadfast love endures forever" (repeated no less than 26 times). Though other psalms have antiphons (e.g., Pss 24 and 118), none has them in such number. A Qumran manuscript (11QPs[a]) gives Ps 145 a similar recurring refrain, "Blessed be the LORD and blessed be his name forever and ever." Jewish tradition refers to Ps 136 as the "Great Hallel."

"Give thanks to the LORD/God" (vv. 1-3, 26) opens and closes the psalm. The same phrase also opens and closes Ps 118 (118:1, 29). This and other similarities support the argument, already made at Ps 135, that Pss 111–18 and 135–36 were meant to frame the Songs of Ascents. Contrary to most hymns, Ps 136 invites no specific group. Possibly, the group already named in Ps 135:1-2, 19-21 is summoned here as well. Virtually all hymnic invitations provide a motive for giving praise which is introduced by the conjunction "for" *(kî)*. Psalm 136 mentions as a motive *"for* he is good" once (v. 1) and *"for* his steadfast love endures forever" twenty-six times. Each of the deeds in verses 4-25 is apparently considered an instance of "his steadfast love." "Steadfast love" *(ḥesed)* refers here to an obligation willingly assumed by one partner in a covenant toward the other. In the covenant, Israel assumed obligations toward the Lord. The psalm focuses on the Lord's free and loving obligation toward Israel, seeing in each deed an instance of that love. The divine names (totaling four) are revealing. Though Yahweh (NRSV: "the LORD") occurs only once (v. 1), titles indicating sovereignty over the other gods appear three times: "the God of gods" (v. 3), "the Lord *[ʾādôn]* of lords" (v. 3), and "the God of heaven" (v. 26). Psalm 135 explicitly asserted the Lord's superiority "above all gods" (Ps 135:5).

Though the structure is simple (invitatory, list of divine acts, repetition of invitatory), the exposition of divine acts is complex. Each new stage of divine activity is introduced by the participle form of the verb ("one who does such and such"): verses 4*a*, 5*a*, 6*a*, 7*a*, 10*a*, 13*a*, 16*a*, and 17*a*. A change in syntax in verse 21 introduces the last event in the recital: The verb is in the past tense ("and gave their land"). The change marks the end of the recital of creation-exodus-conquest. Further syntax changes in verse 23 (visible even in NRSV) send signals that the poem is interpreting the ancient recital for the current situation. It is important to note that the distinction drawn by most translations between "creation" (vv. 4-9) and "redemption" (vv. 10-22) finds no support in the text. The psalm narrates a single series of divine actions, beginning with creation and ending with deliverance and guidance in the present situation. Since the psalm is tightly unified, the divisions below are solely for convenience of analysis.

Exegetical Analysis

Give thanks to the Lord (vv. 1-3)

In the Bible, people do not give thanks by saying "thank you" but by telling others of the person's great deeds and benefits. Most people even today do the same. To say to others, "Look at this great book that Aunt Sally just gave me!" is a more instinctive reaction to a gift than to say directly to Aunt Sally, "Thank you for this nice book." By stating at the very beginning that Yahweh is God of gods and Lord of lords, verses 1-3 make clear that all the great deeds described in verses 5-25 could be done by no other power.

The Lord who creates the world and Israel (vv. 4-26)

Verse 4 is transitional. In form, it belongs to verses 5-22; in content it continues the theme of verses 1-3, the sole sovereignty of the Lord, "who *alone* does great wonders." "Wonders" (as in Pss 72:18 and 86:10) are deeds demonstrating to the nations that the Lord is sole deity. In most biblical cosmogonies, the created universe consists of heaven, earth, and the waters (vv. 5-6). This psalm gives special attention to the heavenly bodies (sun, moon, and stars), drawing, it seems, from Gen 1:16-18. Psalm 136 goes further than Genesis, however, in asserting that the stars rule over the night. Control of the heavenly lights show God's complete control over human life, for the lights define day and night as well as the sacred calendar.

At verse 10 a participle marks a new stage (vv. 10-12): God strikes down the Egyptian firstborn and leads the Israelites out of Egypt with "a strong hand and an outstretched arm." The latter is a signature phrase of the exodus traditions (e.g., Exod 6:6; Deut 4:34; 26:8). Like Ps 135, Ps 136 selects one key incident, the killing of the firstborn (Exod 11; 12:29-32), to stand for the entire Egyptian oppression and liberation. The next stage (vv. 13-15), introduced again by a participle ("who divided"), singles out the passage through the Red Sea: the Lord splits the sea, leads Israel through it, and overthrows Pharaoh and his troops (Exod 14–15). Leading the people through the wilderness is given only one line (v. 16). Like Ps 135, Ps 136 sees the exodus primarily as two events: liberation through overcoming Pharaoh in Egypt (vv. 10-14, cf. Ps 135:8-9) and the giving of land through overcoming kings in Canaan (Ps 136:17-22; cf. Ps 135:10-12). Sihon and Og are more fully described in Num 21:21-35 and Deut 3:1-7. The clause "and *gave* their land" in verse 21 breaks the series of participles that had begun each verse. The exodus is over and Israel is in the land. "Heritage," repeated for emphasis as in Ps 135:12, is the land of Canaan viewed as an inheritance of the tribes. "His servant Israel" is a title of honor, implying that the Lord of lords has chosen a particular people for service (cf. Ps 135:4).

In verse 23, changes in syntax (visible even in NRSV) and in grammatical person (from third to second) suggest the poem is coming to its climax. The poem shifts from recital of the past to interpreting events contemporary to the psalmist, "us in our low estate" (v. 23). With faith and daring, the singer asserts that the Lord who created the world and Israel still remembers (NRSV: "remembered," v. 23) us in our trouble. "To remember" implies compassion toward human beings (e.g., Pss 20:3; 25:7; 74:2) and awareness of the covenantal relationship (e.g., Pss 78:39; 106:45). "Gives food" (v. 25) is a common idiom for feeding. The phrase "all flesh" means all living beings, suggesting the food will be so abundant that every living being will be sated. Verses 23-25 develop the last event of the recital, Israel resident in the land of Canaan. God rescues Israel from those who want to drive them from the land and feeds them with food from fertile Canaan. The final line forms an inclusio with the first summons to give praise to the Lord.

Theological and Ethical Analysis

The words "thank you," even when spoken to God, can seem to be abrupt and formal. The psalmists perhaps felt the word was an unsatisfactory response, and found a way to savor God's works rather than employ a fixed and formal response. Drawing on the traditional story of creation and the exodus-conquest, Ps 136 makes it possible for a community to respond in dialogue to the great works of God. Lest the deeds be taken for granted, it interposes the refrain "for his steadfast love endures forever" to accompany each deed. After listing the mighty acts of God and eliciting praise for each of them, the psalm proceeds to show how the ancient acts affect the psalmist's own community (vv. 23-25). The Lord who effortlessly brought the world and our people into being is with us in our time of need.

Psalms teach people how to pray as well as offer texts for prayer. This psalm shows pray-ers how to keep together God and God's works and see in each work "his steadfast love." The psalm quietly insists on the Lord's uniqueness. It begins ("the God of gods" and "the Lord of lords") and ends with the same insistence ("the God of heaven," v. 26). God in this psalm is not, however, the God of the deists—the architect of the universe—but the one who created "his servant Israel" and is always there when Israel is in need.

PSALM 137

Literary Analysis

Psalm 137 stands on its own, unrelated to neighboring poems. Though distinctive for its style and artistry in the Psalter, it nonetheless fits into a recognizable genre—communal lament.

Like several of the preceding Songs of Ascents (Pss 122:6; 123:3; 125:4; 126:4), its petition (v. 7, "Remember, O LORD") is not introduced until the need has been clearly set forth (vv. 1-7)—the people's distress over the destruction of the Temple. The stanzas, verses 1-3, 4-6, 7-9, have approximately the same number of Hebrew words. The first stanza is framed by "Zion" (vv. 1*a*, 3*c*), which occurs only in this stanza; thereafter only "Jerusalem" is used for the holy city (vv. 5, 6, 7). "Zion" is the climax of verses 1 and 3. The second stanza opens with the lament word "how" (*'êk*, cf. 2 Sam 1:25, 27; Isa 14:12; Jer 48:39) followed by a rhetorical question. The psalmist swears an oath not to mention Zion to the captors. Stanza 3 is a curse on the enemies of Jerusalem—Edom and Babylon.

Exegetical Analysis

We cannot sing the songs of Zion (vv. 1-3)

With an impressive economy of words, the author allows the singers ("we") to tell their story and share their feelings. "By the rivers of Babylon" deftly shows how far from arid Palestine the people are. Their distance from Zion and its worship brings tears, as in Ps 42:3,

> My tears have been my food
>   day and night,
> while people say to me continually,
>   "Where is your God?"

To be away from Zion is suffering enough, but their captors taunt them, asking for the songs of Zion. Such songs (e.g., Pss 46, 48, 76, 84, 122) told of the grandeur of the city: how the Lord defeated enemy kings there, made it a center of fertility, and installed the Davidic king in its midst. Such claims are too painful to speak of now, especially to those who would only laugh at them. NRSV "mirth" is best rendered "songs of joy" (NIV), the rhetorical figure of abstract for concrete.

May my hand wither and tongue freeze if I ever sing those songs (vv. 4-6)

"How" in a rhetorical question introduces a lament, for example, "How the mighty have fallen, / and the weapons of war perished!" (2 Sam 1:27). The psalmist uses a self-imprecation: May I suffer such and such if I ever do this deed. Let hand and tongue, the very means of making music, cease to function if I ever forget Jerusalem. Chiasm in an ABBA pattern binds the stanza together:

A   If I *forget you,* O Jerusalem,
  B   let my *right hand* wither!
  B   Let my *tongue* cling to the roof of my mouth
A   if I do not *set* Jerusalem *above my highest joy.*

As "Zion" opened and closed stanza 1, "Jerusalem" opens and closes stanza 2. There is wordplay in verse 5, for *šākaḥ* is a homonym for two different verbs, "to forget" and "to wither." The singer vows never to expose the songs of Zion to contempt by singing them in a foreign land to a foreign audience. Not to sing the songs does not imply the singer has forgotten Zion. Psalm 137 is a psalm of longing, seeking at bottom one thing: to take part in the celebrations of the city as the dwelling of Yahweh.

May the Lord repay Edom and Babylon for their attacks (vv. 7-9)

The singer asks God to remember against Edom its attack on Jerusalem. "To remember" to the debit or credit of someone is an idea found also in Ps 132:1; Neh 6:14; 13:29. Edom, a country south of the Dead Sea, was an ally in the Babylonian destruction of the city (Lam 4:21; Ezek 25:12-14; 36:5; Obad 8-14). Its foundations will be destroyed. If Edom is to be punished, how much more Babylon, the chief agent of Jerusalem's ruin and the very people who are eager to ridicule the grand songs of Zion. NRSV "you devastator" (v. 8*a*) is a correction of the Masoretic Text "doomed to destruction," which addresses Babylon as already suffering destruction. By the poetic justice that frequently operates in the Bible, Babylon will suffer what it forced others to suffer. Its attempts to eradicate Israel will come back on its own head. The psalm makes Edom and Babylon larger than life; they represent the enemies of God, not just of Israel and Jerusalem. In the New Testament, Babylon is a symbol of the great enemy of God (Revelation). As an entity completely opposed to God's kingdom, Babylon must be eradicated. Its children, guarantors of its continued existence, must be destroyed. That wish is the last utterance of the singer.

Theological and Ethical Analysis

Psalm 137 has the distinction of having one of the most beloved opening lines and the most horrifying closing line of any psalm. If the poem ended at verse 6, it would be in the top ten. Alas for its popularity, it ends with verse 9. One can understand, if not approve, the singer's vehement wish. The Babylonians have destroyed Zion, the dwelling of the sole God Yahweh. Not satisfied with physical destruction, some Babylonians seek further to damage the Lord's glory by ridiculing the songs that declare Zion unconquerable. Babylon seems to represent the injustice in the world. The singer is unable to abstract evil from its embodiment and prays that the people be removed root and branch from God's beautiful universe. How can modern readers interpret the poem? It is too easy to lop off the final verses or even to dismiss the psalm in its totality. The singer's longing for Zion is not merely nostalgia for the good old days. The singer longs for the presence of the Lord in a particular place, Zion, which is now destroyed; its worshipers are dispersed. Passion for the Lord's justice is what pains the singer and inspires the longings expressed in the poem, both negative and positive.

The poem should be appreciated as part of the legacy of Israel, expressing unforgettably a significant, albeit painful, part of the story. More important, it is the cry of a singer who believes in God's presence in a particular place and among a particular people but must face up to the gap between sacred tradition (the Zion

Songs) and painful present (exile from Zion). With an artist's passion, the singer refuses to do anything that diminishes the Lord's glory and vows to put Jerusalem above any personal interest. A single poem expresses longing for Zion and a passion for justice. Pray-ers today will leave out the final verse as unacceptable to a modern audience.

PSALM 138

Literary Analysis

Psalm 138 is the first in a collection of Davidic psalms (Pss 138–45). In genre, it is an individual thanksgiving: giving thanks and report of the rescue (vv. 1-3), an invitation to others (in this case the kings of the world) to praise and give their obeisance (vv. 4-6), and a statement of confidence in the Lord's future favor (vv. 7-8). The divisions of three stanzas (each of decreasing length) accurately reflects the logic of the piece. Psalm 138 is not a typical individual thanksgiving, however. Among its unusual features are speaking "before the gods" (v. 1), the exceedingly generalized report of rescue (v. 3), and the worldwide scope of the thanks the psalmist wishes to be offered (vv. 4-6). These features transcend the purposes of an individual giving thanks for a rescue. Though indeed modeled on a poem acknowledging a specific rescue, the psalm gives thanks that the Lord has been a splendid patron throughout the psalmist's life. So splendid has the Lord's patronage been that every other "god" is put to shame (v. 1) and kings should rush to offer obeisance. A thanksgiving becomes a confession. Keenly aware of the unique power and goodness of the Lord, the psalmist cannot be silent while other gods are given the credit, and kings (and their nations) give them honor they do not deserve. It is obvious, the psalmist thinks, that the Lord is the only God worthy of worship and trust. In the final verses, the psalmist vows to trust in the proven Helper in time of need.

Exegetical Analysis

I praise the Lord who always hears me (vv. 1-3)

Emphasizing the act of thanksgiving rather than the act of rescue, the singer gives thanks before the gods, in the direction of the Temple, on account of God's steadfast love and faithfulness. Only after these protestations does the psalmist describe the rescue (v. 3) and then in conventional terms, "when I called, you answered me." NRSV "on the day I called" is too literal, wrongly giving the impression that the deliverance was a singular event; the phrase rather is the Hebrew idiom for "when." The fixed pair "call" and "answer" is common in the Psalms (e.g., Pss 3:4; 22:2; 86:7). Here the two verbs describe a relationship; the psalmist is the one in the relationship who habitually calls out in need, and God is the one who answers. Just as some individual laments focus more on the relationship with God than on the particular trouble, so this thanksgiving focuses more on God's fidelity than on a specific deliverance.

May the kings of the earth praise you (vv. 4-6)

NRSV "All the kings of the earth shall praise you" (v. 4a) is a possible translation, which is also adopted by NJPS and NAB because verse 4b seems to be a statement rather than a wish. Preferable, nonetheless, are NIV and REB, which interpret verse 4a as a prayer, "May all the kings of the earth praise you, O LORD / when they hear the words of your mouth." Experience has taught the psalmist that the Lord alone is truly powerful and worthy of the worship of all the nations. Let the kings who rule them join their praise to that of the psalmist, for the "glory of the LORD" is manifest (v. 7). The kings should not regard the invitation to give thanks as merely a recommendation, however, for the Lord scrutinizes human conduct and keeps the haughty at a distance.

I am confident you will continue your help (vv. 7-8)

As verse 3 sums up the past relationship as the psalmist's experience (calling and the Lord answering), so verse 7 sums up the psalmist's hope: Though I walk in the midst of trouble, you will protect me against enemies. The words recall Ps 23:4,

> Even though I walk through the darkest valley,
>   I fear no evil;
> for you are with me;
>   your rod and your staff—
>   they comfort me.

Throughout verses 7-8, the singer's eyes stay fixed on God. Apart from verse 7a, all the verses have God as subject, showing how profound is the reliance on the divine patron.

Theological and Ethical Analysis

Just as some laments were more concerned with the relationship to God than with deliverance, so also this thanksgiving puts the relationship ahead of any rescue. To be able to call out and be heard by the Lord of the universe is indeed worthy of celebration. The psalmist wishes that all might rely on the greatest patron of all and resolves to live as a trusting client.

Psalm 138 moves beyond details to go directly to the Lord. Psalm 138 helps pray-ers to appreciate the Lord's generosity and protection as patron. Though enthroned on high, the Lord gladly hears and looks upon the lowly. To be heard out, especially when one is in trouble (v. 3), is surely a great thing. To be seen by friendly eyes (v. 6a) is equally great, all the more so because such attention and sympathy are unmerited. They are acts of grace. The psalm reveals a generous God; it also reveals a great-souled singer who knows how to receive.

PSALM 139

Literary Analysis

Psalm 139, one of the great poems of the Psalter, is unique. It is unrelated to the psalms that surround it and belongs to none of the traditional psalm genres. Some scholars class it as a lament. Although it begs the Lord to kill evildoers (vv. 19-20), it lacks the other essentials of a lament. It is not a thanksgiving, for it reports no rescue and gives no praise. A third suggestion is that it is the prayer of an accused person facing an ordeal such as that described in Num 5:11-31. Such ordeals were used when evidence for a crime was lacking. The accused was brought "before the Lord" (Num 5:16) and made to drink a potion and swear an oath of innocence. If the accused were innocent, the drink had no ill effects, but if the accused were guilty, the drink would poison the oath taker. In this hypothesis, Ps 139:1, 24 invite divine scrutiny and verses 19-20 ask God to slay the false accusers. Is the hypothesis valid? Though it is conceivable that Ps 139 was remotely inspired by an ordeal, the poem's individuality and subtlety make it unlikely it was used in such proceedings. Also unsatisfactory is the hypothesis of scribal additions to account for the seemingly abrupt petition in verses 19-22, for textual evidence for such an addition is lacking. Because of the difficulty of identifying the genre of Ps 139, commentators have tended to devote their attention to its details rather than to the poem as a whole.

Commentary on this psalm ought to begin with observations on style. The subjects of the verbs in the stanzas alternate between "you" (God) and "I" (the psalmist): "you" dominates verses 1-6 and 13-18, and "I" dominates verses 7-12 and 19-24. NRSV stanzas reflect this structure. In the second half of the poem (vv. 13-24), the distinction between "you" and "I" is less sharp, for example, verses 14 and 18 have "I" as subject, and verses 19-20 have "you" as subject. A clear shift in sentiment appears in verse 19. The verb "to know" occurs six times (vv. 1, 4, 14, 23) and the cognate noun "knowledge" occurs once (v. 6), adding up to seven occurrences of the Hebrew root "to know." The psalmist's knowledge of God will change in the poem. The divine name occurs seven times: "LORD" three times, "God" (*'ĕlôah*) once, "God" (*'ēl*) once, and the independent pronoun "you" (God) twice. "Search me" with two occurrences of the verb "to know" appears both in verses 1 and 23, forming an inclusio that brings the poem to an end.

Moving from style to content, one is struck by three features: the highly personal discourse, the ambiguous feelings of the psalmist (at least initially) toward the divine presence, and the fierce petition at the end that God kill the wicked. Highly personal discourse appears also in the "problem" Pss 49 and 73 in which the psalmist faced a personal problem and worked through it to a satisfying solution. In Ps 49 the problem is the protection that wealth seems to offer, and in Ps 73 the problem is the prosperity of the wicked. In the course of each psalm, the psalmist comes to a new understanding of God. In Ps 139, the problem seems to be God, whose searching eye and universal presence seem to diminish rather than liberate the psalmist: "you hem me in . . . , / and lay your hand upon me" (v. 5). Further reflection brings a solution to the problem: the realization that God is a bountiful creator operating from within and involved in every aspect of life. Filled with wonder (vv. 14, 17-18), the psalmist exclaims, "I am still with you" (v. 18b). The solution is similar to those of Ps 49, "God will ransom my soul from the power of Sheol, / for he will receive me" (v. 15), and Ps 73, "You guide me with your counsel, / and afterward you will receive me with honor" (v. 24). A third poem that contributes to the understanding of Ps 139 is Ps 104, for it too abruptly prays at its end, "let sinners be consumed from the earth, / and let the wicked be no more" (v. 35). In both psalms, pondering God's skilled and caring governance leads the psalmist to express revulsion at sin and pray that God destroy sinners. Only against the background of beauty and majesty, it seems, can sin be recognized as the disfiguring horror that it is.

Though there are four stanzas (vv. 1-6, 7-12, 13-18, 19-24), the psalm more basically divides into two halves: verses 1-12 and 13-24. In a sense, the psalmist experiences God's presence power as two moments, one in verses 1-12 and a second in verses 13-24. In the first experience, God's presence is unsettling, for God seems an omniscient and omnipresent outside force, hemming in the psalmist (vv. 1-12). In the second experience, God is revealed as an insider, the one who created the psalmist and accompanies every stage of the psalmist's life. Though this thought, too, is overwhelming, it is reassuring and consoling (vv. 13-18). Only after experiencing the full scope of God's action and goodness does the psalmist comprehend his or her own place and the malice of human rebellion. From that comprehension the psalmist begs to play an active role in ridding the world of sinners (vv. 19-24).

Exegetical Analysis

First experience of God: God as subject (vv. 1-6)

God is the subject of the verbs. The verbs convey God's powerful scrutiny that extends to every action and thought. At this stage in the process, such divine knowledge is intimidating. When the psalm ends and the process is complete (vv. 23-24), the psalmist will actually delight in being known, so as to learn God's ways and avoid sin. "Sit down" and "rise up" (v. 2) form a merism, naming the ends of the spectrum as a figure for the entire spectrum. Verses 1-4 reflect Hebrew psychology: The heart was the organ of thinking and deciding ("my thoughts," v. 2b), the source of action ("sit down," "rise up," "my path") and of speech ("a word is on my tongue"). All these organs of action and reflection come under the scrutiny of the all-seeing Lord. No wonder the psalmist feels the hand of the Lord (v. 5) and finds such knowledge "too wonderful" (verbal root *pl'*). The same verbal root is repeated twice in verse 14 ("wonderful," "wonderfully").

First experience of God: the psalmist as subject (vv. 7-12)

The psalmist is the subject of every verb in verses 7-9. A shift takes place in verse 10, however, when "your hand shall lead me, / and your right hand shall hold me fast." Though the words can have a positive meaning (as in Ps 73:23), they are not positive in this context, for God lays hold of the psalmist, who is contemplating flight from God's presence. The psalmist is the subject of one last verb, "If I say" (v. 11a). The darkness that might have offered a hiding place turns out to be fully lit to God; light and darkness have no effect on God. An unforgettable picture: the psalmist planning to flee only to realize God's very being makes all such plans foolish. God's hand will grasp the cleverest planner.

Second experience of God: the psalmist sees God afresh (vv. 13-18)

Up to now, the psalmist has experienced God as an outsider scrutinizing every action and present in every place the psalmist might go. Though awestruck (v. 6), the psalmist was intimidated and even angry at being hemmed in. Verses 13-18 shift the perspective from outside to inside, from large- to small-scale. Exclaiming "It was you who formed my inward parts," the psalmist comes to the realization that the divine power that can loom over and constrict life also gives life and shapes it in the maternal womb. Delicacy, growth, and "maternal" involvement also characterize God's work. Verse 14 is significant, for the psalmist praises God, "for I am fearfully [nôrā'ôt] and wonderfully made." Nôrā'ôt, which here refers to the psalmist's own creation, elsewhere refers to the great deeds of the Lord like those celebrated in Pss 65:5; 106:22; and 145:6. God's creation of the psalmist is as wondrous in its own way as other great deeds of God.

Verses 17-18 are the psalmist's response. Advancing beyond verses 6 and 14, the psalmist declares "I am still with you," using the language of intimacy and fidelity found also in Gen 28:15 and Isa 41:10. The preposition "with" signals the advance. No longer feeling alone and judged, the psalmist knows God is near and has been near from the beginning. Omnipotence and omnipresence are complemented by nearness and personal care.

O Lord, kill the wicked and search my heart for any evil (vv. 19-24)

Why the sudden move from appreciating the Lord to praying the Lord to kill the wicked? Psalm 104 offers the best hint. After surveying God's beautiful creation, the singer exclaims, "Let sinners be consumed from the earth, / and let the wicked be no more" (v. 35). Contemplating the majesty and the delicacy of creation, the psalmist realizes there is only one thing marring it—sin. It does not belong; it must be uprooted. Psalm 139:19-20 mentions the violent and rebellious side of sin. A literal English rendering of verses 21-22 is misleading. "Hate" and "loathe" refer to concrete actions rather than to attitudes, as in the commandment to love the neighbor in Lev 19:17-18; 33:34. One can render verses 21-22: "Should I not fight those who fight you? . . . With all my energy I fight against them. They have become my enemies" (Zenger 1996, 32-33). Having glimpsed personally the rule of God, the psalmist prays that it be fully realized. To this end, the psalmist invites God's scrutiny to see if there is anything within that opposes it. Once frightened about the scrutiny of God in the first part of the psalm, the psalmist now invites it for the sake of the reign of God.

Theological and Ethical Analysis

Psalm 139 records how God comes to be revealed to human beings. First, the psalmist experiences God as all-powerful and all-present. Profoundly true yet unsettling because the picture is incomplete. Then comes an experience that complements and fills out the first: God working gracefully in the mother's womb, all attention and love, shaping a marvelous human being. The psalmist appreciates the grandeur of the God now known and trusted and even conceives the desire to join in the divine work. Psalm 139 gives a new meaning to the familiar phrase "the reign of God."

A traditional criticism of belief in God is that it infantilizes human beings, making them dependent and taking away their initiative. This psalm belies such criticism. It leads the believer to the majestic God who might conceivably lessen human dignity, and then leads the believer to the loving God who gives each person dignity and purpose. God cannot be caught in one glimpse. One must return again and again to the God so grand and so loving and allow God to reveal Godself.

Psalm 140

Literary Analysis

Psalm 139 ended with the psalmist (who is David according to its superscription) at war with the enemies of God (Ps 139:19-24). Psalm 140 begins with "David" (named in the superscription) pleading for deliverance from those enemies. Being a friend and client of the Lord can place one in conflict and peril. The complaint mentions evildoers and slanderers whose plots against the psalmist are about to turn into war. The psalmist prays to be ready when their assault begins. "In its form more bold than beautiful," wrote Franz Delitzsch of Ps 140 in his celebrated commentary. The elements of an individual lament (or petition) are here: petitions (vv. 1, 6, 8, 9-11) expressed in positive terms (save me!) and negative terms (punish them!), complaint (vv. 2-3, 5, 8), and statement of trust (vv. 12-13). Complaint is mixed with petition. Like other individual laments, Ps 140 dramatizes the prayer's situation as an innocent and loyal client of the Lord beset by enemies who are also enemies of God. The question is thus posed to God: where are you, O my patron who does justice?

The structure is clearly marked. Verses 1-3, 4-5, 6-8, and 9-11 stand out as distinctive by their syntax, content, and word count (each has 23 Hebrew words; vv. 6-8 contain 24). Verses 12-13, the statement of trust, has two-thirds that number of words. Stanzas 1 and 2 (vv. 1-3 and 4-5) are paired by their syntax. Each begins with similar petitions and descriptions of enemies: "deliver me . . . from evildoers; / protect me from those who are violent, / who plan evil things," (vv. 1-2a); "Guard me . . . from the hands of the wicked; / protect me from the violent / who have planned my downfall" (v. 4). Though parallel in form, stanza 2 shows progression of thought from stanza 1. Verses 2-3 describe the wicked doing evil in general terms; verses 4c-5 describe the wicked doing evil against "me" (the psalmist). Stanza 2, moreover, employs a tricolon (v. 5) to attain a climactic effect. Stanza 3 is marked as distinct by its initial verb "I say" (v. 6a) and by its protestations of affection and loyalty to the Lord. The stanza ends with a negative petition containing two occurrences of "not" (*'al,* v. 8). As previous stanzas began with a petition or protestation followed by a complaint, stanza 4 begins with a complaint (v. 9*a*) followed by a petition (vv. 9*b*-11). Like stanza 3, this stanza ends with a negative petition containing two occurrences of "not" (*bal,* vv. 10*b*-11). The final stanza, the statement of trust, is clearly marked by the verb "I know" as the first word. Coherence between the stanzas is assured by repetitions of key words: "LORD" occurs seven times; the Hebrew words "violence," "protect," "tongue," "lip," and "head" all occur three times. By poetic justice, the very evil that the malefactors planned to inflict on the righteous at the beginning (slander and traps, vv. 3, 5) will (the psalmist hopes) be visited on the malefactors themselves (vv. 9-11).

Exegetical Analysis

Deliver me from violent slanderers (vv. 1-3)

As noted, verses 1-3 and 4-5 are remarkably parallel in style, syntax, and number of words. The main difference between the two stanzas is that the complaint in verses 2-3 is about evildoers generally, whereas in verses 4*c*-5 it is about evildoers attacking "me," the psalmist. What is the reason for the difference? Perhaps because the psalmist wants God to see that the evildoers are first and foremost *God's* enemies. God must act primarily for the sake of justice. Opponents of the psalmist must be exposed as opponents of divine justice. "Violent" (*ḥāmās,* lit. "violence," vv. 1, 4, 11) connotes physical attack. "Tongue" (v. 3) is a formidable weapon, for slander destroys one's good name and place in the community. Verses 9*b* and 11 pray that slanderers have no place in the community.

Deliver me from those who seek to trap me (vv. 4-5)

Slight stylistic variations, visible even in translation, differentiate stanza 2 from stanza 1: The complaint is in the form of a tricolon (v. 5), and it mentions the psalmist as the object of the enemies' malice. As vicious speech was the dominant metaphor of malice in stanza 1, so a trap is the metaphor of stanza 2. Enemies plot "to push my feet" (v. 4c, NRSV: "planned my downfall") and hide a trap along the road. Setting a trap is a common metaphor for attack in the Psalter (e.g., Pss 9:15; 31:4; 35:7). In an agrarian society, animal and bird traps were familiar and thus a vivid symbol of sudden and unforeseen malice. Against such premeditated and violent assaults the psalmist prays to be protected.

I pray to you my God: Stop them! (vv. 6-8)

The verb "I say" (v. 6) shifts the voice from petition to confession. With the freedom of a loyal client, the psalmist demands that the divine patron listen to the plea while at the same time affectionately recalling past assistance (v. 7). NRSV "you covered my head" (v. 7) means you protected my head. A just God cannot allow the wicked to attain their goals! (v. 8).

Complaint and petition (vv. 9-11)

Previous sections began with petitions or confessions and moved to complaint. This section begins with complaint and moves to petition. The Lord will oversee the process of poetic justice. As the Lord shielded the head of the psalmist, the enemies, unaware of their own vulnerability, lift up their heads and invite retribution. May they be flung into pits in punishment for the pit they dug for the psalmist (cf. v. 5). Let their own words overwhelm them in punishment for the words of their earlier slander (cf. v. 3).

Statement of trust (vv. 12-13)

"I know that," in initial position, like the phrase "I say" in verse 6a, clearly marks the shift from petition back to confession. "I know that" states belief in God's fidelity (cf. Pss 20:6; 56:9; 135:5; Jonah 4:2). "Needy" and "poor" designate those whom the Lord always helps; the psalmist wishes to be among their number. "Surely" emphasizes the psalmist's triumphant hope that the righteous will be rescued.

Theological and Ethical Analysis

Humility, shrewdness, and rhetorical skill are on display in this poem. Aware that the world is God's, the psalmist seeks to persuade the just Lord to act from self-interest, that is, to ensure that the world remains just. For this reason, the Lord must punish all evildoers, especially those who attack the poor and needy, among whom is the psalmist.

Almost by definition, human beings are needy and poor, in some cases overwhelmingly so. When one is in the depths, it is difficult to find a firm standpoint from which one can call upon the Lord. Psalm 140 helps pray-ers name their enemy and name their God. Taking account of the confusion that can overwhelm a sufferer, the psalm leads the pray-er methodically through petition, complaint, and hope. A sufferer has to have the opportunity to express all three aspects. Only to express hope is unrealistic; only to petition neglects one's prior relationship to God; only to complain stays focused on one's own pain. This psalm keeps all the elements of a prayer in balance. Using this prayer, a sufferer can safely come before the Lord.

Psalm 141

Literary Analysis

Psalms 140–43, all individual laments, are connected by common themes and words. Examples are Ps 140:6, "give ear, O Lord, to the voice of my supplications," which recurs, slightly varied, in the first lines of Pss 141–43. In Pss 141–42, the divine name occurs four times: "Lord" *(YHWH)* three times and "Lord" *('adōnāy)* once.

Though textual corruption in verses 5-7 makes precise

interpretation impossible, the conventions of the lament genre suffice to indicate that a supplicant begs to be ranked among the righteous (vv. 1-4) whose prayers for protection prove effective (vv. 8-10). Verses 5-7 seem to say that the psalmist is willing to submit to the discipline that makes one faithful, which in the Bible means willingness to be taught and rebuked by others. Underlying the prayer is the common biblical assumption of the two ways, that is, that people's actions ultimately put them into one of two classes, the wicked and the righteous. The wicked cannot count on God's protection; their prayers will go unheard. The psalmist dreads this state and asks God to "set a guard over my mouth" (v. 3a) and to keep the wicked at bay (v. 4).

Given the textual uncertainty, the NRSV stanza divisions (vv. 1-2, 3-4, 5-7, 8-10) are reasonable. "LORD" occurs in the first colon of stanzas 1, 2, and 4; the last stanza has the fuller divine name, "LORD, my Lord" (v. 8a, NRSV: "O GOD, my Lord"). Stanza 1 (vv. 1-2) asks simply to be heard, and stanza 2 asks to be kept from sin and sinful companions (vv. 3-4). Stanza 3 apparently expresses willingness to undergo the discipline that makes one truly a friend of God (vv. 5-7). Stanza 4 expresses total trust in God and hope of protection from enemies.

Exegetical Analysis

Hear my prayer (vv. 1-2)

Like the usage in Pss 4:1, 3; 99:6, the phrase "when I call to you" (v. 1b) means "as often as I call upon you," referring not to prayer for a onetime need but to daily prayer. Equivalently, the verses ask for a relationship with the Lord who "hears," that is, who acts eagerly on behalf of the singer. Verse 2 expands the request: may such prayer be as favorably regarded "before you" like ritual in the sanctuary performed by the priests. According to Exod 30:6, the priests offered incense every morning "in front of the mercy seat that is over the covenant, where I will meet with you." According to Exod 29:38-42, the evening sacrifice was burned at the entrance of the tent of meeting "before the LORD" (v. 42). May the psalmist's prayer similarly rise up before the Lord.

Protect me from my sinful inclinations and from evil companions (vv. 3-4)

In biblical Wisdom literature, the most important human organ is the mouth (alternately, tongue or lips). Words express the inner self more surely than any other organ. Therefore they can stand for all human activity. Prayer for a guard over the mouth includes a guard over the hands and feet as well. Let no evil in the heart ever be expressed in act. Next, the psalmist prays to avoid evil companions. Wisdom literature contains many warnings against bad companions (e.g., Prov 22:24; 23:17-18; 24:1, 19-20). Proverbs 22:24 is an excellent example, for it contains a motive: "Do not associate with an angry person, / do not accompany a hothead, / lest you learn his ways, and spring a trap upon yourself" (my translation). "Eat of their delicacies" means share their fellowship, as in Ps 41:9, "my bosom friend in whom I trusted, / who ate of my bread." The psalmist does not want to be separated from God by their corrupting influence.

I resolve to stand fast as the wicked go to destruction (vv. 5-7)

Unfortunately, textual corruption makes the entire section uncertain. This commentary follows the NRSV emendations. Desiring to be admitted to the ranks of the righteous and preserved from the company of the wicked, the psalmist willingly accepts the sometimes harsh discipline of the righteous. The point is made paradoxically in verse 5 and also in Prov 27:6, "Trustworthy are the blows of a friend, / dangerous, the kisses of an enemy" (my translation). Verse 6b in NRSV does not make sense. NSV "pleasant" can have the nuance "acceptable" as in Prov 6:24, which suggests that Ps 141:6b should be translated, "all will learn that my prayers were heard" (i.e., acceptable to God). Verse 7 announces that the wicked will die violently and there will lie unburied, a terrible fate in that culture.

Trust in the Lord who will provide an escape from the wicked (vv. 8-10)

Apparently in the company of the wicked (albeit unwillingly), the psalmist's eyes turn toward the Lord. Alluding perhaps to the traps mentioned in the preceding psalm (Ps 140:5, 10b), the psalmist prays that justice be done: Let the wicked fall into the very traps they set for me, and let me escape.

Theological and Ethical Analysis

The psalmist ardently desires to be the Lord's loyal servant, but is unusually sensitive to the obstacles to that ideal. The first obstacle lies within, in the human heart. Like Jeremiah (5:23; 17:15; 23:17), the psalmist is aware of the perversity of the heart and prays that the perversity never be expressed in word or deed. The second obstacle lies without, in the corrupting influence of the culture (evil companions, v. 4). Positively, one must submit to discipline, which means learning from others. In the process of growth that the psalmist embraces, the most important thing is to walk with one's eyes on the Lord (v. 8).

Psalms ask for many things. Some are emergency calls in the midst of danger. Others, like Ps 141, ask for something permanent. These need be no less passionate than the emergency calls. The psalmist is well aware of the evil in his or her own heart and of the baneful influence of the contemporary culture. Prayer is needed lest one fall victim to one's own indifference and to one's culture. May God accept such prayer as surely as the smoke of evening sacrifice. This psalm expresses faith that God will accept the gesture and answer the prayer.

PSALM 142

Literary Analysis

Like Pss 140–43, Ps 142 is an individual lament ascribed to David in the superscription. It has special links to Ps 143: "faint spirit" in 142:3 and 143:4; "save me" in 142:6 and 143:9; "pursue" in 142:6 (NRSV: "persecutors") and 143:3. J. Clinton McCann Jr. suggests that Ps 142 is the center of a collection of David psalms (139–43) that is framed by Pss 138 and 144–45.

Customary elements of the lament genre appear: petition (vv. 1-2, 4*a*, 6-7), complaint (vv. 3*cd*, 4*bcd*, 6*cd*), mention of enemies (vv. 3*cd*, 6*c*), and statement of trust (v. 7*cd*). Special emphasis is given to the weakness (v. 3*a*) and defenselessness (vv. 4, 6*cd*) of the singer, whose sorry state is proposed as a motive for the Lord to act. Other psalms emphasize the violence and injustice of the enemies as a motive for God to act and also stress the client's loyal service to the divine patron. Psalm 142, however, says nothing about the singer's innocence or loyalty. The psalmist's desperate need becomes a claim for divine assistance. According to the superscription, David recited this prayer "when he was in the cave," which can apply to incidents related in 1 Samuel 22–24 when Saul was pursuing David as an outlaw. The plea, "save me from my persecutors" (Ps 142:6*c*), may have suggested to a scribe convinced of David's authorship of the psalms that he wrote it while fleeing Saul.

No one outline immediately imposes itself on the reader. Not surprisingly, translations vary in their stanza divisions. NJPS and NAB have no stanzas; NRSV has four. The poet does offer some guidance, however: Grammatical person shifts from third to second in verse 3*b*; "I cry to the LORD" in verse 1*a* is repeated almost verbatim in verse 5, and these two verses are the only ones in which the divine name appears; the independent second-person singular pronoun "you" appears in similar settings in verses 3*b* and 5*b*; repetition marks verses 1-2: "with my voice I cry to the LORD; / with my voice I make supplication to the LORD / . . . before him / . . . before him." Of the above observations, the most significant is the repetition of verse 1*a* in verse 5*a*, for it shows that verse 5*a* begins the second half of the poem. Only in the second half does the singer display intimate feelings toward the Lord (v. 5).

Exegetical Analysis

I cry to the Lord, for no one else cares or is powerful (vv. 1-4)

Stiffness and repetition mark the opening verses. Verse 1*b* virtually repeats verse 1*a*; only the verb is different; "before him" is repeated in each colon of verse 1*cd*. Perhaps the psalmist is numbed by the suffering, only finding the words to describe the danger in verse 3*cd*, where the familiar metaphor of the trap appears. Not only is there a trap hidden on the path the psalmist travels, but the psalmist must walk it alone (v. 4). In a touching plea, the psalmist asks God to look at his or her right hand. The right hand was the traditional place for a loyal and helping friend (cf. Ps 109:31). No one is there. No one cares. Danger lurks and the psalmist is all alone.

I cry to the Lord, who is my refuge and my portion (vv. 5-7)

Verse 5 repeats the opening line with the important difference that the psalmist addresses God for the first time in the psalm in personal terms, "my refuge" and "my portion in the land of the living." Both metaphors have to do with place. "My refuge" occurs in the psalms in juxtaposition to mighty rock (Pss 62:7; 91:2; 94:22). "Portion" here means a share in land, as when Joshua distributes seven portions of the land to various groups (Josh 18:5, 6, 9). To declare God as one's refuge is an impressive act of trust. It is equally impressive to declare God as one's portion, for in an agrarian society one's land or portion provided the necessities of life. From the land came one's food and clothing. In Num 18:20, "the LORD said to Aaron: You shall have no allotment in their land, nor shall you have any share among them; I am your share and your possession among the Israelites." Psalm

141:4 declared that the psalmist had no friend or helper, surely a pitiable state. In verse 5, the psalmist hopes God will be that true friend. A series of verbs in the imperative mood follow in quick succession: "give heed to my cry," "save me," "bring me out of prison." The motive in the first two petitions is to alleviate the psalmist's suffering, "for I am brought very low" and "they are too strong for me." But with the last request, the motive is God-centered, "so that I may give thanks to your name" (v. 7b). Leaving the isolation of prison, the psalmist hopes to join the company of "the righteous," that is, those who enjoy the friendship of the Lord.

Theological and Ethical Analysis

Individual laments help people to express their sufferings before God. Psalm texts teach people to speak to God and even to become fluent as they bring more and more of their lives to God. Psalm 142 illustrates how one grows in the capacity to pray. At first, the psalmist describes the work of prayer, listing complaints and troubles for the Lord, displaying his or her need and lack of resources. Such care and fidelity lead to another stage, where one calls God "my refuge" and "my portion in the land of the living" and looks forward to giving further praise to the Name. Psalm 142 demonstrates that one can grow in familiarity with God in prayer.

Where is the turning point in this prayer? Surely, it is in verse 5 when the pray-er takes a chance, moving from description of suffering and lack of resources to depending on God, "my refuge" and "my bit of land." Lack of resources becomes less intimidating. Hope of being with the righteous community (v. 7) takes over and animates the psalmist. Prayer that is constant and honest helps one grow in familiarity with God.

PSALM 143

Literary Analysis

Like the preceding three psalms, Ps 143 is an individual lament. It has especially close links to Ps 142, as pointed out in the first paragraph in the commentary on Ps 142. Especially strong are the links in Ps 143:4, 8, and 11. Psalm 143 is one of the seven penitential psalms of the church, the others being Pss 6, 32, 38, 51, 102, and 130. These psalms had a special place in the lenten liturgy during the Middle Ages.

Old material has been incorporated into the poem. To mention only a few examples, "for the enemy pursued me" (v. 3*a*) is found also in Ps 7:5; Ps 77:4-7 is similar to Ps 143:4-7; "do not hide your face from me" (Ps 143:7*c*) recalls Pss 27:9 and 69:17. Despite its borrowing and use of common motifs, Ps 143 is a fresh poem. It insists on basing all dealings with God on the divine faithfulness and righteousness (v. 1). One must avoid any claim of equality and rely completely on the mercy of God (vv. 1-2). Only after establishing this ground rule does the psalmist mention the danger, pursuit by enemies (vv. 3-4). The psalmist remembers the days when God was favorable and begs for the return of those days (vv. 5-7). Petitions follow one another in rapid succession (all are the first words in the colon): "let me hear of your steadfast love," "teach me," "save me," and "teach me." Such petitions seek more than deliverance from the enemy of verse 3*a* as verses 8-10*b* make clear. Another cluster of petitions for deliverance follow in verses 11-12 (all in second or third place in the colon). The final words in the poem are "for I am your servant." The psalmist's argument has made much use of the venerable words for God: "faithfulness," "righteousness," and "steadfast love."

Exegetical Analysis

In your righteousness, hear my prayer (vv. 1-4)

Having one's prayer heard in the psalms means that one is accepted by God as well as delivered from a specific danger. Like other psalmists, this one has a strategy: that God act because of God's virtues ("faithfulness" and "righteousness") rather than the psalmist's, for "no one living is righteous before you" (v. 2*b*). "Faithfulness" and "righteousness" are one of several word pairs (1 Sam 26:23; Ps 40:10) that the Bible uses for God's "essence." As is well known, the Bible avoids describing God's essence through adjectives (Exod 34:6 is a famous exception), preferring instead to describe God's actions on earth. Nonetheless, some attention is paid to the divine nature, and word pairs are one way of doing so. The psalmist wants God to act from within, so to speak, rather than from without (in response to the psalmist's conduct). With this ground rule established, the psalmist can mention the immediate danger—pursuit by enemies. As in other laments, the danger is described in general terms; specifics can be supplied by pray-ers who will use the text. The language of distress is traditional (cf. Ps 7:5; Lam 3:6). Enemy pursuit has affected the singer who feels depressed and unable to cope (v. 4).

I remember the days of favor and my spirit fails (vv. 5-7)

Formal similarities between verses 1-4 and this section reinforce the judgment that verses 5-7 form a distinct section. With verse 5, "I remember" changes the topic from petition to remembering past times. In both sections, positive petitions (vv. 1, 7) are followed by negative petitions introduced by "not" (vv. 2*a*, 7*c*). Verse 8 begins a new section, for each bicolon in verses 8-10 begins with a verb in the imperative mood with the attached suffixed for "me."

As in Ps 77:5-6, the singer remembers the days when the Lord acted favorably, and that memory inspires fresh pleas. In verse 6, the singer stretches physically toward God ("my hands" and "my soul") in the hope that God will reciprocate: "answer me quickly," "do not hide your face." Without a favoring glance from the Lord's face, the singer feels doomed (v. 7*d*).

Show me your love and your way; save me from my enemies (vv. 8-10b)

As noted, each bicolon begins with a verb in the imperative mood with the attached suffix "me," indicating a new section. Verse 8 asks to "hear of your steadfast love," that is, to see evidence that the Lord acts from a covenantal commitment to the singer rather than simply reacting to the singer's virtue. As in verse 1, the motive for God to act is simply that the singer trusts (v. 8*b*). "Morning" is the time when God's justice typically appears (e.g., Pss 5:3; 46:5). Though verse 9 still asks to be rescued from enemies, as in verse 3, the other petitions ask for greater knowledge of God and fidelity. The psalmist asked in verse 1 that God deal with him or her according to God's fidelity and righteousness. Now the psalmist asks to know this loving God so as to become a more faithful servant (cf. vv. 2*a*, 12*c*).

Lead me on a level path and destroy my enemies (vv. 10c-12)

A shift in syntax signals a new section. All the verbs but the last are placed at or near the end of the colon. "Your good spirit" occurs elsewhere only in Neh 9:20 in a reference to the Lord's sharing Moses' spirit with the seventy elders (Num 11:16-30). In Ps 143, "your good spirit" is a way of speaking about divine guidance. "Level path," like the use of "level" in Pss 26:12 and 27:11, is a metaphor for trouble-free living; no obstacles stand in the path one walks. The requests in the last three verses are all to be rescued from life-threatening danger. In verse 11, the psalmist once more appeals to the divine character, expecting God to act "for your name's sake," "in your righteousness," and "in your steadfast love."

Theological and Ethical Analysis

The prayer is much more than a request for deliverance from a particular problem. To be sure, the psalmist asks at the beginning (v. 3) and at the end (vv. 9, 11-12) for rescue from pursuing enemies. The underlying request, however, is that the Lord act out of love and fidelity for a loyal servant. Only when the Lord acts generously and lovingly can the psalmist act as a good servant; otherwise enemies from without and discouragement from within (vv. 4, 6, 7a) will spell ruin. Because the psalm is so aware of the grace in the relationship to God, it can serve as a model text for anyone who wishes to be a good servant in the midst of personal limits and trouble from outside. The poem is realistic about attacks from outside and discouragement from within. The psalm turns pray-ers toward the Lord who acts from fidelity and love and before whom one can stand confidently as an *unequal* partner.

PSALM 144

Literary Analysis

David's name in the superscription of Ps 144 is especially appropriate for this psalm, for it is a royal prayer, begging the Lord to come with storm weapons and rescue him (vv. 1-8, 11). Anticipating such a rescue, the king gives thanks in advance (vv. 9-10) and looks forward to the effects of the victory in national life: abundance of children, fertility, and safe and happy cities (vv. 12-15). In composing the piece, the poet used traditional material. Verses 1-2 share material with Ps 18:2, 34, 46-47; Ps 144:5-8 has much in common with Ps 18:7-19. Psalm 144:3-4 shares themes with Ps 8:3-4, though the vocabulary in each is distinctive. Because of what they consider wholesale borrowing by Ps 144, some scholars term it "anthological style," that is, composed by citing verses and even sections from sacred literature.

Anthological style characterizes late Second Temple Judaism, when certain books were becoming "scripture," to be revered and quoted. This commentary, however, regards the psalm as preexilic or early exilic, because of the lively role of the king; the psalm assumes he is a vigorous and independent agent of the Lord. Commonalities with other psalms do not of themselves prove dependence, for psalms use a common store of traditions and phrases, as one would expect in the case of liturgical writings. The abruptness of verses 3-4 and 12-15 in the poem is only apparent. The implied narrative in verses 1-2 virtually demands verses 3-4 as its complement, and verses 12-15 illustrate in agrarian terms the peace that the king hopes the Lord's victory will introduce.

Exegetical Analysis

Blessed be the Lord who strengthens me all unworthy (vv. 1-4)

"Blessed be the LORD" is a formula of blessing God, that is, praising God for a beneficial act, in this case choosing the king as servant. The Davidic king's authority is rooted in the Lord's cosmic victory. Psalm 89:1-37 fill in the story: The Lord selects a king to oversee the newly created universe. As noted in the commentary there, verse 19 should be read: "I have set a leader over the warriors, I have exalted one chosen from the faithful." In Ps 144:1-2, the king blesses God for something very specific: the Lord's election of him as king, which means equipping him for the wars the king must wage for the Lord. The affective dimension of the relationship is intense as can be inferred from the titles the king uses in verses 1-2. Though the metaphors are military, they also confess that the Lord is the king's ultimate refuge. Even as the king willingly accepts the royal office and even glories in its challenges, he is awed by the love and honor shown him by the Lord. How can an all-holy God entrust to a lowly mortal such a noble task? Such is the import of verses 3-4, which fit perfectly into the dramatic logic of the psalm. Psalm 8 is similar, for there a human being (not a king) is likewise awed by the attention and care of the Lord.

O Lord, come as Storm God and rescue me (vv. 5-8)

Having accepted the royal office and now lost in wonder at the gracious choice, the king realizes the many battles that ahead will only be won with the Divine Warrior, his patron deity. Thus he prays for the coming of the God whose thunder shakes the mountains and whose lightning-arrows make enemies flee (vv. 5-6). In a wonderful mixture of cosmic language ("mighty waters," v. 7*b*) and historic language ("the hand of foreigners [NRSV: "aliens"] v. 7*c*), the king describes himself as imperiled and desperate for help. "Mighty waters" seems to refer to the waters of chaos. Such mixing of language is a reminder that the king's authority is grounded in the Lord's creation victory. Foreigners who speak lies (v. 8) are kings who use every means possible to unseat the Davidic king.

Anticipatory thanks to the victorious Lord (vv. 9-11)

Why the sudden shift from petition that the Lord rescue the king to the king singing a new song? Verse 11, which continues to pray for the king's deliverance, indicates the king is promising a new song when deliverance comes. "New song" elsewhere is a response to God's creation of the world or the nation Israel (Pss 96:1; 98:1; 149:1; Isa 42:10). "New" refers to the act celebrated, not to the novelty of the song. Meanwhile, the king remains under siege from enemies who would destroy Israel (v. 11).

Prayer for Israel's future generations, domestic animals, and its cities (vv. 12-14)

As already noted, many scholars regard verses 12-14 as a later addition and evidently would be happy if verse 11 ended the poem. Though one must take seriously such views, the juxtaposition of victory and fertility is not at all unusual. Psalm 72, for example, celebrates the king for his role in fertility as well as victory. In an agrarian society, political peace and agricultural fertility cannot be separated. The king protects the land from invaders and blesses its fertility.

Theological and Ethical Analysis

A proper understanding of election, authority, and service are crucial for a strong and healthy community. Some people grasp authority to enjoy its benefits; others reject it because they want no part of community life. In this psalm, the king in prayer faces the Lord who appointed him to the office. (Kingship is here conceived chiefly in terms of military leadership.) A variety of responses to the appointment is possible: reluctance to be chosen (Exod 3–4; Judg 6:11-27; Jer 1:4-10), unquestioning acceptance (Isa 6; 40:1-11), or refusal (Jonah). In Ps 144, the king accepts the call generously, awed and delighted that the Lord of the universe would choose him as a servant. With such sentiments David accepted the Lord's call in 2 Sam 7. The king expresses delighted surprise (vv. 3-4) and prays that the Lord reign over Israel and over the world (vv. 5-15). Putting aside both fear and ambition, the king prays only that the Lord's will be done.

Modern pray-ers will understand that the king represents the people to God and God to the people. In his unqualified acceptance of his vocation, he speaks for the congregation; they too are called by God to support and pray for the reign of God. Many obstacles stand in the way of such acceptance: egotism, a privatistic style, and indifference toward the kingdom of God. This prayer shows the Davidic king accepting in faith his noble vocation. A community today can imitate his generosity and acceptance of their vocation by praying this psalm. Christians can also view the psalm as foreshadowing Christ as son of David and son of God, delighting in the role and eager to do the will of God.

PSALM 145

Literary Analysis

Psalm 145 ends the Davidic collection (Pss 138–45) with a hymn of praise, and so prepares for the hymns (146–50) that conclude the Psalter in praise and thanksgiving. Psalm 145 is an acrostic poem. Though the line beginning with *nun* (n) dropped out of the Masoretic Text through scribal miscopying, the line is preserved in the Septuagint and a Qumran scroll (11QPs[a]). Virtually all modern translations (including NRSV, v. 13*cd*) quite properly include it.

Like most acrostic poems, Ps 145 has an inherent logic in addition to the structure provided by the successive letters of the alphabet. The singer's own voice is prominent throughout, vowing "*I* will extol you" (vv. 1-2), reaffirming the vow (vv. 5-6), and concluding with "*my* mouth will speak the praise of the LORD" (v. 21). In verses 3-7, one generation tells the next of the acts of the Lord, which are portrayed as objective acts. Verse 8, "the LORD is gracious and merciful," reminds the reader of the divine governance responsible for those acts (vv. 11-13) and the divine generosity toward human beings (vv. 10-20). The final verse (v. 21) reprises the first.

Exegetical Analysis

I will praise you, my Lord (vv. 1-2)

In this final poem of the Davidic collection, the singer's voice is strong, insisting on telling of the Lord's wonderful works so that all will respond with admiration and praise. The title "my King" (v. 1) points forward to the four occurrences of "kingdom" in verses 11-13, which should be understood as an act (ruling) rather than a state (kingdom). "Your name" refers to the way in which God is revealed in the world; it is parallel to "My God and King" in verse 1*a*. "Your presence" is an English equivalent to "your name." Verses 1-2 are linked by repetition of the phrases "I will bless" and "your name forever and ever."

People praise the splendor of your works (vv. 3-7)

Verses 3-7 differ from the verses following in their focus on the majestic and powerful in the works of God. The singer presides as "one generation shall laud your works to another," as in the process of education described in Ps 78:4 (cf. Exod 13:8, 14; Deut 6:20):

> We will not hide them from their children;
> we will tell to the coming generation
> the glorious deeds of the LORD, and his might,
> and the wonders that he has done.

Education is very concrete. Instead of abstract instruction, parents show their children how they too belong to the community founded and guided by the Lord. The children experience the effects of the mighty deeds of old that are constantly renewed.

The Lord is gracious and merciful (vv. 8-21)

In verse 8, which cites the famous confession of God's attributes in Exod 34:6, the singer turns toward God's rule over human beings. Characterizing that rule is compassion; the two related Hebrew words *raḥûm* and *reḥem* occur in verses 8-9 (NRSV: "merciful" and "compassion"). Personalizing the divine "works," the poet has them give thanks (v. 10a) along with "your faithful" (v. 10b), that is, Israel. NRSV "kingdom" (*malkût*, similarly translated in REB and NIV) occurs four times in verses 11-13. The word is better rendered "reign" (NAB) or "kingship" (Delitzsch, NJPS). In verses 11-12, *malkût* is twice placed in parallelism with "power, might," and in verse 13, it is placed in parallelism with "dominion." "Kingdom" means primarily a politically organized community or a sovereign state with a monarch. The meaning does not fit Ps 145. Israel tells of the Lord's dominion to the nations (vv. 11-12). Verses 13c-20 give specific instances of how the divine rule operates: by upholding the weak (v. 14), feeding the hungry (vv. 15-16), and answering the cries of the poor (vv. 18-20). To uphold the falling and raise up those who are bowed down (v. 14) can be an act of justice as well as compassion, for biblical justice is often deciding *between* two claimants, putting one party down and raising up the other. Verses 13c-16 have become a traditional table blessing. The final line (v. 21) is an inclusio of verse 1; the first-person voice of the singer returns, and three words are repeated from verse 1, "bless," "name," and "forever and ever."

Theological and Ethical Analysis

As the Psalter nears its end, doxology begins to predominate. As leader of the liturgical community, the singer in Ps 145 invites praise of God's wonderful works, rejoicing in the fact that older members tell of the works to younger members (v. 4) and that the whole community repeats those wonders to the nations (v. 12). The singer is especially concerned to interpret the kingship of the Lord (vv. 11-12) as compassionate and generous rule (vv. 13c-20).

Psalm 145 invites pray-ers to view the world in a celebratory way. Even before one examines any one aspect of the universe, one can, like the poet, decide to extol the name of the Lord (vv. 1-2). As the priest-poet Gerard Manley Hopkins put it in *God's Grandeur,* "The world is charged with the grandeur of God. It will flame out, like shining from shook foil." Though the psalm mentions the traditional works of God such as creation or the exodus, its real interest is the day to day governance of the universe, "your reign" (vv. 11-13, NRSV: "your kingdom"). Psalm 145 holds up to pray-ers a dynamic universe issuing from a caring, generous, and compassionate Lord. Mercy is as much an ingredient of royal rule as justice.

PSALM 146

Literary Analysis

Psalms 146–50 form the concluding doxology to the entire Psalter. Each poem begins and ends with "Praise the LORD!"

(traditionally, Hallelujah). Each of the preceding four books of the Psalter ended in a brief doxology: Pss 41:13; 72:18-19; 89:52; and 106:48, and it is fitting that the entire Psalter end in a great surge of praise. In Ps 146 themes of the preceding psalms appear: the kingship of the Lord (Ps 146:10; cf. Ps 145:11-13) and the Lord as "keeper" (Ps 146:6, 9 [NRSV: "watches over"]; cf. Psalm 121:4; 145:20). Like the immediately preceding poem, Ps 146 begins with the singer declaring the intention to give praise. Differently from Ps 145, where the singer led the community in robust praise, this singer engages in an inner dialogue ("Praise the LORD, O my soul!" Ps 146:1*b*) before addressing the community in verse 3. Praise has a more distinctively personal origin than in Ps 145, arising as it does from the psalmist appreciating the vanity of human resources (vv. 3-4) and the multiple ways in which the Lord governs the world (vv. 5-9).

Thought and structure are relatively clear. Verses 1-4 state the singer's intention to praise (vv. 1-2), which is set in opposition to the alternative of relying on powerful human beings for protection and patronage (vv. 3-4). Contrasts are maximized for rhetorical effect: singular number and positive exhortation (vv. 1-2) versus plural number and negative admonition (vv. 3-4). Verses 5-10 begin with a beatitude declaring happy those who make the Lord their help (v. 5) and then lists the virtues of the Lord in the participial construction common in hymns (e.g., "the one who makes heaven and earth"). After the ninth such participle ("watches over the strangers," v. 9*a*), the poet switches to a finite verb ("he brings to ruin," v. 9*c*).

Exegetical Analysis

Bless the Lord, O my soul! Do not trust in human help (vv. 1-4)

Beginning with a self-exhortation to praise the Lord, the psalmist resolves to give such praise as long as he or she lives. The psalmist is bound and determined to live a life marked by praise of God. Deliberately contrasted to the psalmist's praising style is trust in powerful humans. "Trust" in verse 3 is the standard verb for trust in God. One cannot place one's trust in powerful humans and God at the same time. To be sure, humans in high places can offer help to their family and friends, but they cannot offer basic and ultimate help. Why? Because they are as subject to death as anyone else. Their plans perish when they do (v. 4). In a moment, the psalm will recite the participles praising the one "who made heaven and earth" (v. 6*a*) and the one who "will reign forever / . . . for all generations" (v. 10*ab*).

Happy are those whose help is the creator and righteous ruler of the world (vv. 5-10)

Verse 5, literally, "happy is the one whose help is the God of Jacob" (NRSV makes the subject plural), shifts from the plural number of verses 3-4 to the singular number of verses 1-2. Like many texts in Wisdom literature, the psalm contrasts the righteous individual (singular number) with the wicked group (plural number). One who trusts in God is happy because the Lord who offers help is above any power. What is distinctive about the nine hymnic participles in verses 6-9 is that they do not mention the exodus or other great events of Israel's history. The psalm goes directly from creation (v. 6*ab*) to the Lord doing justice, for example, giving food to the hungry, setting prisoners free, and upholding the widow and the orphan. Psalms 135 and 136 are more typical of hymns, for they mention Israel and its history immediately after creation. Why does Ps 146 not follow the customary sequence of events in historic recitals? The answer seems to be the singer's decision to praise the Lord rather than to trust princes (vv. 1-3). The internal dialogue that began the psalm (v. 1*a*) was a genuine deliberation, pondering where to go for help in a crisis. Finally, the psalmist decided to trust in the Lord rather than in powerful people. The hymn is the result. All the Lord's actions mentioned in verses 6-9 are actions that rescue beleaguered individuals. To mention the exodus, guidance in the wilderness, and conquest would not have been relevant to the psalmist's situation. The final verse (v. 10) states that the Lord will *always* exist and exert power, whereas human helpers, even the most powerful and kindly, are creatures of a moment and cannot count on being there for one. Verse 10*c* forms an inclusio with verse 1*a*, just as one expects in a hymn.

Theological and Ethical Analysis

One can give praise to the Lord by reciting the traditional acts done on behalf of Israel. Such is the procedure of Pss 105–6, 135–36, and 145. Or one can do what Psalm 146 does: praise the Lord as savior of the poor, which is equivalent to entrusting oneself in the Lord when in peril. To the psalmist, God should be remembered as the one who always stands on the side of the poor. Social justice and prayer are here united. One senses freedom and joy in the singer who has consciously rejected purely human solutions in order to place complete trust in the God of the poor.

PSALM 147

Literary Analysis

Psalm 147 is one of the five hymns that conclude the Psalter. Each of its three sections (vv. 1-6, 7-11, and 12-20) begins with an invitation to praise the Lord and then lists the divine acts for which praise is to be given. Normally in hymns, the conjunction "for" *(kî)* introduces the list as in Pss 95:3 and 96:4. In Ps 147, "for" plays such a role only in verse 13; it is implied in the other sections. As is usual in the Bible, praise is given for specific divine actions.

At first reading, the three sections of Ps 147 do not display any pattern. Verses in which God creates natural phenomena (vv. 4, 8-9, 16-18) stand next to verses in which God brings Israel back from exile (v. 2), tends the downtrodden (vv. 3, 6), and sends forth his word to Israel (vv. 13, 18-20). Though it does not mention the exodus-conquest as in other hymns, this poem does mention the new exodus: the restoration of Israel after the exile (v. 3), and the giving of statutes and ordinances to the people (vv. 15-19). Section 1 (vv. 1-6) lists as reasons for praise the Lord's restoration of Jerusalem and gathering of exiles along with the healing of various casualties (presumably of the exile). Section 2 (vv. 7-11) lists as reasons the Lord's control of natural phenomena for the benefit of humans, adding a comment about the necessity of revering the Lord (vv. 10-11). Section 3 (vv. 12-20) invites Jerusalem to give praise and gives the reason: to Israel alone has the Lord entrusted his powerful word.

Do these seemingly disparate items add up to a coherent hymn? The answer is yes. First, the juxtaposition of creation and governance of Israel is common in the Bible. In Ps 136, for example, God's creation of the world (vv. 4-9) flows seamlessly into God's actions on behalf of Israel (vv. 10-22). Though modern people make a sharp distinction between "nature" and "history," the Bible does not (see Clifford 1994, pp. 158-62). Psalm 147 tells of the restoration of Jerusalem and its healing as a single work. Stanza 2 tells of the Lord making the land fertile (paralleling the healing of the people in stanza 1) and ends with an encomium of those who revere the Lord. Stanza 3 invites restored Jerusalem to give praise for the one thing it has alone among the peoples—the word of the Lord. There is, therefore, a pattern. The singer invites Israel to thank God for rebuilding it (stanza 1), enabling them to respond (stanza 2), and giving them his precepts. The date of the psalm is in the postexilic period. It explicitly speaks of gathering the outcasts of Israel (v. 2), and its concern with the word of God was a particular concern of Second Temple Judaism.

Exegetical Analysis

Praise the Lord who builds up Jerusalem (vv. 1-6)

The clause following "praise the LORD" has unusual syntax. Instead of the expected "for" *(kî)* introducing the actions for which one gives thanks, the Hebrew word is used in another sense, "*How* good it is." Perhaps the poet deliberately scrambled familiar words for the sake of variety. At any rate, the poet exclaims how wonderful it is to praise God. NRSV: "he is gracious" (v. 1c) can be rendered with equal plausibility "how pleasant is fitting prayer!" Building up Jerusalem is the first divine act described, and all subsequent acts in stanza 1—healing, binding, lifting up, casting down—elaborate that building up. God's numbering the stars (v. 4) is a work of creation like God's stretching out the heavens in Isa 51:16 (cf. 42:5; 45:12; 51:13):

> I have put my words in your mouth,
>   and hidden you in the shadow of my hand,
> stretching out the heavens
>   and laying the foundations of the earth,
>   and saying to Zion, "You are my people."

Creating the heavens and rebuilding Zion are parallel works. Psalm 147:5 continues the theme of creation, for divine power and understanding are shown in creation in Jer 10:12; 51:15; and Job 26:12.

Praise the Lord who makes the land fertile (vv. 7-11)

Verse 7 hymns God as one who makes the earth fertile with rain (v. 8) and ensures that even the least animals have enough food from the soil. Not stated but implied by God's feeding the animals is that God will ensure that every human has enough to eat. Because exilic biblical literature deals mostly with spiritual loss, modern readers may underrate the physical devastation of the exile. Forced depopulation created hordes of displaced persons, and many of them were diseased and starving. In such troubled times, it took great faith to praise God for making the earth able to feed every creature. Exactly in the middle of the poem (measured by word count), verses 10-11 turn attention to a new topic: how Israel is to respond to the Lord who builds up Jerusalem. The answer: not by their strength (v. 10) but by their "fear" and hope (v. 11). "Fear the Lord" is an unsatisfactory translation; the Hebrew phrase means to revere Yahweh alone, which means obeying Yahweh's will and performing the appropriate rituals and honors. "Hope in his steadfast love" (v. 11*b*) means to rely on the Lord to rebuild and nurture Jerusalem. This invitation is fleshed out in stanza 3.

Praise the Lord, O Jerusalem, for the word given to you alone (vv. 12-20)

Verse 2 praises God for building up Jerusalem and verses 8-9 praise God for providing food for all creatures. Verses 12-14 elaborate both expressions: God protects Zion, blesses its children, grants peace to its borders, and provides food for its inhabitants. All these gifts, it is implied in verse 15, come through God's powerful word. The nature of that word is illustrated by heavenly phenomena, which, like the word, are sent from heaven. Isaiah 55:10-11 similarly compares rain and snow to the word of God. As God sends snow, frost, and hail before which no human can stand, with equal ease God sends his word that is too powerful for any human to resist. Verses 15-20 have seven terms for the word of God ("command," "word" [3 times], "statutes, "ordinances" [twice]). Also powerful is God's "wind" (*rûaḥ*, v. 18*b*) that makes the massive waters trapped in the ice flow freely. "Wind" can mean "spirit" (of God), and the poet plays on both meanings. Verses 19-20 specify the meaning of the divine word; it is the word the Lord gave at Sinai and now gives to the people in fresh measure. The word made them distinctive then (cf. Deut 4:5-8) and makes them distinctive now, for "[God] has not dealt thus with any other nation" (v. 20*a*). Concern with the word of the Lord was a feature of Second Temple Judaism. "Praise the LORD!" in verse 20 reprises the opening invitation in verse 1.

Theological and Ethical Analysis

How does one rebuild after a catastrophe, especially when the catastrophe was caused by the stupidity and sin of one's ancestors?

There are only two possible strategies: exit or voice. One can leave or one can participate. The second is the strategy of the psalm, for it raises its voice in praise of the God who rebuilds Jerusalem and heals its inhabitants. Was the psalm written in the depths of the exile, or was it written when rebuilding was well under way or even long completed? It is impossible to say. What is important is that the psalmist expects *God* to rebuild Jerusalem, not human resources. More is needed than God rebuilding, however, for Israel must respond if there is to be relationship. And that relationship will be built on the firmest of foundations, God's word. It reveals Godself, defines Israel's common life, and enables Israel to respond.

Though it may have originated in a particular moment in history, the psalm is of perennial relevance. The Lord is always building up Jerusalem, feeding its inhabitants, strengthening its gates. One can never give sufficient praise to such a generous God. The Lord's acts are never one-way, however. They invite a response. They are always "ethical" in this sense. The Lord's word is self-communicating, not only showing people the right path but also enabling them to speak in response. Rebuilding Zion shows a generous God. Speaking a word to Zion shows a loving God.

PSALM 148

Literary Analysis

Each psalm in the series (146–50) begins and ends with "Praise the LORD!" (*hălĕlû yāh* = traditionally rendered "hallelujah"). Psalm 148 employs the verb "to praise" twelve times! The divine name "LORD" occurs four times and "the name (of the Lord)" three times. Possibly the number twelve is the sum of multiplying three ("name") and four ("LORD"). These numbers give an idea of the formality of Ps 148. Like other hymns, it names those invited to give praise, for example, "Praise the LORD, all you nations" (Ps 117:1 and "Make a joyful noise to the LORD, all the earth," Ps 100:1). Most hymns name the invited group in a line or two and concentrate on describing the divine acts that are the object of praise. Psalm 148, on the contrary, spends most of its time listing the invited groups. Verses 1-4 list the inhabitants of the heavenly world, and verses 7-12 list the inhabitants of the earthly world. The divine acts meriting praise are mentioned only briefly in verses 5-6 and 13*bc*, introduced by the conjunction "for" *(kî)*, "*for* he commanded and they were created" (v. 5*b*) and "*for* his name alone is exalted" (v. 13*b*).

Psalm 148 is arranged in two panels of nearly equal length: verses 1-6, "Praise the LORD from the heavens," and verses 7-14, "Praise the LORD from the earth." "Heaven and earth" is the Hebrew idiom for "universe," as in Gen 2:1, "Thus the heavens and the earth were finished, and all their multitude." Creatures of the heavens, animate ("his angels," "his host") and inanimate ("sun and mood," "stars," "highest heavens," "waters"), are invited to give praise. The motive for giving praise is that the Lord created them and assigned them all their tasks (v. 5). Similarly, creatures of earth, human ("kings," "princes," "men and women," "old and young together") and nonhuman ("sea monsters and all deeps," weather phenomena, "mountains and all hills," animals), are invited to give praise. The motive for praise is that the Lord's name and glory are exalted above heaven and earth (v. 13), that is, that the Lord is the supreme deity. Creation is implied because the Lord became the supreme deity by creating the universe. All creatures must pay due homage to their creator. How does verse 14 fit into the hymn? Some scholars regard it as an addition, for the tricolon in verse 13 seems to them a perfect conclusion, and Israel seems an afterthought. Israel need not be mentioned in every hymn, as Ps 150 shows. Though the view has some merit, no textual evidence supports it. One should accept verse 14. In context, it affirms that the Lord of the universe has chosen ("strengthened") and exalted one people. The Lord of the universe is not distant, therefore, but has made an entry into the universe through one people. The date of the poem is the Second Temple period. It may have inspired the Song of the Three Youths in Dan 3, which is found in Greek and Latin manuscripts between

Dan 3:23-24. Its first part is similar to Pss 96 and 97 and the second part (beginning with "Bless the Lord") resembles Ps 148 in inviting inanimate as well as animate nature to bless the Lord.

Exegetical Analysis

Praise the Lord from the heavens (vv. 1-6)

"Praise the LORD!" frames this psalm (vv. 1 and 14) as it does every one from 146–50. Verse 1 identifies the location of the praise ("from the heavens," "in the heights") as verse 7a will shortly do ("from the earth"). In the heavens, heavenly beings ("angels," "his host") offer unceasing and perfect worship (cf. Ps 103). Personifying the heavenly elements, the psalmist has them join the chorus as well. "Highest heavens" is, literally, "heaven of heavens"; the syntax is like "song of songs" meaning "the sublime song." Hebrew cosmology assumed that the earth was a disk floating on a cosmic sea over which was a vast ocean. Even that vast ocean is summoned to give thanks. The motive for praise is that "he commanded and they were created." Creation was by word as in Gen 1. Creating means assigning tasks or destinies, and verse 6 speaks of this further organizing of the heavenly bodies. There is persistent Hebrew wordplay between "heavens" (šāmayim) and "name" (šēm).

Praise the Lord from the earth (vv. 7-14)

As the first section began with angels and concluded with cosmic waters (v. 4), the second section in good chiastic fashion (ABBA) begins with cosmic waters and concludes with human beings. Verses 7b-8 invite those elements especially impossible for humans to control: sea monsters and weather phenomena. These should give praise, for they are under "his command" (v. 8b; cf. Ps 147:16-18). Human beings come next on the list: first kings and princes (v. 11), then every human being as indicated by "men and women," "old and young" (v. 12). Like his angels and his host, human beings are invited to praise the name or the self-manifestation of the Lord (v. 13). Verses 5-6 and 13 propose the same motive for praise: the Lord's creation and maintenance of the universe. Verses 5-6 stress the eternal order and fixed nature of the heavens ("forever and ever," "cannot be passed"), whereas verse 13 stresses the supremacy of the Lord Yahweh over all else ("his name alone is exalted"). Verse 14, the final verse, shifts attention to the Lord's people, Israel. The following paraphrase may be helpful: The Lord has given strength to his people, given renown to all his faithful, the children of Israel, the people close to him. Only against the background of Israel's devastation in the exile can the verse be understood, for it describes the restoration of Israel. If the Lord's name and glory are above heaven and earth (v. 13), restored Israel has been given some of that glory. If readers do not understand the prior devastation of the Lord's people, verse 14 can seem self-centered and narrow.

Theological and Ethical Analysis

Psalm 148 sees the world as coherent and ordered, as in Gen 1. Both heaven and earth, arranged symmetrically, give praise to the Lord. The whole world, so to speak, is liturgical, constructed so that each of its multiple aspects is oriented to the Lord who brought it into being. Though moderns tend to think of worship as the response of rational creatures to their God, this psalm rather regards worship as virtually inherent in the world's structure. Even before any human being decides to worship, the world is already engaged in worship of the Lord. The emphasis on the parallelism of heavenly and earthly worship characterized patristic views of liturgy. In modern churches, this outlook is particularly at home in the Orthodox church. Viewing planetary life as coherent and inherently ordered to transcendence, Ps 148 is a good text for ecological spirituality. But is God only a recipient of heavenly and earthly praise? Verse 14 contains the answer to the question, though it requires careful consideration lest it be misunderstood as a claim of privilege. To be sure, the glory of the Lord has been given to a particular people. Other biblical passages about Israel and the nations provide a fuller context: The Lord of the universe is not content with receiving praise but wishes to enter into a relationship with kings, young men and women alike, old and young together. Israel has a mysterious relationship to that divine desire. The people "close to him" represent the Lord to the world in an inviting way.

PSALM 149

Literary Analysis

Psalm 149 is the fourth in the series of hymns that conclude the Psalter. Each psalm in the series begins and ends with "Praise the LORD!" Of all the concluding poems, the sentiments of Ps 149 offer the most difficulty to interpreters and devout readers alike. How can one have the praises of God in one's throat and a two-edged sword in one's hands? Why should one execute vengeance on the nations and bind kings with fetters? Why should these acts be "glory for all his faithful ones" (vv. 6-9)? To understand Ps 149, one needs to appreciate its debt to Pss 146–48 (especially the last) and to Ps 2. Of the immediately preceding psalm, one verse has been especially important, Ps 148:14. Of its twelve words, Ps 149 uses all but two: "raise up," "his people," "praise," "his faithful" (twice), "all," "people/children of," and "to praise." Why does Ps 149 draw so heavily on this verse and this psalm? Psalm 148 summoned the universe—heaven and earth—to acknowledge the Lord's sovereignty, and emphasized that *every* human being was summoned, including kings, princes, and rulers (Ps 148:11-13). It singled out one people, Israel, as special among all the nations (Ps 148:14). Psalm 149 will develop that very theme: Israel has a special calling to proclaim the sovereignty of the Lord to the nations and their kings.

The second influence is Ps 2. An editor of the Psalter seems to have matched the second psalm to the second-to-last psalm. Psalm 2 tells how "the kings of the earth . . . / and the rulers" conspired against "the LORD and his anointed, saying, / 'Let us burst their bonds asunder'" (Ps 2:2-3), and how "the decree of the LORD" (Ps 2:7) made the king the Lord's son and enabled him to subdue the nations with an iron rod (Ps 2:8-9) so they might serve the Lord (Ps 2:10-11). The king is the instrument of the Lord's rule. Such also is the theme of Ps 149, though with an important difference. When Ps 149 was written (the Second Temple period), the king was gone from public life and (according to some texts) his role of representing the Lord's sole kingship to the nations was transferred to the people. Isaiah 55:3cd clearly states the transferral of the Davidic office to the people: "I will make with you [plural, the people] an everlasting covenant, my steadfast, sure love for David." In Ps 149, Israel enthusiastically embraces its role in promoting the Lord's reign in the world. If kings resist, Israel will shatter their arrogance by its proclamation that Yahweh is the Lord of the world (as in Ps 2). To proclaim that the Lord is king is to unmask all other kings as false; the proclamation in a sense is an act of war against those kings who do not acknowledge their sovereign. Like the king in Ps 2, Israel in Ps 149 represents the kingship of the Lord to the nations. The difference between king and people is not so great as might appear, for the Davidic king was in a sense the voice of the people. The military language in verses 6-9 is, therefore, metaphorical. Israel's fidelity and public praise are weapons that advance the rule of the Lord (the kingdom of God).

The literary structure is established by the two sets of invitatory verses. Verses 1-3 and 5 invite hearers to give praise, using verbs in the imperative and jussive (exhortatory) mood. As is usual in hymns, the invitatory verses 1-3 are followed by the conjunction "for" (v. 4a) that names the motive for praise (the Lord's victory for his people). The second invitation to give praise (v. 5) contains no motive, evidently appropriating the motive already expressed in verse 4. There are, then, two stanzas, verses 1-4 and 5-9. The first stanza invites praise for the Lord's victory. The second also invites praise and then equates it with weapons of war against the rebellious kings.

Exegetical Analysis

Sing a new song to the Lord! (vv. 1-4)

"Praise the LORD!" opens and closes the hymn. The "new song" (v. 1), which the people are invited to sing, elsewhere is a response to God's creation of the world or Israel (Pss 33:3; 96:1; 98:1; 144:9; Isa 42:10). "New song" here similarly responds to the Lord's creation, for Israel is "glad in its *Maker*" (v. 2*a*). The victory (v. 4*b*) celebrated in this hymn has established Yahweh as king, for "the children of Zion rejoice in their king" (v. 2*b*). The deed for which the poem gives thanks is nothing less than the creation of the world and of Israel; this grand act establishes the kingship of Yahweh. No wonder the Lord's own faithful (v. 1*c*) give thanks with such a burst of emotion: singing, exulting, playing musical instruments, and dancing. In winning the victory, the Lord had Israel in mind, "for the LORD takes pleasure in his people" (v. 4*a*).

Let your praises proclaim the Lord's victory to kings and nations (vv. 5-9)

As noted, the invitation to exult and sing in verse 5 parallels in brief form the longer invitation to give praise in verses 1-3. As the first invitation was uttered "in the assembly of the faithful" (v. 1*c*), so the second one is uttered "on their couches" (v. 5*b*), a phrase that has caused much discussion. As is recognized by many scholars, "couch" (or bed) symbolizes private expression (as opposed to public expression) in Pss 4:4; 6:6; 36:4; and Hos 7:14. In Ps 36:4, "they plot mischief while on their beds," means secret or private intent. In Ps 149:5*b*, the phrase "on their couches" refers to praise expressed in private, which complements the public praise expressed in "the assembly of the faithful" (v. 1*c*). Public and private is a merism meaning every moment. At all times, Israel gives praise to the Lord.

Verses 6-9 are the most controverted part of Ps 149. How can the people sing God's praises and wield a sword at the same time?

The answer is that wielding a sword (and the other military actions in vv. 7-9) is a metaphor for proclaiming the Lord's sovereignty over kings and nations as explained above under "Literary Analysis." In verse 6, the conjunction "and" ("*and* two-edged swords in their hands") turns the statements of colon A and colon B into a comparison: Praising God is like wielding a sword. Proverbs 26:9 is an example of "comparative *and*": "A thorn lands on the hand of a drunkard *and* a proverb lands on the mouth of a fool" (cf. Prov 17:3; 25:3; 26:3, 9; Job 2:11). Worship furthers the Lord's reign as a military campaign furthers the reign. It is the honorable task of Israel (the "glory for all his faithful ones," v. 9*b*) to embody the sovereignty of the Lord and make it visible and audible in the world. Israel's witness unmasks false kingdoms and invites the nations to join in their praise. Verses 6*b*-9 assume, exactly as Ps 2 does, that the kings (representing the nations) will resist the Lord and will only do homage after being defeated. NRSV "vengeance" (v. 7*a*) is better rendered "retribution" for the kings' refusal to recognize their true suzerain. The "judgment decreed" is the divine decision manifested in the victory, making Yahweh the supreme king. Kings rule only by the Lord's sufferance.

Theological and Ethical Analysis

The poem vigorously affirms the kingdom of God in its active sense of God reigning or ruling. A true Israelite is aware of the kingdom and shouts it from the housetops. Some modern readers would perhaps be more comfortable if that reign were expressed in less bellicose terms and if the mediating role of one nation were less emphasized. Such modern accommodations to good taste and civility would, alas, make Ps 149 quite unbiblical. The warlike tone and exaltation of one nation need not spoil the poem as modern prayer, however. Properly interpreted, they make the poem more real and engaging. First, divine kingship is active—daily governance and administration of justice. Evil is powerful and entrenched, so the Bible assumes, and a just ruler must have the means to contain its institutional and individual expressions. Biblical justice, it should be remembered, is frequently interventionist, actively upholding an aggrieved party and putting down arrogant oppressors. Psalm 149 imagines a "worst-case scenario"—defiant and unjust kings—to dramatize the reality of the Lord's rule. Second, one nation is selected for the sake of all the nations. The chosen people are called to recognize the Lord's total sovereignty; their obedience and worship alerts all the nations to that true sovereignty. Woe to the special people if they do not revere the Lord and give praise in the sight of the nations.

Though the language is open to misunderstanding, Ps 149 is a favorite of Christians. In churches with a liturgical tradition of morning and evening prayer, it has long been a fixture in the morning prayer of Sunday. It is easy to see why. The psalm expresses the vocation of the church with vigor and memorable phrases, inviting Christians to give witness to the kingdom of God. The holy people rejoice in the great victory that has made the Lord the King of the universe, and they pray that the rule will be recognized by every king and nation.

Psalm 150

Literary Analysis

The final psalm in the Psalter, and final hymn in the five-hymn series (146–50), opens and closes, like the others, with "Praise the Lord!" (*hālĕlû yāh*, traditionally "hallelujah"). The same verb in the imperative mood, "praise him," begins all the verses except the final one (*hālĕlûhû*, in v. 1*b*, simply "praise,"*hālĕlû*). The verb occurs thirteen times in this final outburst of celebration. Each of the five books of the Psalter ends with a doxology (Pss 41:13; 72:18-19; 89:52; 106:48) and it is only fitting that one grand doxology conclude Book 5 and the entire Psalter.

The poem contains the usual hymnic elements, though they are arranged in unconventional ways. The invitatory is stretched out, extending, in fact, through the whole poem. The poem is one long invitation to give praise. Instead of the customary mention of musical instruments, verses 3-5 list virtually every instrument in the Psalter to create a full symphony. The motive for praise is not introduced by the usual conjunction "for." Instead, verse 2 mentions "his mighty deeds" and "according to his surpassing greatness," summarizing the works that other hymns describe in detail. The group summoned to give praise, whom most psalms name almost immediately, is not revealed until the end, and it is of vast range: "everything that breathes." The delay in naming those invited, and the unique group, emphasizes the universal sweep of the poem. It goes beyond the holy people to the entire human race, even to the animal kingdom! The vast reach of the poem is a reminder that the call of one people is made in view of God's commitment to all.

Most scholars correctly date the psalm well into the Second Temple period. It is very possible that was specifically composed to conclude the Psalter; the poet might have had an eye on Ps 2.

Exegetical Analysis

There are thirteen occurrences of the divine name in six verses if one counts the independent third-person singular pronoun: "LORD" three times *(Yāh)*, "God" *('ēl)*, "him" nine times (the suffixed third-person pronoun -*hû'*). The place where praise is to be given is "his sanctuary" (v. 1), which could be either the Jerusalem Temple or the heavenly Temple. Since the earthly Temple in Jerusalem was regarded as a copy of the heavenly Temple, it is probable that "everything that breathes" (v. 6) refers to creatures in heaven and on earth. "Firmament," the vast space under the heavenly vault, indicates that worship cannot be confined to a small building in a particular city. The Lord's grandeur can only be adequately praised in the amphitheatre of the cosmos. "His mighty deeds" (v. 2) include creation of the world and all its inhabitants. They include as well "nature," that is, the natural wonders of the world, beautiful, awe-inspiring, and beyond human control.

Every instrument of the orchestra joins the human voice in giving praise. Verses 3-5 are the largest collection of references to musical instruments in the Psalter. Trumpet, originally a ram's horn *(šôpār)*, is the most frequently mentioned instrument in the Bible. It was used in military contexts and in liturgy as in the transport of the ark to Jerusalem (2 Sam 6:15). The biblical harp (v. 3*b*) had ten strings (Pss 33:2; 92:4) of unequal length; it was played with the hand. The lyre had four to eight strings and was played with a plectrum. The tambourine was a percussion instrument, a handheld drum often played by women; it was struck by hand rather than by sticks. Exodus 15:20 has the same phrase, tambourine and dance. Perhaps the phrase means "tambourine used for dancing." Pipe (v. 4*b*) is somewhat uncertain. "Cymbals" are copper or bronze percussion instruments. Found all over the ancient Near East, they came in various sizes, from saucer-like plates to small disks fastened to two fingers of the hand (King and Stager 2001, pp. 290-98).

With verse 6, the syntax changes. No longer beginning "praise him," verse 6 begins "let everything that breathes praise the LORD!" Delayed till now, the group summoned to give praise is finally named: "everything that breathes." The delay gives emphasis, underscoring the limitless range of those called to acknowledge God's beneficence. Musical instruments, the products of human ingenuity, support and extend the human voice in its God-given task.

Theological and Ethical Analysis

Psalm 1 declares happy those who recite the divine words of the Psalter. "Happiness" comes not only because the psalms satisfy the deepest desires of the human heart but also because the psalms turn one toward God, the Lord of the universe. More perhaps than any other psalm, Ps 150 urges again and again that every living being is to respond wholeheartedly to God in the vast cathedral of the cosmos. The very designation of those invited— "everything that breathes"—is a reminder that one's very being, one's breath, is owed to God. Musical instruments—percussion, strings, trumpets, flutes—are there to help each person speak and sing the heartfelt praise that is due to God, the Lord of lords.

SELECT BIBLIOGRAPHY

WORKS CITED

Barré, Michael, and John S. Kselman. 1983. New Exodus, Covenant, and Restoration in Psalm 23. Pages 97-127 in *The Word of the Lord Shall Go Forth: Essays in Honor of David Noel Freedman in Celebration of His Sixtieth Birthday*. Edited by Carol L. Meyers and Michael Patrick O'Connor. Winona Lake, Ind.: Eisenbrauns.

Barré, Michael. 1985. Fasting in Isaiah 58:1-12: A Reexamination. *Biblical Theology Bulletin* 15:94-97.

———. 1988. "*'rṣ (h)ḥyym*-'The Land of the Living?' " *Journal for the Study of the Old Testament* 41:37-59.

———. 1995. Hearts, Beds, and Repentance in Psalm 4,5 and Hosea 7,4. *Biblica* 76:53-62.

Clifford, Richard. 1979. Style and Purpose in Psalm 105. *Biblica* 60:420-27.

———. 1980. Psalm 89: A Lament over the Davidic Ruler's Continued Failure. *Harvard Theological Review* 73:35-48.

———. 1981. In Zion and David A New Beginning: An Interpretation of Psalm 78. *Traditions and Transformations: Turning Points in Biblical Faith*. Edited by Baruch Halpern and Jon D. Levenson. Winona Lake, Ind.: Eisenbrauns. 121-41.

———. 1994. *Creation Accounts in the Ancient Near East and in the Bible*. Catholic Biblical Quarterly Monograph Series 26. Washington, D.C.: Catholic Biblical Association.

———. 2000. What Is The Psalmist Asking for In Psalms 39:5 and 90:12? *Journal of Biblical Literature* 119:59-66.

Crow, L. D. 1992. The Rhetoric of Psalm 44. *Zeitschrift für die Alttestamentliche Wissenschaft* 104:394-401.

Dalley, Stephanie 1989. *Myths from Mesopotamia: Creation, the Flood, Gilgamesh and Others.* Oxford: Oxford University Press.

Freedman, David Noel. 1999. *Psalm 119: The Exaltation of Torah.* Biblical and Judaic Studies 6. Winona Lake, Ind.: Eisenbrauns.

Keel, Othmar. 1978. *The Symbolism of the Biblical World: Ancient Near Eastern Iconography and the Book of Psalms.* Translated by Timothy J. Hallett. New York: Seabury.

King, Philip J., and Lawrence E. Stager. 2001. *Life in Biblical Times.* Library of Ancient Israel. Louisville: Westminster John Knox.

Kselman, John S. 1987. Psalm 3: A Structural and Literary Unity. *Catholic Biblical Quarterly* 49:572-80.

———. 1997. Psalm 36. Pages 3-17 in *Wisdom, You Are My Sister: Studies in Honor of Roland E. Murphy on the Occasion of His Eightieth Birthday.* Edited by Michael L. Barré. Catholic Biblical Quarterly Monograph Series 29. Washington, D.C.: Catholic Biblical Association.

Levenson, Jon D. 1987. The Sources of Torah: Psalm 119 and the Modes of Revelation in Second Temple Judaism. Pages 559-74 in *Ancient Israelite Religion: Essays in Honor of Frank Moore Cross.* Edited by Patrick D. Miller, Paul D. Hanson, and S. Dean McBride. Philadelphia: Fortress.

Roberts, J. J. M. 1977. Of Signs, Prophets, and Time Limits: A Note on Psalm 74:9. *Catholic Biblical Quarterly* 39:474-81.

Soll, Will. 1991. *Psalm 119: Matrix, Form, and Setting.* Catholic Biblical Quarterly Monograph Series 23. Washington, D.C.: Catholic Biblical Association.

Stager, Lawrence E. 1997. Jerusalem and the Garden of Eden. Pages 183-94 in *Eretz-Israel.* Frank Moore Cross volume. Edited by Baruch A. Levine. Archaeological, Historical, and Geographical Studies 26. Jerusalem: Israel Exploration Society, 1999.

Weinfeld, Moshe. 1991. What Makes the Ten Commandments Different? *Bible Review* 6:35-41.

Wilson, Gerald. 1992. The Shape of the Book of Psalms. *Interpretation* 46:129-42.

Zenger, Erich. 2000. Zion as Mother of the Nations in Psalm 87. Pages 123-60 in *The God of Israel and the Nations: Studies in Isaiah and the Psalms.* Norbert Lohfink and Erich Zenger. Collegeville, Minn.: Liturgical Press.

COMMENTARIES

Allen, Leslie C. 2002. *Psalms 101–150.* Revised. Word Biblical Commentary 21. Waco, Tex.: Word Books. Excellent on language and literary structure of the psalms.

Alonso Schökel, Luis, and Cecilia Carniti. 1980. *Salmos: Traducción, introduciones y comentario.* 2 vols. Navarra, Spain: Editiorial Verbo Divino. Sensitive to the psalms as poems and to their theology and relation to the New Testament.

Anderson, A. A. 1972. *Psalms 1–72. Psalms 73–150.* The New Century Bible Commentary. Grand Rapids, Mich.: Eerdmans. Balanced, provides a sense of earlier scholarship.

Augustine, Saint. 2000–2003. *Expositions of the Psalms.* Vols 15-18 of The Works of Saint Augustine III. Edited by John Rotelle. Hyde Park, N.Y.: New City Press. The great sermons of the church father are available in several editions.

Brueggemann, Walter. 1984. *The Message of the Psalms: A Theological Commentary.* Minneapolis: Augsburg. In addition to exegesis, he offers provocative theological reflection.

Calvin, John. 1979. *Calvin's Commentaries.* 22 vols. Grand Rapids, Mich.: Baker Book House. Calvin's commentary on Psalms (5 volumes in this edition) is unusually personal and especially revered among his works. Selections: 1999. *Heart Aflame: Daily Readings from Calvin on the Psalms.* Phillipsburg, N.J.: P & R Publishing.

Craigie, Peter. 1983. *Psalms 1–50.* Word Biblical Commentary 18. Waco, Tex.: Word Books. Strong on comparison with extrabiblical material, especially Ugaritic literature.

Dahood, Mitchell. 1965–1970. *Psalms.* 3 vols. Anchor Bible 16–17A. Garden City, N.Y.: Doubleday. More of a word study than a standard commentary. Though it contains some interesting suggestions, it is only for specialists.

Davidson, Robert. 1998. *The Vitality of Worship: A Commentary on the Book of Psalms.* Grand Rapids, Mich.: Eerdmans. Fine all-purpose commentary. Good analysis with homiletical reflections.

Delitzsch, Franz. 1991. *Psalms*. Vol. 5 of *Commentary on the Old Testament* by C. F. Keil and F. Delitzsch. Translated by James Martin. N.p., 1872. Reprint, Grand Rapids, Mich.: Eerdmans. Justly celebrated for its grasp of the Hebrew text. Too dated for ordinary reference.

Ehrlich, Arnold. 1905. *Die Psalmen*. Berlin: M. Poppelauer. Like Dahood, a specialized study of the Hebrew vocabulary rather than a commentary. Specialists only.

Feuer, Avrohom Chaim. 1996. *Tehillim: Psalms; A New Translation with a Commentary Anthologized from Talmudic, Midrashic and Rabbinic Sources*. 5 vols. ArtScroll Tanach Series. Brooklyn: Mesorah Publications. Excerpts from the Jewish commentary tradition.

Gerstenberger, Erhard S. 1988, 2001. *Psalms*. 2 vols. Forms of the Old Testament Literature 15, 19. Grand Rapids, Mich.: Eerdmans. Useful assessment of psalms according to their genre or type with large bibliography. For the scholar.

Gunkel, Hermann. 1968. *Die Psalmen: Göttinger Handkommentar zum Alten Testament*. Göttingen, 1929. Reprint, Göttingen, Germany: Vandenhoeck & Ruprecht. Gunkel founded modern historical-critical psalm study. Though Gunkel has a feel for religious poetry, his volume is for scholars.

Hossfeld, Frank Lothar, and Erich Zenger. 2000. *Psalmen 51–100*. Herders Theologische Kommentar zum Alten Testament. Freiburg, Germany: Herder. Combines critical scholarship and theological concerns. Especially interested in the formation of the smaller collections within the Psalter.

Kirkpatrick, A. F. 1951. *The Book of Psalms*. The Cambridge Bible for Schools and Colleges. Cambridge: Cambridge University Press. Tremendous amount of information. Historically oriented.

Kraus, Hans-Joachim. 1988–1989. *Psalms*. 2 vols. Translated by Hilton C. Oswald. Minneapolis: Augsburg. Esteemed for its form-critical astuteness, it needs to be supplemented by Gerstenberger, for the German edition is 1961. For the scholar.

Mays, James L. 1994. *Psalms*. Interpretation. Louisville: Westminster / John Knox Press. Mays, a renowned expositor, explores the psalms as statements of faith..

McCann, J. Clinton, Jr. 1996. Psalms. Pages 639-1280 in Vol 4 of *The New Interpreter's Bible*. Nashville: Abingdon. An excellent and balanced commentary.

Schaefer, Konrad. 2001. *Psalms.* Berit Olam Series. Edited by David W. Cotter. Collegeville, Minn.: Liturgical Press. Particularly astute on the structure of the psalms. Underlines the theological ideas.

Seybold, Klaus. 1996 *Die Psalmen.* Handbuch zum Alten Testament I/15. Tübingen: J. C. B. Mohr. Technical. A scholarly commentary that presumes that the Psalms were revised and supplemented over several centuries.

Stuhlmueller, Carroll. 1983. *Psalms.* 2 vols. Wilmington, Del.: Michael Glazier. A much used commentary by a revered Roman Catholic scholar.

Tate, Marvin E. 1990. *Psalms 51–100.* Word Biblical Commentary 20. Waco, Tex.: Word Books. A good commentary, judicious and strong in analysis.

Weiser, Artur. 1962. *The Psalms.* Old Testament Library. Translated by Herbert Hartwell. Philadelphia: Westminster Press. Slightly dated, it underlines the role of the covenant renewal festival, sometimes excessively.

Westermann, Claus. 1989. *The Living Psalms.* Translated by J. R. Porter. Grand Rapids, Mich.: Eerdmans. Commentary on selections by a well-known German scholar.

FOR FURTHER STUDY

Anderson, Bernhard W., and Steven Bishop. 2000. *Out of The Depths: The Psalms Speak to Us Today.* 3d ed., Rev. and expanded. Louisville: Westminster John Knox. Widely used as a textbook for psalm study.

Bonhoeffer, Dietrich. 1974. *Psalms: The Prayer Book of the Church.* Translated by James H. Burtness. Minneapolis: Augsburg Fortress. Memorable commentary by one of the great heroes of the modern church.

Brown, William P. 2002. *Seeing the Psalms: A Theology of Metaphor.* Louisville: Westminster John Knox. Important study of the imagery of the psalms.

Childs, Brevard. 1976. Reflections on the Modern Study of the Psalms. Pages 377-88 in *Magnalia Dei, the Mighty Acts of God: Essays on the Bible and Archaeology in Memory of G. Ernest Wright.* Edited by F. M. Cross. Garden City, N.J.: Doubleday. An influential essay on reading the psalms from a canonical perspective, that is, from their being part of Christian Scripture.

Crenshaw, James L. 2001. *The Psalms: An Introduction.* Grand Rapids, Mich.: Eerdmans. Fine introduction to the psalms by a well-known scholar and writer.

SELECT BIBLIOGRAPHY

Day, John. 1992. *Psalms*. Old Testament Guides. Sheffield, England: Sheffield Academic Press. Useful to the scholar as well as to the layperson.

Greenberg, Moshe. 1983. *Biblical Prose Prayer: As a Window to the Popular Religion of Ancient Israel*. The Taubman Lectures in Jewish Studies, 6th ser. Berkeley: University of California Press. Broader than the title might suggest, this little book perceptively studies blessing and other themes important in the Psalter.

Gunkel, Hermann. 1998. *An Introduction to the Psalms: The Genres of the Religious Lyric of Israel*. Translated by James D. Nogalski. Mercer Library of Biblical Studies. Macon, Ga.: Mercer University Press. Though Gunkel's approach has been fully incorporated into modern scholarship, his study is still valuable.

Holladay, William. 1993. *The Psalms through Three Thousand Years: Prayerbook of a Cloud of Witnesses*. Minneapolis: Augsburg Fortress. Learned chapters on the formation of the Psalter, the influence of the psalms in Christianity and Judaism, discussion of some current issues. Unique.

Kugel, James L. 1995. *The Idea of Biblical Poetry: Parallelism and Its History*. Baltimore: Johns Hopkins University Press. Reprint of 1981 edition. A comprehensive study of parallelism in biblical poetry.

Levenson, Jon D. 1986. The Jerusalem Temple in Devotional and Visionary Experience. Pages 32-61 in *Jewish Spirituality: From the Bible through the Middle Ages*. Edited by Arthur Green. New York: Crossroad. A valuable treatment of the Temple in Jewish religious experience.

Lewis, C. S. 1964. *Reflections on the Psalms*. New York: Harcourt. Broad reflections on the palms by the great Christian thinker and apologist.

Limburg, James. 1992. *Psalms for Sojourners*. Minneapolis: Augsburg. Uses examples of each genre to acquaint the reader with "the strength, the passion, and the fire" of the psalms.

Lohfink, Norbert. 2003. *In the Shadow of Your Wings: New Readings of Great Texts from the Bible*. Collegeville, Minn.: Liturgical Press. Detailed and theologically rich treatments of Psalms 1, 36, 46, and 109.

Lohfink, Norbert, and Erich Zenger. 2000. *The God of Israel and the Nations: Studies in Isaiah and the Psalms*. Collegeville, Minn.: Liturgical Press. Includes essays on Psalms 25, 33, 87, and 90–106.

Mays, James Luther. 2002. The God Who Reigns: The Book of Psalms. Pages 29-38 in *The Forgotten God: Perspectives in Biblical Theology; Essays in Honor of Paul J. Achtemeier on the Occasion of His Seventy-fifth Birthday.* Edited by A. Andrew Das and Frank J. Matera. Louisville: Westminster John Knox. Close study of an important and neglected theme: the portrayal of God in the Psalter.

The Midrash on Psalms. 1959. Yale Judaica Series 13. 2 vols. Translated by William G. Braude. New Haven, Conn.: Yale University Press. Excellent translation.

Miller, Patrick D. 1986. *Interpreting the Psalms.* Philadelphia: Fortress. Important essays on interpreting the psalms today followed by rigorous and perceptive analysis of ten psalms.

———. 1994. *They Cried to the Lord: The Form and Theology of Biblical Prayer.* Minneapolis: Fortress. Careful analysis of various types of biblical prayers with special attention to the Psalter.

Mowinckel, Sigmund. 1967. *The Psalms in Israel's Worship.* 2 vols. Nashville: Abingdon. Important arguments for liturgical influence on the psalms. For scholars.

Murphy, Roland E. 2000. *The Gift of the Psalms.* Peabody, Mass.: Hendrickson. An excellent introduction followed by succinct commentary on each psalm, all within 176 pages.

Nowell, Irene. 1993. *Sing a New Song: The Psalms in the Sunday Lectionary.* Collegeville, Minn.: Liturgical Press. A very competent study of the responsorial psalms in the Roman Catholic liturgy. Deals with their meaning in relation to all the readings.

Pleins, J. David. 1993. *The Psalms: Songs of Tragedy, Hope, and Justice.* Maryknoll, N.Y.: Orbis Books. Excellent introduction with attention to the psalms and social justice.

Sarna, Nahum M. 1995. *On the Book of Psalms: Exploring the Prayers of Ancient Israel.* New York: Schocken Books. A fine introduction by a renowned Jewish scholar.

Seybold, Klaus. 1990. *Introducing the Psalms.* Translated by R. Graeme Dunphy. Edinburgh: T & T Clark. An extremely useful introduction, which includes discussion of some technical aspects.

Smith, Mark S. 1987. *Psalms: The Divine Journey.* New York: Paulist. A very helpful entry into the world of the psalms using the image of journey.

Zenger, Erich. 1996. *A God of Vengeance? Understanding the Psalms of Divine Wrath.* Louisville: Westminster John Knox. An outstanding discussion of the problem in the psalms. Breaks new ground.

INDEX OF PSALMS
ACCORDING TO TYPE

Some classifications are uncertain.

Psalm   *Type*

BOOK ONE

1	Torah Psalm
2	Royal Psalm
3	Individual Lament
4	Individual Lament
5	Individual Lament
6	Individual Lament
7	Individual Lament
8	Hymn
9–10	Individual Lament?
11	Declaration of Trust
12	Community Lament
13	Individual Lament
14 (= 53)	Declaration of Trust
15	Admission to Worship
16	Declaration of Trust
17	Individual Lament
18	Appointment of the King and Thanksgiving
19	Torah Psalm
20	Royal Prayer for Victory

21	Royal Thanksgiving
22	Individual Lament
23	Declaration of Trust
24	Hymn: Enthronement
25	Individual Lament
26	Individual Lament
27	Declaration of Trust
28	Individual Lament
29	Hymn
30	Individual Thanksgiving
31	Individual Lament
32	Individual Thanksgiving
33	Hymn
34	Individual Thanksgiving
35	Individual Lament
36	Declaration of Trust
37	Wisdom Psalm
38	Individual Lament
39	Individual Lament
40	Thanksgiving and Petition
41	Individual Thanksgiving

BOOK TWO

42–43	Individual Lament
44	Community Lament
45	Royal Wedding Song
46	Song of Zion
47	Hymn: Enthronement
48	Song of Zion
49	Wisdom Psalm
50	Covenant Renewal Liturgy
51	Individual Lament
52	Declaration of Trust
53 (= 14)	Declaration of Trust
54	Individual Lament
55	Individual Lament
56	Individual Lament
57	Individual Lament
58	Community Lament

INDEX OF PSALMS ACCORDING TO TYPE

INDEX